THE CHURCH,

THE FALLING AWAY,

AND

THE RESTORATION

BY

J. W. SHEPHERD

Editor of
"Handbook on Baptism," "Queries and
Answers," "Salvation of Sin"
"What is the New Testa-
ment Church?"

GOSPEL ADVOCATE COMPANY
Nashville, Tenn.
1977

Published by Gospel Advocate Co.
P.O. Box 150
Nashville, TN 37202
www.gospeladvocate.com

First Published: 1929

ISBN 0-89225-504-8

CONTENTS

Preface 3

PART ONE

THE CHURCH

What Should the Church of the Present Be?........ 5
The Church and the Temple....................... 9
Infant Baptism 16
Conditions of Membership....................... 25
Agencies 28
Conditions 28
Conditions of Continued Membership.............. 29
The Worship 32
The Apostles' Teaching 36
The Fellowship 38
Breaking Bread 39
Prayers 40
Singing 40
Polity 42
The Word of God................................ 42
Names 43
Congregational Independence 44
Elders 45
Deacons 47
Evangelists 47

PART TWO

THE FALLING AWAY

The Falling Away Predicted...................... 49
The Falling Away 54
The Confessional 63
Indulgences 67
John Tetzel 69

PART THREE
THE REFORMATION IN EUROPE

John Wyckliffe 74
Translates the Bible Iinto English.................. 75
William Tyndale 79
Erasmus Arrives in England 80
Tyndale Translates the Bible Into English........... 82
Goes to Hamburg 84
Bishop of London Supplies Money.................. 86
Betrayed and Murdered........................ 88
Martin Luther 89
A Friend Indeed 90
Becomes a Monk 91
Makes a Pilgrimage to Rome 94
Professor of Theology at Wittenburg................ 96
The Ninety-five Theses 97
Debates With John Eck and Burns the Papal Bull......100
Before the Diet of Worms........................103
Under Imperial Ban............................110
A Change Comes Over Luther.....................112
Retains What Is Not Forbidden....................115
Origin of Protestantism 116
The Reformation in Switzerland 122
The Reformation in England 126
Changes Made by Edward VI.....................129
"Bloody Mary" 131
Elizabeth, the Protestant Queen 133
The Reformation in Scotland 138
The Independents 138
Haldane and Aikman 141
The Scotch Baptists 142
The Separetists 144

PART FOUR
THE RESTORATION MOVEMENT IN AMERICA

Spiritual Unrest in Many Places....................148
Barton W. Stone 153
Confronted by Many Difficulties 153
Ordained to the Ministry 157
Remarkable Meeting at Cane Ridge 160
"A Time of Distress" 163

Last Will and Testament........................166
The Witnesses' Address 167
Practices Modified in Many Particulars 169
"Shakerism" 170
The Work Prospers 171
Thomas Campbell 175
Conflict With the Seceders 175
The Declaration and Address 180
Alexander Campbell 188
Subject and Act of Baptism Settled 188
The Redstone Association 195
A Wider Field 199
The Campbell-McCalla Discussion 203
Visits the Kentucky Baptists 207
John Smith 209
Soul Struggles 210
Desires to Preach 213
Terrible Calamity 215
Preaches at Crab Orchard 215
The Christian Baptist 217
Fetters Cast Off 218
Resolves to Preach the Simple Gospel.............220
"Ancient Order"—Baptists in Kentucky 224
Walter Scott 231-236
A Sincere Truth Seeker 232
Turning Point in His Life 235
Reformers in Other States—John Wright..........246
Herman Christian Dasher 249
The Christians and Reformers Unite 251

PREFACE

An effort is made in the following pages to set forth what the New Testament church was when it came into the world through the preaching of inspired men; how it was led into apostasy; and an account of some of the many attempts to restore it to its original purity and simplicity.

In proportion as any religious work becomes a potent force in affecting the welfare of mankind, its early history becomes interesting and important. This is especially true of the very beginning of its history where those influences which have molded its character are most clearly seen. It is due to the world no less than to the heroic men who were chief actors in such a movement, that the motives which inspired them, the principles which guided them, and the forces which opposed them, together with the results of this conflict, should be set down accurately for the information and for the benefit of those who are seeking the truth

If the writer did not most profoundly believe that this effort to restore the New Testament church was one of those providential movements designed by Jehovah to correct existing evils, and to purify religion from its corruptions that the gospel may run and be glorified in the earth, then he would feel but little interest in its history and achievements. But recognizing, as I do, the hand of God in this remarkable movement of the nineteenth century, it is believed that an important service is being rendered by putting on record the causes which gave birth to it, and the influences which by action and reaction have made it what it is. If God overrules in human affairs, and teaches men by means of history, then he who faithfully records historic facts fulfills an important service in the education of men. This is pre-eminently true of that kind of history which deals with the struggles of the human mind and heart to know God, and to understand his will concerning human redemption.

It is of the very greatest importance to the successful carrying forward of the Lord's work that the younger generation should become thoroughly acquainted with the spirit which animated, and the principles which controlled the men who, under God, gave the primary impulse to this great work. They should become familiar with the conflicts of those early days and with the tremendous sacrifices made by those valiant men and women who loved the truth more than popularity, more than ease, more than wealth, friends, and family ties. It is only as we shall be able to perpetuate this love of truth, this freedom from the bondage of tradition and inherited opinions, that we shall be able to carry forward, successfully the work they inaugurated.

We need the same dauntless heroism, the same faith in God, the same zeal for truth and the same underlying principles which characterized them and who have transmitted to us the responsibility of carrying forward the work which they began. If this volume which is now sent forth shall serve to inspire the workers who are to succeed us with the same passion for pure apostolic Christianity, with the same spirit of loyalty to Christ, which marked the beginning of their work, the purpose of the writer shall have been fulfilled.

J. W. SHEPHERD.

Birmingham, Ala.. July 25, 1929.

PART I.

The Church.

CHAPTER I.

WHAT SHOULD THE CHURCH OF THE PRESENT BE?

That the church is the bride of Christ is clearly expressed in the following: "Wherefore, my brethren, ye also were made dead to the law through the body of Christ; that ye should be joined to another, even to him who was raised from the dead, that we might bring forth fruit unto God" (Rom. 7: 4). "For I am jealous over you with a godly jealousy: for I espoused you to one husband, that I might present you as a pure virgin to Christ" (II Cor. 11: 2). In these passages the bride evidently means the church. That the bride will remain till the Bridegroom comes there can be no reasonable doubt; that she has ever waited his coming is equally certain. She has been in great distress, being driven into the wilderness and deprived of much of her glory, but she has ever looked for the coming of her espoused. In what condition the Bridegroom will find her is a question about which there has been much speculation. Unless we believe that the Bridegroom, when he comes, will find his bride in dishonor—living in fornication with the world—we may not measure the church by human standards. That the bride will be found wearing the name of the Bridegroom and living in chastity when he comes to claim her, there is no room for reasonable doubt. The world may be deeply defiled by crime, but the church will be arrayed in her robes of righteousness. Hence, while the church may have its impurities, as everything composed of humanity has, it must at least be uncontaminated to the extent of fidelity to Christ. This may cut off much of what the world calls the church, but not what God regards as the church.

This has ever been the case since the apostasy, and will doubtless so continue to the end.

In the days of the apostles, God had a people in Babylon, but while they were in Babylon they were not of Babylon. Hence the Lord says: "Come forth, my people, out of her, that ye have no fellowship with her sins, and that ye receive not her plagues" (Rev. 18: 4). God doubtless has a people in Babylon now; but they and Babylon are two distinct things. God's church is not composed of the Babel of sectarianism. Just who God's people are who may now be in Babylon it is not my purpose to determine. God has revealed to us the things that pertain to his church—the faith, the practice, and the promises—and with these it is my purpose to deal. Here, all is faith and assurance; beyond this, all is opinion and fruitless speculation. Concerning those in Babylon we have but one living direction. "Come forth, my people, out of her." To this we should give faithful heed. For to console people in the Babylon of sectarianism, and to reconcile them to their bondage, we have no divine right; but to deliver them from it is a divine obligation. Therefore God's church is an institution separate and distinct from the Babel of denominationalism.

In determining, then, what the church should be, it will be necessary to ascertain the characteristics of the apostolic church. If the church of the present day be essentially different from the apostolic as a matter of preference, it can not be the church of which God is the author. Hence it can not be a divine institution, neither can it be the the virgin bride of Christ. It follows, therefore, that the church must possess the following characteristics:

1.   IT MUST BE A DIVINE INSTITUTION

At the beginning the church was a divine institution, and it can not cease to be divine and still be the church of God, for God does not begin with the divine and end with the human. Beginning in the spirit the things of God are not made perfect in the flesh. A divine institution must have for its organization and essential features divine authority, for the world can not make an ordinance or an institution divine. It must be specially appointed of God. No human institution, therefore, nor combination of institutions for which there is no special divine appointment, can ever constitute the church of God, for it is of God and not of men. Hence the church must be in all its essential features of specific divine appointment. These appointments are all found in the New Testament; therefore, the church to be a divine institution must be fashioned after that model.

2. IT MUST BE GOVERNED WHOLLY BY DIVINE AUTHORITY.

The church was governed wholly by divine authority at the beginning. Should it substitute human for divine authority it would cease to be the church of God. A substitute for a divine thing can never itself be divine; therefore, anything substituted for the church as it was in the beginning is not that church. Just as certainly therefore, as Christ will own and accept his church when he comes again, so certainly will it be governed by his authority. Christ will accept only the church which he established. That which he established was governed wholly by divine authority: therefore the church of today must be so governed.

3. IT SHOULD HAVE ONLY THE NAMES IT HAD AT THE BEGINNING.

In the New Testament there are various names applied to the church and to its members. All these names have their significance, for the Holy Spirit never used them by accident, and for these names, and for these only, is there divine authority. The true church of to-day will be governed by divine authority; therefore, only these will the church accept. This with it is not simply a matter of taste, but of loyalty to Christ. Names unknown to the New Testament have come of the apostasy.

4. IT MUST HAVE THE FORM OF GOVERNMENT GIVEN TO THE CHURCH IN THE BEGINNING.

It must necessarily be true, since it recognizes only the same authority. The church of to-day could not disregard the government of the New Testament church and still be the same church. Its congregations are not bound in the coils of an ecclesiasticism as merciless as it is unscriptural. Its bishops are not diocesan, but congregational. There are not a plurality of churches, under one bishop, but a plurality of bishops in one church. Its government is not in the hands of a legislative body, but it is under the legislation of Christ, executed by the several congregations.

5. IT HAS THE UNITY OF THE CHURCH OF THE NEW TESTAMENT.

This conclusion is reached from several considerations. (1) Since the church is governed only by divine authority, has the same form of government that it had in the beginning, and wears only the names found in the New Testament, the unity that characterized the first church follows as a consequence. (2) The destruction of the unity of the church was the work of the apostasy; hence when the church is reclaimed from the apostasy it will be freed from this disunion. (3) There can be no doubt that Christ's prayer for the unity of his people can now be fulfilled as it was at the beginning. This unity can never exist through denominational walls. There were no denominational walls between the Father and the Son, neither was there any between the first disciples. Hence, if that prayer is answered in the restoration of the church, and it must be, there must be the same unity that characterized the church in the beginning.

CHAPTER II.

THE CHURCH AND THE TEMPLE

Under the Patriarchal and Jewish dispensation there were numerous animal sacrifices by divine appointment. Not only so, but the people generally, who knew not the true God, have, all down the ages, poured sacrificial blood upon altars innumerable. This must have come about by the perversion of divinely-appointed sacrificial institutions, or from the felt need of fallen man for some way of mediation and of approach to God. That the need was felt by true worshipers is not open to doubt, for if sacrifice were devised by man, it would only have arisen from a sense of that need; and, on the other hand, if ordained of God, it could only have been acceptably offered under a consciousness thereof.

Sacrifices, altars and priests have generally stood together; and so long as they have been upon divine lines have been highly beneficial. But it has been alleged that priests have been a curse rather than a blessing to the nations, and I am not prepared to dispute the allegation. But neither God nor the Bible is responsible, because the priesthood as instituted by the Jews was a good and not an evil to that people; while, on the other hand, the priestly system has no place in Christianity. The priests of heathendom and of Christendom are not of God. Then how widely different, how completely opposite, is the unpriestly worship of the Church of Christ from the sacerdotal ceremonies of the Jewish economy. There we find the costly temple, in the construction of which were gold, silver, precious stones and costly fabrics in unrestricted abundance; sacred places over which the people may not pass, and which the feet of priests and Levites only may tread; ceremonials which bring death to those who touch them with other than priestly hands; altars and fires, blood and incense, and priests, all of divine ordering, so that we read:

Then the king and all the people offered sacrifice before Jehovah. And King Solomon offered a sacrifice of twenty and two thousand oxen, and a hundred and twenty thousand sheep. So the king and all the people dedicated the house of God. And the priests stood, according to their offices; the Levites also with instruments of music of Jehovah, which David the King had made to give thanks unto Jehovah (for his loving kindness endureth forever), when David praised by their ministry; and the priests sounded trumpets before them; and all Israel stood.   Moreover Solomon hallowed the middle of the court that was before the house of Jehovah; for there he offered and burnt offerings, and the fat of the peace offerings, because the brazen altar which Solomon had made was not able to receive the burnt offering, and the meat offering, and the fat·

So Solomon held the feast at that time seven days, and all Israel with him, a very great assembly, from the entrance of Hamath unto the brook of Egypt.   And on the eighth day they held a solemn assembly: for they kept the dedication of the altar seven days, and the feast seven days.   And on the three and twentieth day of the seventh month, he sent the people away unto their tents, joyful and glad of heart for the goodness that Jehovah had showed unto David, and to Solomon, and to Israel his people.   (II Chron. 7: 4-10.)

The significance, and richness, and glory of that economy surpassed anything that the world had ever seen; but in the fullness of time it was superseded by a higher and more glorious dispensation, concerning which the Apostle Paul wrote:

And such confidence have we through Christ to God-ward: not that we are sufficient of ourselves, to account anything as from ourselves; but our sufficiency is from God; who also made us sufficient as ministers of a new covenant; not of the letter, but of the spirit: for the letter killeth, but the spirit giveth life.   But if the ministration of death, written, and engraven on stones, came with glory, so that the children of Israel could not look steadfastly upon the face of Moses for the glory of his face which glory was passing away: how shall not rather the ministration of the spirit be with glory?   For if the ministration of condemnation hath glory, much rather doth the ministration of righteousness exceed in glory.   For verily that which hath been made glorious hath not been made glorious in this respect, by reason of the glory that surpasseth.   For if that which passeth away was with glory, much more that which remaineth is in glory.   (II Cor. 3: 4-11.)

Shall we, then, look for still greater material splendor and wealth in temples, vestments, altars and instruments of music?   If not, why not?   And still, if not, why did the like exist under the former and inferior economy?   We should look for nothing of the sort, nor suffer its intrusion upon the Church of Christ, and that for one reason, sufficient without others equally good—the former economy, in all its ceremonials, was typical of spiritual blessings then to come.   There was a perfect typical system most expressive and opposite, but rendered useless when its antitypes appeared.   The cross took the place of the altar; the High Priest of our confession came in the room of the Aaronic priesthood, "the sacrifice of praise," "that is the fruit of our lips," set aside the praise by trumpets, psaltery and cymbal. These were good and expressive in their day and place.   "A shadow of things to come; but the body is Christ" (Col. 2: 17).   "For the law having a shadow of good things to come, not the very image of the things, can never with the same sacrifices year by year, which they offer continually, make perfect them that draw nigh.   Else would they not have ceased to be offered?" (Heb. 10: 1).   So we see that the Holy Spirit very aptly informs us that "the body" or substance, is Christ's, and when he came and filled to the full the types and shadows of the law, they passed away in their entirety, giving place to higher institutions, by means of which the worshipers could be made perfect.   "And not only so," as a ripe Bible student very forcefully says, "but just in proportion as these abandoned shadows are intruded into the church and worship of God they become injurious and more or less substitutes for the realities of which, in their day and place, they were the proper types and symbols. Consequently, in setting in order, by the apostles, of the Church of Christ, the temple and its worship were in no degree taken as models, and this is highy reasonable, inasmuch as the existence together of the type and the antitype would be completely inadmissible.   Nothing could have been easier than for the apostles to have adopted priestly, or modified priestly vestments.   There could have been no manner of difficulty in burning incense as an act of praise or worship.   It can not be supposed but that, long before the close of the apostolic ministry, they could have used and enjoined the use of instrumental music.   But no! Nothing of the kind; no trace even of a leaning, or of a desire, in that direction. The things of the shadows were done with, and those of the substance took their place."

That the church is not modeled after the temple, but after the synagogue, is established beyond doubt by the testimony of the learned men in the denominational world. If objection be made to the inconsistency of denominational scholars putting forth such views, I answer that it is a well-known fact that men do confess truths that they fail to carry into effect; but the truth is not weakened thereby, but rather derives additional weight from the fact that it forces confession, even against the interests and associations of those who utter it. But however that may be, they write the truth abundantly clear.

The first witness I introduce is "Richard Watson," who the McClintock and Strong Cyclopedia says "gave the first systematic treatment of Wesleyan theology. His Institutes, though not the legal, have been the moral and scientific standard of Methodist doctrine." All aspirants to the Methodist pulpit are required to study "Watson's Theological Institutes." He says:

The course of the synagogue worship became indeed the model of that of the Christian Church. It consisted in prayer, reading and explaining the Scriptures, and singing psalms; and thus one of the most important means of instructing nations, and of spreading and maintaining the influence of morals and religion among people, passed from the Jews into all Christian countries. . . . The mode of public worship in the primitive church was taken from the synagogue service; and so, also, was its arrangements of offices. . . . Such was the model which the apostles followed in providing for the future regulation of the churches they had raised up. They took it, not from the temple and its priesthood, for that was typical, and was then passing away. But they found in the institution of the synagogues a plan admirably adapted to the simplicity and purity of Christianity, . . . and which was capable of being applied to the new dispensation without danger of Judaizing. (Theological Institutes, pages 640, 683, 684.)

Lyman Coleman, Presbyterian, who was "eminent in solid abilities, in accurate scholarship, in stores of accumulated learning, and in extended usefulness," says:

He (Jesus) was a constant attendant upon the religious worship of the synagogue, and, after his ascension, his disciples conformed their acts of worship to those of the synagogue. They consisted in prayer, in singing and in the reading and exposition of the Scriptures, as appears from the writers of the New Testament, from the earliest Christian fathers, and from profane writers of the first two centuries. (Ancient Christianity Exemplified, page 94.)

The eminent scholar of the Church of England, G. A. Jacob, in his "Ecclesiastical Polity of the New Testament," which is used as a text-book in some of the Episcopal theological seminaries in this country, says:

In the temple was the priest consecrated according to a precise regulation, and a sarcedotal succession laid down by God himself, with the altar and its sacrifices at which he officiated, the incense which he burned, the holy places into which none might enter but those to whom it was especially assigned. In the synagogue was the reader of the Scriptures, the preacher or expounder of religious and moral truth, the leader of the common devotions of the people, unconsecrated by any special rites, and unrestricted by any rule of succession; with a reading desk or pulpit at which he stood, but with no altar, sacrifice or incense, and no part of the building more holy than the rest. And without attempting now to dwell upon all the remarkable contrasts thus displayed, it may suffice to say that the temple exhibited in a grand combination of typical places, persons and actions. God dwelling with man, reconciling the world unto himself in the person and work of Christ; and pardoning, justifying and graciously receiving those who come to him through the appointed Saviour; while the synagogue exhibited a congregation of men, already reconciled to God, assembled as devout worshipers for prayer and praise, for instruction in divine knowledge, and edification in righteous living. And the two systems—the one gorgeous and typical, the other simple and real; in one, God drawing near to man, in the other, man drawing near to God—never clashed or interfered with each other; were never intermingled or confounded together. In the temple there was no pulpit, in the synagogue there was no altar. . . . They (apostles) retained and adapted to Christian use some Jewish forms and regulations; but they were taken altogether not from the temple, but from the synagogue. The offices which they appointed in the church, and the duties and authority which they attached to them, together with the regulations which they made for Christian worship, bore no resemblance in name or in nature to the services of the priesthood in the temple. The apostles had been divinely taught that those priests and services were typical forms and shadows, which were centered, and fulfilled, and done away in Christ; and to reinstate them in the Church would have been in their judgment to go back to the bondage of "weak and beggarly elements" from the liberty, strength and rich completeness of the Gospel dispensation. They saw that as the ordinances of the temple represented the work of God wrought out for man, not man's work for God to continue them after that work was finished in the life and death of Jesus, would be in effect so far to deny the efficacy of the Saviour's mission, and to thrust in the miserable performances of men to fill up an imagined imperfection in the Son of God. (Ecclesiastical Polity, pages 96-98.)

The apostles, therefore, by the directions of the Holy Spirit adopted official arrangements similar to those of the synagogue, and discarded those of the temple, in the institution of church offices, and plainly showed by this circumstance that no priestly powers or duties were attached to their ministrations. Another argument which leads to the same conclusion is deduced from the condition of the members of the Church as it appears in the New Testament, and the equality of standing in Christ, which Christians possessed. The way of access to God being open to all without distinction through the priesthood of Christ, there was nothing for a priest to do—no sacerdotal work or office for him to undertake.

On this phase of the subject, Mr. Jacob has said some very pointed things, and I will call on him to give testimony. He says:

A distinct proof that the office bearers in the Church of the Apostles were not, and could not be priests, or perform any sacerdotal duties, is seen in a condensed form in the epistle to the Hebrews, and is found at large in the whole of the Old and the New Testaments, of which that epistle, as far as the subject reaches, is so valuable an epitome. We there learn that from the very nature of the priestly office, it is necessary for those who hold it to be specially called and appointed by God, either personally by name, or according to a divinely instituted order of succession; and that, since the patriarchal dispensation, only two orders of priesthood have ever had this necessary divine sanction granted to them. The two orders are the order of Aaron and the order of Melchisedek. The priests of the former order belonged to the Jewish dispensation only, and have indisputably passed away.   The only priest after the order of Melchisedek, even mentioned in the Bible, is our Lord Jesus Christ—the "priest upon his throne," without a successor, as he had none before him, in the everlasting priest-hood of his mediatorial reign.   This argument appears to me to be conclusive.   It appears to me that the epistle to the Hebrews shuts out the possibility of there being any other priest in the Church besides Christ himself.   But this does not so appear to a large number of our clergy.   Bishops as far back as the third century claimed to be successors or vice-gerents of Christ on earth; and our presbyters do not hesitate to declare that they are priests after the order of Melchisedek To my mind and feeling this is an impious claim; but counten-anced as they are by numberless past and present examples, good men are not conscious of impiety in making it.   But, then it is necessary to ask the "priests" for their credentials.   Where is the record of their divine appointment to the sacredotal office?   In what part of the New Testament, and in what form of words, is the institution of such priests, and the manner of their succession, to be found?   And to such inquiries no satis-factory answer has been or can be given.   (Ibid, pages 102-104.)

CHAPTER III.

INFANT BAPTISM

Another point in which the Church of Christ and the Jewish Covenant are at exact opposites is that of infant membership. In the Apostolic Church baptism preceded membership, and faith was prerequisite to baptism, consequently there was not, neither could be any place for infant membership. On this account we have in the New Testament neither precept for, nor example of, infant baptism, but on the contrary, much that renders it totally incompatible with apostolic teaching.

But we are reminded by the advocates of infant baptism that in some sense baptism stands to its subject and the Church as circumcision did under the Abrahamic covenant. They emphasize that as an unquestioned fact, and seem to think there ought to be something in it, somewhere or somehow, in favor of infant baptism. Some claim that circumcision initiated into the Church under the former dispensation, and that baptism is initiative now; and that infants were formerly initiated by circumcision, and should now be initiated by baptism. Others hold that circumcision was a declaration of church membership under the Jewish dispensation; and that baptism is a declaration of membership now: and that as circumcision was extended to infants, so baptism should be extended. They further claim that infants were put in the Church which was established in the family of Abraham; that the Church of the old dispensation is identical with that of the new; that no law has since been enacted to put them out; and that they were then initiated by circumcision and that, as baptism has superseded circumcision, infants should now be initiated by baptism.

To some this is a strong and satisfactory argument, but a few plain, simple facts should decide the question whether the Church of the new covenant is identical with that of the old and that baptism takes the place of circumcision:

(1) "The covenant of circumcision" (Acts 7: 8) was a covenant with Abraham and to him "that is born in thy house, and he that is bought with thy money" (Gen. 17: 12, 13); while the new covenant embraces believers in Jesus Christ, without respect to Abraham's flesh or money. (See II Cor. 5: 16, 17; Gal. 3: 26-29; Heb. 8: 8-12.)

(2) Male children alone were subjects of circumcision. If baptism took the place of circumcision, none but the males should be baptized; but the advocates of infant baptism contend that infants should be baptized regardless of sex, flesh or money.

(3) If baptism came in the place of circumcision, persons already circumcised could not be baptized. If the one came in the place of the other, the two could not exist at the same time in the same person. But all the Jews that had been circumcised on believing in Christ were baptized. The children of Jewish Christians were still circumcised. Is it possible that pedobaptists are so blinded in their contention for infant baptism that they can not see this?

That there is a point of similarity between circumcision and baptism there is no doubt, for Paul says: "In whom ye were also circumcised with a circumcision not made with hands, in the putting off the body of the flesh, in the circumcision of Christ, having been buried with him in baptism, wherein ye were also raised with him through the faith in the working of God, who raised him from the dead" (Col. 2: 11. 12). In circumcision the foreskin of the flesh was cut off by the hands; so in baptism the sins were put off, and this putting off the sins was called "a circumcision not made with hands."

The Mosaic law given to the fleshly family of Abraham typified to some extent the spiritual family of God. Circumcision marked those born of the flesh as members of the kingdom of Israel; baptism marks those begotten of the Spirit as members of God's spiritual kingdom. To affix the spiritual mark to the fleshly birth is to do violence to the figure and to introduce those born of the flesh into the spiritual kingdom. Now faith is the first manifestation of the spiritual begetting, and only those begotten of the Spirit and manifesting it in faith can be introduced into the spiritual kingdom, or should have the mark of God's spiritual child. To place the mark of the birth of the Spirit upon one born of the flesh is to mislead and deceive that child and make the impression that it is one of God's spiritual children when it is not. The Spirit of God always connects the fleshly mark with the fleshly birth into the fleshly kingdom, and the spiritual mark (baptism) with the spiritual birth into the spiritual kingdom. Hence the Holy Spirit says: "Go ye therefore, and teach all nations, baptizing them into the name of the Father, and of the Son, and of the Holy Spirit" (Matt. 28: 19). "Go ye into all the world, and preach the Gospel to the whole creation. He that believeth and is baptized shall be saved; but he that disbelieveth shall be condemned" (Mark 16: 15, 16). "Repent ye, and be baptized every one of you in the name of Jesus Christ unto the remission of your sins" (Acts 2: 38). "And now why tarriest thou, arise, and be baptized and wash away thy sins, calling on the name of the Lord" (Acts 22: 16). Only those capable of believing, repenting and of thus showing that they are begotten of the Spirit, are fit subjects for baptism. To bestow the mark of the spiritual birth on those born of the flesh is to break down and carnalize the kingdom of God.

The prophet says:

Behold, the days come, saith Jehovah, that I will make a new covenant with the house of Israel, and with the house of Judah: not according to the covenant that I made with their fathers in the day that I took them by the hand to bring them out of the land of Egypt: which my covenant they brake, although I was a husband unto them, saith Jehovah. But this is the covenant that I will make with the house of Israel after those days, saith Jehovah: I will put my law in their inward parts, and in their hearts will I write it; and I will be their God, and they

shall be my people.   And they shall teach no more every man
his neighbor, and every man his brother, saying, Know
Jehovah: for they shall all know me from the least of them
unto the greatest of them, saith Jehovah: for I will forgive
their iniquity, and their sins will I remember no more. (Jer.
31: 31-34.)

This shows that a new covenant different from that he
made at Sinai would be made.   That was a fleshly covenant with the house of Israel, into which they were born
by a fleshly birth; but in the new covenant the law was to
be written on their hearts, and all were to know him, from
the least to the greatest.   That is, all must know the law
of God, accept it in their hearts before they could become
members of the Church of God.   So Paul asks: "What
then is the law?   It was added because of transgressions,
till the seed should come to whom the promise hath been
made" (Gal. 3: 19).   The seed that was to come was Christ,
and this plainly shows that because of the transgression this
law was to continue only until Christ should come.   Then
the new spiritual covenant was to go into force, and the
members of it were all to believe in Christ.

The following significant contrast is drawn by the
Apostle Paul: "Ye are our epistle written in our hearts,
known and read of all men; being made manifest that ye
are an epistle of Christ, ministered by us, written not with
ink, but with the Spirit of the living God; not on tables of
stone, but in tables that are hearts of flesh.   And such confidence have we through Christ to Godward: not that we
are sufficient of ourselves, to account anything as from ourselves; but our sufficiency is from God, who also made us
sufficient as ministers of a new covenant; not of the letter,
but of the spirit: for the letter killeth, but the spirit giveth
life.   But if the ministration of death, written and engraven
on stones, came with glory, so that the children of Israel
could not look steadfastly upon the face of Moses for the
glory of his face; which glory was passing away: how shall
not rather the ministration of the spirit be with glory?   For
if the ministration of condemnation hath glory, much rather
doth the ministration of righteousness exceed in glory.   For

verily that which hath been made glorious hath not been made glorious in this respect, by reason of the glory that surpasseth. For if that which passeth away was with glory, much more that which remaineth is in glory" (II Cor. 3: 2-11). In this the Ten Commandments, written upon the tables of stone, is contrasted with the law of Christ, written in the hearts of God's children. The law written on stones is called "the letter" that "killeth." It convicted of sin, but had no power to deliver from it. The sins were rolled and rolled year by year until Jesus came and shed blood, not only for our sins but for "the redemption of the transgressions that were under the first covenant that they that have been called may receive the promise of the eternal inheritance.

The letter to the Hebrews was written to show the change from the old covenant to the new, and to show the immense superiority of the new to the old. To turn back from the spiritual law and the Church of Christ to the fleshly law and institution of Judaism is called falling "away from grace." "Ye are severed from Christ, ye who would be justified by the law; ye are fallen away from grace" (Gal. 5: 4).

Since it is so very evident that there is no ground whatever for infant baptism based on the arguments on the analogy of circumcision and the identity of the covenants it is quite appropriate to close this article with quotations from two great pedobaptist scholars. Dr. Jacob Ditzler, claimed to be the best debater the Methodist Church has produced, says ·

I here express my conviction that the covenants of the Old Testament have nothing to do with infant baptism" (Graves-Ditzler Debate, page 694).

Moses Stuart, Congregationalist, Professor of Sacred Literature in Andover Theological Seminary, called "The Father of Biblical Literature in America," says:

How unwary, too, are many excellent men, in contending for infant baptism on the ground of the Jewish analogy of circumcision! Are females not proper subjects of baptism? And again, are a man's slaves to be all baptized because he is? Are they church members of course when they are so baptized? Is there no difference between ingrafting into a politico-ecclesiastical community, and into one of which it is said that "it is not of this world?" In short, numberless difficulties present themselves in our way, as soon as we begin to argue in such a manner as this. (Old Testament Canon, § 22, page 369.)

In the investigation thus far we have learned that under the old covenant infants were included, so were slaves, taken in war or bought with money. The covenant was with a nation, involving national laws and customs, and promising national and temporal blessings. The duly recognized, as embraced under that covenant, were not thereby entitled to eternal life. As the entire flesh of the nation, for national purposes, was included, the infants of that nation, from the moment of birth, stood in covenant relation with God and the covenant people. There was no ceremonial by which they entered into that relationship—they were born into it. They came not in by circumcision, for the male infant, continuing uncircumcised, was not said to be debarred from entering, but was to be "cut off" from the people which implies previous covenant relationship.

But all this is reversed under the new covenant. No one nation is chosen, but the people of the covenant are to be those who respond to a call made to all nations. No family is chosen, but the blessing is offered to each of all the families of earth. No infant is either invited or excluded, except as it comes to faith in, and obedience to, the Son of God. The covenant blessings are not national and eternal, based upon a living and active faith. As a consequence, infants are not, and could not possibly be embraced in the new covenant; and as the Church of Christ, as to its divinely-ordained membership, consists of those who have thus believed in him, infants are not and can not be in the Church of Christ, therefore are not subjects of baptism, for all who are Scripturally baptized enter into the church.

We now turn our attention to the remaining methods by which the practice of infant baptism could be proven. They are: (1) Express command of an inspired man; or, (2) by an example from Scripture where an inspired man baptized infants, or where it was done in his presence, by his consent and approval. Inasmuch as it is admitted by renowned pedobaptists that there is neither express command for or example of infant baptism in the New Testament, I will make no attempt to answer the arguments to prove it, but let the most learned of their number speak for themselves. This is legitimate and has the divine sanction, for Jesus said: "Out of thine own mouth will I judge thee" (Luke 19: 22); and Paul, in meeting opposition to his preaching, said: "As certain even of your own poets have said" (Acts 17: 28); and again: "One of themselves, a prophet of their own, said" (Titus 1: 12).

Henry Alford, one of the most variously-learned clergymen that the Church of England has produced, says:

The language of the Bible is against them; and, on their own ground, which is a very sore perplexity. There is one escape, and that is a perfectly effectual one; but they are unwilling to avail themselves of its assistance. They might declare, and they ought to declare, that infant baptism was a practice unknown to the apostles; that not only does the New Testament not give one single expression which plainly and necessarily implies that infants were baptized in the apostolical churches, but it can be fairly argued from a passage in chapter 7 of I Corinthians that such a practice could not have existed at Corinth. The recognition that the baptism of adults was the only baptism known to the apostles would clear every difficulty on this point out of the way of the Low Churchmen. It is natural that the sacred writers should assume that men who, at great worldly sacrifice, not free from risk of life, came forward to profess the Christian faith by a solemn initiatory rite, possessed the frame of mind which that fact implied —that they were honestly changed and renewed beings. And then it would be easy to pass on the conclusion that the baptismal service of the Church of England has been constructed on the language of the Bible, and that the embarrassment has proceeded not from a mistaken view of baptism, but from the application of the words used by Scripture of an adult person to an unconscious and, so to say, mindless infant. (Contemporary Review, Vol. 10, page 329.)

Joseph Ager Beet, one of the finest scholars that the English Wesleyan Methodist Church has produced, Professor of Systematic Theology in the Wesleyan Theological College, Richmond, England, says:

It must be at once admitted that the New Testament contains no clear proof that infants were baptized in the days of the apostles. (Christian Baptism, page 28.)

Albert Taylor Bledsoe, of whom it has been truthfully said, "He was one of the most candid and trustworthy writers that the Methodist Church has produced," says:

It is an article of our faith, that "the baptism of young children (infants) is in any wise to be retained in the church, as one most agreeable to the institution of Christ." But yet, with all our searching, we have been unable to find, in the New Testament, a single express declaration, or word, in favor of infant baptism. We justify this rite, therefore, solely on the ground of logical inference, and not on any express word of Christ or his apostles. This may, perhaps, be deemed, by some of our readers, a strange position for a pedo-baptist. It is by no means, however, a singular opinion. Hundreds of learned pedobaptists have come to the same conclusion; especially since the New Testament has been subjected to a closer, more conscientious, and more candid exegesis than was formerly practiced by controversalists. (Southern Review, Vol. 14, page 334.)

John Calvin, the founder of the Presbyterian Church, says:

As Christ enjoins them to teach before baptizing, and desires that none but believers shall be admitted to baptism, it would appear that baptism is not properly administered unless when preceded by faith. (Harmony of the Evangelists, Vol. 3, page 38.)

Heinrich August Wilhelm Meyer, German Lutheran, the "prince of New Testament exegetes," says:

The baptism of the children of Christians, of which no trace is found in the New Testament, is not to be held as an apostolic ordinance; but it is an institution of the church, which gradually arose in post-apostolic times in connection with the development of ecclesiastical life and of doctrinal teaching, not certainly attested before Tertullian, and by him still decidedly opposed, and although already defended by Cyprian, only becoming general after the time of Augustine in virtue of that connection. (Commentary on Acts 16: 15, page 312.)

August Wilhelm Neander, Lutheran, who is unanimously conceded to be by far the greatest of all ecclesiastical historians, and is surnamed "the father of modern church history," says:

Baptism was administered at first only to adults, as men were accustomed to conceive baptism and faith as strictly connected. We have all reason for not deriving infant baptism from apostolic institution somewhat later, as an apostolical tradition serves to confirm this hypothesis.   (Church History, Vol. 1, page 424.)

Moses Stuart, a Congregationalist, called "the father of Biblical literature in America", says:

On the subject of infant baptism I have said nothing. The present occasion did not call for it; and I have no wish or intention to enter into the controversy respecting it.   I have only to say that I believe in both the propriety and expediency of the rite thus administered; and therefore accede to it ex animo.   Commands, or plain and certain examples, in the New Testament relative to it, I do not find.   Nor, with my views of it, do I need them.   (Mode of Christian Baptism, pages 189, 190.)

But I have given enough; it is a thing made out that infant baptism was not an apostolic practice.   So, indeed, have all the scholars who have thoroughly investigated this subject conceded.   I know of no subject which seems to be more clearly made out, and I can not see how it is possible for any candid man who examines the subject to deny this.

CHAPTER IV.

CONDITIONS OF MEMBERSHIP

As we have already learned that infant baptism was not an apostolic practice, we will give it no further attention at present. The conditions of membership in the apostolic Church naturally divide themselves into two classes— those of admission into the Church and those of continued membership.

CONDITIONS OF ADMISSION

Concerning admission into the Church it is said in connection with its establishment that "the Lord added to them day by day those that were saved" (Acts 2: 47). This implies that the Lord saved the people and added them by one and the same process. They were not first saved and then added, nor added and afterward saved, but they were saved in being added, and added by being saved. Hence it was not a formal adding to a local congregation by extending the "hand of fellowship" after salvation from sin, but an adding to the one body of Christ in the obtaining of salvation by obedience to the Gospel. While they were added by the Lord, he added them through certain agencies, both human and divine—the Holy Spirit, the Gospel and the preacher—all present and active in the work. What the Lord did, therefore, he did through these agencies.

In the second chapter of Acts the Holy Spirit gives the directions that God gave to guide sinners into the Church. This being the first time that men were guided into the Church, the directions given would necessarily be more minute and particular in every step than after the way was fully made known to men.

After his resurrection from the dead Jesus said to his disciples, "All authority hath been given unto me in heaven and on earth," to show them that he had the right and authority to speak the words that come next: "Go ye, therefore, and make disciples of all the nations, baptizing them into the name of the Father and of the Son and of the Holy Spirit: teaching them to observe all things whatsoever I commanded you: and lo, I am with you always, even unto the end of the world" (Matt. 28: 19, 20). They were not to go yet, for he had sealed their lips. On the day of his ascension to heaven he said unto them: "Go ye into all the world, and preach the gospel to the whole creation. He that believeth and is baptized shall be saved; but he that disbelieveth shall be condemned" (Mark 16: 15, 16; "but tarry ye in the city, until ye be clothed with power from on high" (Luke 24: 49). So they returned to Jerusalem and waited for the coming of the Spirit who was to unseal their lips and to speak to the world in the name of Jesus. The day of Pentecost came, they were in the temple, when suddenly a sound from heaven filled the house where they were sitting, and they felt themselves moved inwardly by a new power, under which they began to speak to the multitude in the temple, addressing them in all the different languages represented by the nations there assembled. The time had come when they can tell to the world all they know about Jesus fully and freely. And when they had praised God, to the amazement of the people, in all their tongues, Peter arose, now having the keys to the kingdom in his hands, now ready to execute his high commission to open the gates and admit those who were entitled to enter, and for the first time in his life begins to inform men who Jesus is. He delivers a discourse in which he says: "Ye men of Israel, hear these words: Jesus of Nazareth, a man approved of God unto you by mighty works and wonders and signs which God did by him in the midst of you, even as ye yourselves know; him, being delivered by the determinate counsel and foreknowledge of God, ye by the hands of lawless men did crucify and slay: whom God raised up, having loosed the pangs of death."

He quotes language of the prophets to prove this. He then presents the testimony of himself and his fellow apostles to the effect that Jesus had been raised from the dead, and that they had seen him with their eyes and handled him with their hands.   He further states that God had said to Jesus: "Sit thou on my right hand, till I make thine enemies the footstool of thy feet," and closes this powerful argument with this soul-stirring appeal: "Let all the house of Israel therefore know assuredly that God hath made him both Lord and Christ, this Jesus whom ye crucified."

Three thousand of those who stood in the hearing of Peter's voice believed this, felt pricked in their hearts—that sense of guilt which overwhelmed them when they realized that they had been guilty of murdering the Son of the living God, the greatest crime that human being ever committed—and in great agony of soul, they cried out: "Brethren, what shall we do?" to get rid of this pricking of our hearts, to get rid of the awful crime, to get rid of our sins before God and escape its consequences in the day of God's wrath against sin.

Moved by the Holy Spirit, Peter answered: "Repent ye, and be baptized, every one of you, in the name of Jesus Christ unto the remission of your sins; and ye shall receive the gift of the Holy Spirit."   This was God's answer, that enabled them to get rid of their guilt and condemnation at once.   And to assure them still further, he said: "For to you is the promise" (the remission of sins and the gift of the Holy Spirit), "and to your children, and to all that are afar off, even as many as the Lord our God shall call unto him," for the commission was to "all nations," "even unto the end of the world."   But Peter did not stop here, for "with many other words he testified, and exhorted them, saying, "Save yourselves from this crooked generation. Then they that received his word were baptized; and there were added unto them in that day about three thousand souls."

Now, let us see if we can gather from this brief narrative what agencies God used in bringing about the conversion of these people, and what conditions they had to comply with in order to receive the benefits of the redemption which was provided by the blood of Christ.

AGENCIES

1. The Holy Spirit.

2. The apostles, speaking as the Spirit gave them utterance, testifying of the Christ and pleading with sinners, were the leading human agents in this case of conversion, as they are still and ever will be; for though dead they yet speak through the Gospel which they first preached through the Holy Spirit sent down from heaven. As they were agents then through their spoken testimony, so they are agents now through their written testimony. Their words live in all their vitalizing power, and can never be destroyed.

3. The sinners themselves, guilt-stricken and inquiring, had also an agency in this work which so vitally concerned themselves. It was theirs to attend to the things spoken by the apostles, to hearken to the divine counsel, to learn of Jesus, and to receive the truth that they might be made alive. They had the divinely-given power to do this; and they also had the power to reject the Gospel and die, otherwise the apostle could not say, "Save yourselves from this crooked generation"—seize the help God was holding out from heaven.

CONDITIONS

1. They heard (vs. 8, 11, 14, 22, 37).

2. Believed (vs. 30), in accordance with the apostle's appeal to them, otherwise they would not have been pricked in their hearts.

3. They repented.

4. Were baptized in his name. Thus they entered through these divinely-appointed conditions into the enjoyment of the blessings graciously provided for them through the death and mediation.

This was the first time the Gospel in its fullness was ever preached under the guidance of the Holy Spirit, leading men into the Church of God and into the remission of their sins, under the world-wide commission of Jesus, the Lord and Master; for Peter, in giving an account of the conversion of Cornelius, said: "As I began to speak, the

Holy Spirit fell on them, even as on us at the beginning" (Acts 11: 15). On the first occasion, when the world knew not the way, there was of necessity a demand for a fullness and specificness of direction, a careful and distinct enumeration of the steps to be taken in their connection, and the agencies used, that was not needful in after references; after the steps to be taken and the order was once clearly made known, an allusion to one leading step or point or the order called up all of them. These were the steps to be taken, this the rule to be followed, the fixed directions of the spirit of God, sealed by the blood of Christ, worldwide in its application, and to stand to the end of the world. No human power can abrogate, change or modify this commission of the Lord Jesus, this guidance of the Spirit; and I feel sure that no one can have a well-grounded assurance of citizenship in that kingdom until he has complied with the conditions presented in the blood-sealed commission of Jesus Christ, given under the infallible guidance of the Holy Spirit.

This brings us to the discussion of the second division of the subject—

CONDITIONS OF CONTINUED MEMBERSHIP

To all those who entered into the apostolic Church the exhortation was given: "Putting away, therefore, all wickedness, and all guile, and hypocrisies, and envies, and all evil speakings, as new-born babes, long for the spiritual milk which is without guile, that ye may grow thereby unto salvation" (I Peter 2: 1, 2). They were also taught to "let the word of Christ dwell in them richly" (Col. 3: 16). This was necessary in the mind of inspired men because they realized that to be a Christian was to be like God. It was to be like God in the flesh. Jesus Christ was Immanuel —"God with us" in the flesh. He came in the flesh to take on himself all the feelings, temptations, and weaknesses of humanity, to show what and how the Christian should live. With this in mind it is easy to see that with them the Christian was God growing in the flesh up to the stage of maturity in man and perfection under "the law of the Spirit of life in Christ Jesus." In the growth of the Christian there was a constant but gradual growth of all the desires and affections into the likeness of the character affections that move God; a growth in character in the feelings and in thoughts and in actions to the life and character of God. The Christian's life was a continual growth into a nobler life with God. They were to grow in thoughts and feelings, in purposes and actions, into the likeness of God. Solomon said: "For as he thinketh within himself, so is he" (Prov. 23: 7). The thoughts and feelings that a man cherishes in his heart mold and shape the character and make him what he is. A spirit that loves as God loves and seeks to do good and bless as God does will grow into the likeness of God. They were taught that a man must not only think as God thinks; but that the thoughts must grow into permanent principles cherished in the heart; that they must mold the actions to make him act as God acts. Faith in God made them desire to think, feel and act like God, which is the end and accomplishment of the turning to God.

But all who entered into the apostolic Church did not choose to thus develop themselves into the likeness of God and continue in the fellowship with him, for some were put away. There were reasons for this. Since some were and some were not, it follows that there were conditions of continued fellowship. Some have interpreted the parable of the tares (Matt. 13: 24-30)—"Let both grow together until the harvest"—to mean that there is to be no exclusion from the Church, but this is to make parabolic language conflict with plain, unfigurative statements and historical facts, which is not admissible. The Saviour directed that he who would not "hear the church" should be "as the Gentile and the publican" (Matt. 18: 17). Concerning the incestuous man in the church at Corinth Paul said: "For I verily, being absent in the body but present in spirit, have already as though I were present judged him that hath so wrought this thing, in the name of our Lord Jesus, ye being gathered together, and my spirit, with the power of our Lord Jesus to deliver such a one unto Satan for the destruction of the flesh, that the spirit may be saved in the day of the Lord Jesus" (I Cor. 5: 3-5). And to the Thessalonians he gave practically the same directions: "Now we command you, brethren, in the name of our Lord Jesus Christ, that ye withdraw yourselves from every brother that walketh disorderly" (II Thess. 3: 6). The Holy Spirit mentions the following things as the works of the flesh: "Fornication, uncleanness, lasciviousness, idolatry, sorcery, enmities, strife, jealousies, wraths, factions, divisions, parties, envying, drunkenness, revelings, and such like; of which I forewarn you, that they who practice such things shall not inherit the kingdom of God" (Gal. 5: 10-21).

Those guilty of such things "can not inherit the kingdom of God." Such things are disorderly, else they would not deprive one of the kingdom of God. For those that walk orderly enjoy the divine favor. Since such things are disorderly, and the Church is to withdraw from those who walk disorderly, it follows that the Church is to withdraw from all such. Therefore, the congregation that did not do it, disregarded the law and authority of Jesus Christ. Of course, it is understood that an earnest, faithful effort was to be made to bring such offenders to repentance, and an orderly life; but when such efforts failed, they were compelled by the law of Christ to put them away. Consequently the condition of continuing in the membership of the Church of God was an orderly Christian life, as I have already shown.

CHAPTER V.

THE WORSHIP

Of the people under the new covenant the Holy Spirit, through Peter, said: "But ye are an elect race, a royal priesthood, a holy nation, a people for God's own possession, that ye may show the excellencies of him who called you out of darkness into his marvelous light" (I Peter 2: 9). They constitute a nation—not a republic, but a kingdom— so we read: "Unto him that loveth us, and loosed us from our sins by his blood; and he made us to be a kingdom, to be priests unto his God and Father; to him be the glory and the dominion for ever and ever" (Rev. 1: 6, 7). "And madest them to be unto our God a kingdom and priests" (Rev. 5: 10).

A nation or kingdom of priests is equal to a nation or kingdom without priests. And so the whole Church of God is his lot, heritage, "clergy," or priesthood. As a kingdom, not of this world, though in the world. When on trial for his life, Jesus said: "My kingdom is not of this world: if my kingdom were of this world, then would my servants fight, that I should not be delivered to the Jews; but now is my kingdom not from hence" (John 18: 36). Though on earth, not earthly, and its honors and grandeur are not akin to those of the nations of this world. The subjects of this "kingdom" were born, not of blood, nor of the will of the flesh, nor of the will of man, but of God" (John 1: 13); "born of water and the Spirit." They were all the sons and daughters of the Lord Almighty.

Congregated for worship and service they were not only a priesthood, but their edification was committed to the whole body of male members, excluding from ministering therein only those incapable of edifying. There were elders, required to be "apt to teach," not to be the sole instructors of the church, but taking part therein; securing order and propriety on the part of all.

Every member was taught to attend the worship regularly, but this was not the end. Even if every member attended regularly and punctually, this was not to be the end of the teaching, the worship, the service. These were necessary, because without these the end could not be attained. The end was to excite and secure the active and earnest labor of every member in serving God and teaching and helping humanity. One could not serve God without helping others. He was to help them spiritually, morally, intellectually and materially. The end of all the teaching and training of men in the church was that they might bear fruit in doing good to men. Paul said of Christ Jesus: "Who gave himself for us, that he might redeem us from all iniquity, and purify unto himself a people for his own possession, zealous of good works" (Titus 2: 14). They were to cease to do evil and be zealous in good works. "Faithful is the saying, and concerning these things I desire that thou affirm confidently, to the end that they who have believed in God may be careful to maintain good works. These are good and profitable unto men. . . . And let our people also learn to maintain good works for necessary uses, and that they be not unfruitful" (Titus 3: 8-14). The end of the teaching and the worship was to develop the activity and direct the energies of every member in good works. The first element of true good to others was to bring them into proper spiritual relations to God, for without this no good can be enjoyed. But this spiritual harmony with God must show itself in bringing every thought into harmony with the will of God and so direct the bodily energies as to bring all good—spiritual, intellectual and material—to all creatures.

Every member of the Church was to participate in all the services of the church; and the members not only were competent to do all the work pertaining to the church, but they needed this work and service for their own spiritual growth. In this service alone could the Christian find the food and exercise needed for his growing wise and strong in the inner man. The spiritual man could no more grow strong and active without himself doing the worship and work of the church than the body could grow strong while refusing the food and exercise needed for its growth and life. In this service in the church man could alone find the highest development of the soul and the mind and the body. One could no more worship and do the work in the church by proxy and grow spiritually thereby than he could eat and take exercise by proxy and his body grow thereby. The well-being of every member demanded that he should take active part in the worship, the well-being of the church demanded the help of every member that it "may grow up in all things unto him, who is the head, even Christ; from whom all the body fitly framed and knit together through that which every joint supplieth, according to the working in due measure of each several part, making the increase of the body unto the building up of itself in love" (Eph. 4: 15, 16). The point emphasized here is that every member had his work to do, his office to fill, and by this harmonious working of all the parts the body grew into the well-proportioned body of Christ—the Church. The welfare and development of the whole was dependent upon the proper workings of each and every member.

Every child of God, by virtue of his birthright into God's family, a family of priests to God, had the right to perform any and every service connected with the Church of God, limited only by God's directions and by the ability to do it decently and in order. All were encouraged to take part in the service, and in doing the service each member manifested his talent for the work and trained himself for fitness in God's work.

Every dispensation has had its peculiar worship. That of the Jewish dispensation differed from the patriarchal. The worship under the Christian dispensation is radically different from both. The worship which was acceptable under the patriarchal would condemn a Jew; and that which would justify a Jew would condemn a Christian. During the patriarchal dispensation religion was confined to the family. Every one was his own priest, and he could build

his own altar and offer his own sacrific
for his family. (Gen. 4: 4; 8: 20; Job. ,
the priesthood was changed, and confined
Levi (Ex. 28: 1; Num. 25: 11-13), this v
longer permitted by those included in the Sin.
hence no longer acceptable. It is likewise ,   .e
sacrifices offered by the Levitical priesthood c   . to be
acceptable after the death of Christ and the establishment
of the Church. When Christ ascended to the Father the
priesthood was changed. The high priesthood then passed
into the hands of one belonging "to another tribe, from
which no man hath given attendance at the altar. For it is
evident that our Lord hath sprung out of Judah; as to which
tribe Moses spake nothing concerning priests" (Heb. 7:
13, 14). The priesthood being changed, a change of the
worship follows as a necessity. "For the priesthood being
changed, there is made of necessity a change also of the
law" (Heb. 7: 12). While the worship of the three dis-
pensations had some things in common, each had its distinctive peculiarities. Since Christianity is distinguished
from every other religion by its institutions and worship, it
of necessity follows that, in order to its preservation, these
must be strictly observed. Nothing short of this can preserve the Church from degeneracy and final extinction. As
we have already learned, a fundamental feature of the worship in the Church of God is the *Universal Priesthood* of
its membership. All the members of God's family have
became "a royal priesthood," who no longer offer bloody
sacrifices of the law of Moses, but they offer their "bodies
a living sacrifice" (Rom. 12: 1), and the "sacrifice of praise
to God continually, that is, the fruit of lips which make
confession to his name" (Heb. 13: 15). Since all were
priests, all worshiped God without any mediatorship other
than that of the Lord Jesus Christ. They could all come
with equal boldness to the throne of grace. Such clerical
distinction and arrogance as we have at the present time had
no place then.

That the apostles taught the churches to do all the Lord

manded will not be called in question by those who receive the Bible as authority. Whatever, then, the churches did by the appointment or concurrence of the apostles, they did by the commandment of Jesus Christ. Whatever acts of worship the apostles taught and sanctioned in one congregation, they taught and sanctioned in all, because all under the same government of the same King. But the church in Troas met "upon the first day of the week . . . to break bread" (Acts 20: 7), and Paul exhorts the Hebrew brethren to "consider one another to provoke unto love and good works; not forsaking our own assembling together, as the custom of some is, but exhorting one another; and so much the more as ye see the day drawing nigh" (Heb. 10: 24, 25). From the manner in which this meeting of the disciples at Troas is mentioned by Luke, two things are very evident: (1) That it was an established rule of the disciples to meet on the first day of the week; (2) that the primary object of their meeting was to break bread. And Luke also tells us that the Jerusalem church "continued steadfastly in the apostles' teaching and fellowship, in the breaking of bread and prayers" (Acts 2: 42), which shows us that the breaking of bread was a prominent item in those stated meetings. Other corroborating evidences of the stated meetings on the first day of the week for religious purposes are indicated by the instructions Paul gave to the church in Galatia and Corinth: "Now concerning the collection for the saints, as I gave order to the churches of Galatia, so also do ye. Upon the first day of the week let each one of you lay by him in store, as he may prosper, that no collections be made when I come" (I Cor. 16: 1, 2).

As we have seen that whatever the primitive churches did by the approval of the apostles, they did by divine authority, now, as Paul approved their meeting on the first day of the week, it is as high authority as could be required for the practice of meeting to worship on the first day of every week. The items of their worship were:

THE APOSTLES' TEACHING

They believed that the teaching of the apostles was from

God and they constantly and diligently studied it, that they might know and do the whole will of God. The constant study of and the profound reverence for the Word of God were recognized traits of their character. They certainly had the word of Christ dwelling in them richly. Not only was reading the Scriptures a part of all the public worship, it was a daily custom in private life—in the family, the social circle, and even at their toil. On this point I will give the testimony of Lyman Coleman, who has gathered much information on this subject. He says:

No trait of the primitive Christians was more remarkable than their profound reverence for the Scriptures and their diligent study of them. The Word of God, dwelling in them richly and abounding, was their meditation all the day long. Those who could read never went abroad without taking some part of the Bible with them. The women, in their household labors, wore some portion of the sacred roll hanging about their necks; and the men made it the companion of their toil in the field and the workshop. Morning, noon and night they read it at their meals. By the recitals of the narratives of sacred history, by constant reading, by paraphrase, by commentary, and by sacred song, they taught the Scriptures diligently unto their children; talked of these heavenly themes when they sat in their house, when they walked by the way, when they laid themselves down, and when they rose up. One relates with great delight that he never sat at meat with Origen, A. D. 225, but one of the company read to the other. They never retired to rest without first reading the Bible. So diligent were they in this divine employment that "prayers succeeded reading of the Word, and the reading of the Word to prayer." (Ancient Christianity Exemplified, Page 57.)

Augustus Neander says:

The nature of single acts of Christian worship will be evident from what we have remarked respecting its essence generally. As the elevation of the spirit and heart of the united Church of God was the end of the whole, so instruction and edification by uniting in the common contemplation of the divine Word, constituted, from the first, a principal part of Christian worship. The mode in which this was done might, like the form of the church constitution, be closely connected with the arrangement of the assemblies of the Jewish communities in the synagogues. As in the synagogue assemblies of the Jews the reading of portions from the Old Testament formed the basis of religious instruction, so the same practice passed over into the Christian assemblies. The Old Testament was read first, particularly the prophetic parts of it, as referring to the Messiah; next, the gospels, and finally the apostolic epistles. The reading of the Scriptures was of the greater consequence, since it was desired to make every Christian familiar with them. (History of the Christian Church, Vol 1, Page 412.)

THE FELLOWSHIP

The leading idea of this term is that of joint participation. We have fellowship with God because we are made partakers of the divine nature, as we escape the corruption that is in the world through lust. We have fellowship with Jesus Christ because of the common sympathies which his life and sufferings have established between himself and us. To be in fellowship with him means to take part in his poverty and want, to share in his sorrows, his sufferings and self-denial in this world, as well as to partake of the joys and hopes, the consolations and blessedness of this world, and the hopes and glories of the world to come. We have fellowship with one another because of the mutual participation in each other's affections, joys, sorrows and needs. The word as here used includes the contribution which was regularly made on the first day of every week. Paul says: "Upon the first day of the week let each one of you lay by him in store as he may prosper" (I Cor. 16: 2). The small offering of the poor was as much demanded as the greater ones of the rich, and just as acceptable. The regulation governing this was: "For if the readiness is there, it is acceptable according as a man hath, not according as he hath not" (II Cor. 8: 12). God never valued the offerings brought to him by their intrinsic value, but by the sacrifice made by the one making the offering. It was also required that the worshiper should be liberal and cheerful in giving. "He that soweth sparingly shall reap also sparingly; and he that soweth bountifully shall reap also bountifully. Let each man do as he hath purposed in his heart; not grudgingly, or of necessity: for God loveth a cheerful giver" (II Cor. 9: 6, 7). This shows that a cheerful, bountiful offering to God is but a reasonable measure of liberality. God expected this of every worshiper.

BREAKING BREAD

That the churches in apostolic times met on the first day of every week to partake of the Lord's Supper, is well attested by both inspired and uninspired writers. It is plainly stated that the disciples at Troas gathered together to break bread; and what one church did by the authority of the Lord, as a part of his instituted worship, they all did. That they met for this purpose is not to be inferred, for Luke says: "And upon the first day of the week, when we were gathered together to break bread, Paul discoursed with them, intending to depart on the morrow; and prolonged his speech until midnight" (Acts 20: 7). From the way this meeting is mentioned two things are quite obvious: (1) That it was an established custom for the disciples to meet on the first day of the week; and (2) that the primary object of this meeting was to break bread.

All Biblical scholars and church historians, without regard to denomination, generally concede that the apostolic church observed the Lord's Supper on the first day of every week. Out of the many proofs that might be given of this I will give the testimony of only one. Mosheim says:

The first of all the Christian churches founded by the apostles was that of Jerusalem; and after the form and model of this, all the others of that age were constituted. That Church, however, was governed immediately by the apostles, to whom the presbyters and the deacons, or overseers of the poor, were subject. Though the people had not withdrawn themselves from the Jewish worship, yet they held their own separate meetings, in which they were instructed by the apostles and presbyters, offered up their united prayers, celebrated the sacred supper, the memorial of Jesus Christ, of his death, and the salvation he procured. . . . The Christians of this century assembled for the worship of God and for their advancement in piety on the first day of the week, the day on which Christ reassumed his life; for that this day was set apart for religious worship by the apostles themselves, and that, after the example of the Church of Jerusalem, it was generally observed we have unexceptional testimony. (Ecclesiastical History, Vol. I, page 46, 85.)

This testimony is confirmed by the pagan Pliny in his well-known letter to Trajan (about A. D. 100), written while he presided over Pontus and Bithynia.   He says:

> The Christians affirm the whole of their guilt or error to be that they were accustomed to meet together on a stated day, before it was light, and to sing hymns to Christ as a god, and to bind themselves by a sacrimentum, not for any wicked purpose, but never to commit fraud, theft, or adultery; never to break their word or to refuse, when called upon, to deliver up any trust; after which it was their custom to separate, and to assemble again to take a meal, but a general one, and without guilty purpose." (Epistle X, 97.)

PRAYERS

Simplicity characterized everythintg in the primitive worship.   Consequently the prayers of the first Christians were of the most simple and artless character.   They regarded prayer as a quickening spirit, drawing forth the inward inspirations of the soul after God, and accompanied every important act of their public and private life with this holy privilege, and Paul exhorts his readers to "pray without ceasing."   On this subject Lyman Coleman says:

> The prayers of the Church were offered in language the most artless and natural.   Even the most learned of the apologists and early fathers, such as Justin Martyr, Theophilus of Antioch, Clement of Alexandria, Origen, Tertullian, Cyprian, Arnobius, and Lactantius, who were no strangers to the graces of diction, refused all ornamental embellishments in their addresses to the throne of grace, alleging that the kingdom of heaven consists not in words, but in power.   Their prayers were accordingly offered in the greatest simplicity, and as far as possible in the phraseology of Scripture.   This artlessness and elegant simplicity appears in striking contrast with the ostentation and bombast of a later date.   This contrast appears equally great also in the brevity of these prayers.   It was a maxim of the primitive Church that many words should never be employed to express what might be better said in a few." (Ibid, page 316.)

SINGING

Their singing was a real heartfelt service.   The Holy Spirit said: "And be not drunken with wine, wherein is riot, but be filled with the Spirit; speaking to one another in psalms and hymns and spiritual songs, singing and making melody with your hearts to the Lord" (Eph. 5: 18, 19). And again, "Let the word of Christ dwell in you richly;

in all wisdom teaching and admonishing one another with psalms and hymns and spiritual songs, singing with grace in your hearts unto God" (Col. 3: 16).   In this delightful service the whole congregation doubtless took part.   It has been contended, recently, that the singing of the first churches was not congregational, and therefore our congregational singing is as unscriptural and unauthorized as any musical performance in the worship.   The testimony of history is against this statement.   On this subject Philip Schaff says:

The song, a form of prayer, in the festive dress of pietry and the elevated language of inspiration, raising the congregation to the highest pitch of devotion, and giving it a part in the heavenly harmonies of the saints.   This passed immediately, with psalms of the Old Testament, those inexhaustible treasures of spiritual experience, edification and comfort, from the temple and the synagogue into the Christian Church.   The Lord himself inaugurated psalmody into the new covenant at the institution of the holy Supper, and Paul expressly enjoined the singing of "psalms and hymns and spiritual songs" as a means of social edification.   (History of the Christian Church, Vol. I, page 463.)

To the same effect testifies Lyman Coleman:

The prevailing mode of singing during the first three centuries was congregational.   The whole congregation united their voices in the sacred song of praise, in strains suited to their ability.   Their music, if such it could be called, was, of necessity, crude and simple.   Indeed, it appears to have been a kind of recitative or chant.   The charm of their sacred music was not in the harmony of sweet sounds, but in the melody of the heart. . . .   But, however this may be, the most ancient and most common mode of singing was confessedly for the whole assembly; men, women and children blend their voices in their songs of praise in the great congregation.   Such is the testimony of Hilary, of Augustin and Chrysostom.   "Formerly all came together and united in their song, as is still our custom."   "Men and women, the aged and the young, were distinguished only by their skill in singing, for the spirit which led the voice of each one blended all in one harmonious melody." (Ancient Christianity Exemplified, pages 329, 330.)

CHAPTER VI.

POLITY

By the term polity I mean the organic structure and government of the Church. Nothing is more obvious from the New Testament record than the simplicity which characterized its primitive organization. In this particular Christianity was in marked contrast with Judaism. With temple, tabernacle or altars; without priests or Levites, and almost without ceremonies, it made known at once its character and purpose as spiritual and not carnal, as, in fact, a kingdom of God "not of this world." Its only authority was

THE WORD OF GOD

We have already seen that the only creed of the primitive Church was the central truth of God's revelation to man—"Thou art the Christ, the Son of the living God." The whole New Testament is but an expansion of this thought. The early Christians, in confessing their faith in Christ, accepted the whole revelation of God based upon it as their absolute and only authority. The teaching of inspired men was to them what the New Testament is to us, till their teaching was recorded and the necessity for oral inspiration ceased.

The all-sufficiency of the Holy Scriptures is thus expressed by the inspired apostle: "Every scripture inspired of God is also profitable for teaching, for reproof, for correction, for instruction which is in righteousness: for the man of God may be complete, furnished completely unto every good work" (II Tim. 3: 16, 17). This most evidently refers to the Old Testament as a whole—the book that Timothy had known from his childhood. The teaching of Jesus and the apostles in connection with the examples, the teachings, the warnings of the Old Testament Scriptures, are sufficient to thoroughly furnish the man of God with instruction necessary to carrying out all the requirements of God in every relationship of life. Paul's confidence in the sufficiency of the Word of God is also expressed in these words: "And now I commend you to God, and to the word of his grace, which is able to build you up, and to give the inheritance among them that are sanctified" (Acts 20:32). In the Lord's prayer, just before his arrest and tragic death, he said: "Sanctify them in the truth; thy word is truth" (John 17:17).

From what is here stated it is evident that the early Christians were fully convinced that the Word of God in the work of redemption was all-sufficient for the accomplishment of the following things: (1) Teaching. (2) Reproof —conviction of sin. (3) Correction—for setting men upright. (4) Instruction in righteousness. (5) Build men up. (6) Sanctification. (7) Give an inheritance. (8) And perfection in good works.

Since the Bible furnishes all this, it would be difficult to conceive any want it does not supply. It leaves no room for a human creed, nor any other authority in matters of faith. Hence it is a fact, conceded by all Biblical students, that the apostolic Church accepted the Word of God as its absolute and only authority in all religious affairs.

NAMES

Those who became followers of Christ in the early days of Christianity were designated by several names, all of which were significant. They were called "saints" because they had been set apart to the service of God; "brethren," because of their relation as members of a common family; "elect" because they were chosen of God in Christ by the Gospel; "children of God," because of their relation to him as a common Father; "believers," because of their devotion to Christ and of their faith in him; "disciples," because they were learners in the school of their Master; "Christians," because they were followers of Christ and citizens of his kingdom. It was natural, therefore, that the last name should soon become the most prominent and be freely used by the friend and foe in times of persecution. Peter says: "If a man suffer as a Christian, let him not be ashamed; but let him glorify God in this name" (I Peter 4:16). It was the name that united believers in the government of

Christ, and was the most comprehensive of all the names of those given to those who composed the body of Christ. To be called a Christian carried with it all the honors implied in all the other names.   All these names were worn by divine authority, and were evidently given by inspiration.

CONGREGATIONAL INDEPENDENCE

Each congregation was independent of all others in its government.   They sustained a fraternal relation to each other as parts of the body of Christ, but no one was under the ecclesiastical authority of another.   There is no ecclesiastical authority recognized in the New Testament except that of a single congregation, and that only when acting strictly in obedience to the will of Christ.   From such a decision there is no court of appeal.   On this point I submit the testimony of a few distinguished men, who, while they stood identified with an eccleciasticism ruling the individual congregation, admit that no such thing was known to the New Testament.   Mosheim says:

All the churches, in those primitive times, were independent bodies; or none of them subject to the jurisdiction of any other.   For though the churches which were founded by the apostles themselves frequently had the honor shown them to be consulted in difficult and doubtful cases, yet they had no judicial authority, no control, no power of giving laws. On the contrary, it is as clear as the noon-day, that all Christian churches had equal rights, and were in all respects on a footing of equality.   Nor does there appear in this first century any vestige of that consociation of the churches of the same provinces, which gave rise to ecclesiastical councils, and to metropolitans.   But, rather as is manifest, it was not till the second century that the custom of holding ecclesiastical councils first began in Greece, and thence extended into other provinces.   (Ecclesiastical History, Vol. 1, page 72.)

Concerning the churches of the second century, Mosheim says:

During a great part of this century, all churches continued to be as at first, independent of each other, or were connected by no consociation or confederation.   Each church was a kind of small independent republic, governing itself by its own laws, enacted or at least sanctioned by the people.   But in the process of time it became customary for all the Christian churches within the same province to unite and form a sort of larger society or commonwealth; and in the manner of confederated republics, to hold their conventions at stated times, and there deliberate for the common advantage of the whole confederation. (Ibid, page 116.)

Of the independence of the apostolic churches, Prof. Lyman Coleman says:

These churches, whenever formed, became separate and independent bodies, competent to appoint their own officers, and to administer their own government without reference to subordination to any central authority or foreign power. No fact connected with the history of these primitive churches is more fully established or more generally conceded, so that the discussion of it need not ᵇᵉ renewed at this place. (Ancient Christianity Exemplified, page 95.)

From this we learn: (1) That during the first century and the early part of the second the churches were independent; and (2) that so soon as they confederated for the common interest their independency was destroyed and a tyrannical ecclesiasticism established. Much more might be given to establish the face of the congregational independence of the apostolic churches, but as that is so well established and so generally admitted, it does not seem necessary.

ELDERS

In every fully-developed church in opostolic times there was a plurality of elders or bishops. Luke says: "And from Miletus he [Paul] sent to Ephesus, and called to him the elders of the church. And when they were come to him he said unto them, . . . Take heed unto yourselves, and to all the flock, in which the Holy Spirit hath made you bishops, to feel the church of the Lord which he purchased with his own blood" (Acts 20: 17-28). From this we not only learn that there was a plurality of elders at Ephesus, but they were also called bishops, which clearly proves that the terms "elder" and "bishop" are used synonymously." Of Paul and Barnabas it is said: "And when they had preached the gospel to that city [Derbel], and had made many disciples, they returned to Lystra, and to Iconium, and to Antioch, confirming the souls of the disciples. . . . And when they had appointed for them elders in every

church, and had prayed with fasting, they commended them
to the Lord, on whom they had believed" (Acts 14: 21-23).
From this we learn that *elders* were appointed *in every
church*. That there were a plurality of elders in every fully-
developed church is abundantly proved by historical testimony.

The eldership is the most sacred trust of God to his
church. God is the legislator, the only lawmaker of his
people. His authority is absolute, his power omnipotent.
To the elders is committed the work of teaching and enforc-
ing the laws of God and of guarding them against all perversion or corruption by adding to or taking from, or by
bringing in the customs, traditions, or doctrines of men.
No elder can be faithful to God without holding to the faithful word which is according to the teaching, that he may be
able to exhort in sound doctrine, and to convict the gainsay-
ers" (Titus 1: 9). The Holy Spirit through Peter charges
them to "tend the flock of God which is among you, exercis-
ing the oversight, not of constraint, but willingly, according
to the will of God; nor yet for filthy lucre, but of a ready
mind; neither as lording it over the charge allotted to you,
but making yourselves ensamples to the flock" (I Peter 5:
2-4). Their office is to feed the flock on "the Spiritual milk
which is without guile that they may grow thereby unto
salvation." (See I Peter 2: 2.) They are the guardians
of God's heritage, to keep it from being led away from him.

They are to make no rules of their own, as though they
are the lords or rulers over God's house. They have no
authority save to enforce the law of God, and so set an
example of fidelity to God to be followed by the church.
If elders conscientiously confine themselves to the law of
God, they can give account with joy; otherwise with grief.
The spirit in which this is to be done is given by Paul in his
charge to the elders at Ephesus: "Take heed unto yourselves, and to all the flock, in which the Holy Spirit hath
made you bishops, to feed the church of the Lord which he
purchased with his own blood. I know that after my departing grievous wolves enter in among you, not sparing the

flock; and from among your ownselves shall men arise, speaking perverse things, to draw away disciples after them. Wherefore watch ye, remembering that by the space of three years I ceased not to admonish every one night and day with tears, and now I commend you to God, and to the word of his grace, which is able to build you up, and give you the inheritance among all them that are sanctified" (Acts 20: 28-32). This exhortation was given to guide the elders in their work. A fundamental and all-pervading principle of this counsel is that nothing is to be taught or practiced of the precepts of man. The elders are to guard and preserve the purity of God's word, the faith and peace of the church and so promote the salvation of man.

Their labors were confined to the congregation in which they held their membership, and to which they were responsible for their conduct.

DEACONS

There were also a plurality of deacons in every full-developed congregation. Luke tells us (Acts 6: 3) that the Church in Jerusalem selected seven deacons. It is true that they are not here called deacons, but the work to which they were called corresponds to that of the deacons as described by Paul in his letter to Timothy. The work of both is expressed by the same word in the Greek. Paul addressed a letter "to all the saints in Christ Jesus that are at Philippi, with the bishops and deacons." Hence there were a plurality in the Church at Philippi. This being true, and Jerusalem being the Church after which the others were modeled, I conclude that what was true of these churches was true of all the others.

EVANGELISTS

In the New Testament Church there was a class of laborers called evangelists. Their work differed very materially from that of the elders and deacons. Philip, who was one of the seven that were appointed deacons in the Church at Jerusalem, is the first evangelist of which we have any account. He "went down to the city of Samaria, and proclaimed unto them the Christ. And the multitude gave heed with one accord unto the things that were spoken by Philip when they heard and saw the signs which he did. . . . [And] when they believed Philip preaching good tidings concerning the kingdom of God and the name of Jesus Christ, they were baptized, both men and women" (Acts 8: 5-12). Thence he went, in obedience to the instruction of the angel, "unto the way that goeth down from Jerusalem unto Gaza," where he met "a man of Ethiopia," and "preached unto him Jesus. And as they went on their way, they came unto a certain water; and the eunuch said, Behold here is water; what doth hinder me to be baptized? . . . And they both went down into the water, both Philip and the eunuch; and he baptized him." From this we learn that a deacon may soon develop into an evangelist.

Timothy was exhorted to do the work of an evangelist; hence it is legitimate to infer that he was one. From the letters to Timothy and Titus it appears that the general work of an evangelist was to preach the Gospel in other fields than the congregation in which he held his membership, establish churches and take care of them, appoint elders and deacons when such work was appropriate, and to labor for such congregations as needed assistance, whether with or without an eldership.

PART II

The Falling Away

CHAPTER I.

THE FALLING AWAY PREDICTED

The Saviour, when about to leave his apostles, prayed the Father, that as he till then had kept them, so they might be kept when he was no longer personally with them, adding: "I pray not that thou shouldst take them from the world, but that thou shouldst keep them from the evil one" (John 17: 15). And his prayer was answered, for though Jew and Gentile sought their death, yet they were preserved until the church stood forth in the measure of the stature of the fullness of Christ—till the perfect had come. And what a perfection it was! Perfect unfolding of the love of God, so far as that can be comprehended in this life; perfect exhibition of the plan of salvation; perfect deliverance of the faith; perfected canon of Scripture; perfected church policy; perfected hope, blooming with immortality. The last of the apostles were preserved to the church till the entire apostolic work was done. The perfect had thus come, and apostles were no more needed, and have no more been had.

But notwithstanding perfection so varied, the world is not yet brought to the Saviour. This would surprise us did we not know that departure from the faith and order has been as complete and widespread as could be. This sad condition, however, did not come unawares upon the church, for our Saviour himself, and his apostles, foretold the apostasy, and so minutely that its very existence stands out that prophets and apostles "spake from God, being moved by the Holy Spirit."

In the Sermon on the Mount we have this solemn note of warning: "Beware of false prophets, who come to you in sheep's clothing, but inwardly they are ravening wolves. . . . By their fruits ye shall know them" (Matt. 7: 15-20). These false prophets were men who would tear and rend the sheep to satisfy their own greed; coming not only as enemies, but "in sheep's clothing," arising from among the flock.

On careful examination it will be found that the apostles never taught the disciples to look for an unbroken triumph of Christianity. Paul gives warning to the Ephesian elders concerning grievous wolves who would not spare the flock in the following words: "Take heed unto yourselves, to feed the church of the Lord which he purchased with his own blood. I know that after my departing grievous wolves shall enter in among you, not sparing the flock; and from your own selves shall men arise, speaking perverse things, to draw away disciples after them" (Acts 20: 28-30). These grievous, tearing wolves were to arise, not only in the church, but from among the elders. They would care for the fleece, not for the flock; speaking perverse things to draw away from the truth of God. Paul's epistles repeat the warning to the Ephesian elders in various and awful forms. He wrote his second letter to the church in Thessalonica for the express purpose of guarding the church against the expected return of the Lord before the "falling away" in the church, "and the man of sin be revealed, the son of perdition, he that opposeth and exhalteth himself against all that is called God or that is worshiped; so that he sitteth in the temple of God setting himself forth as God" (II Thess. 2: 3, 4). In this it is clearly set forth that a principle was at work in the church that would work out developments and organizations that would set aside the authority of God. The place or perogative of God is to sit as lawmaker, to make laws for his kingdom and his people, and whoever or whatever proposes to legislate, make, repeal or modify the laws of God, add to or take from what God has said, is the man of sin, the son of perdition. Organizations in the church or over the church to do the work that God has committed to individual Christians and the churches are the works of the man of sin.

Concerning false apostles Paul gave this warning: "For such men are false apostles, deceitful workers, fashioning themselves into apostles of Christ. And no marvel; for even Satan fashioneth himself into an angel of light" (II Cor. 11: 12, 14). It was no wonder that false prophets and apostate elders were transforming themselves into apostles of Christ when their master was setting them the example. All who sought to turn people from God's appointments were ministers of Satan, even though they thought they were serving God. The end of all such shall correspond to their works. From this we learn a needful warning in our day, that a man calling himself an apostle, or the successor of the apostles, is no security that Satan is not his prompter. No wonder, then, the apostasy came soon and lasts long.

In the following the apostle again plainly foretells the apostasy: "But the Spirit expressly saith that in latter times some shall fall away from the faith, giving heed to seducing spirits and doctrines of demons, through the hypocrisy of men that speak lies" (II Tim. 4: 1, 2). Every one that teaches that man can in any manner set aside the law and appointments of God, or substitute man's devices for the order of God, is a seducing spirit that turns man from the truth. Seducing spirits carry on their evil work through men who speak lies in hypocrisy.

Again the apostle brings up the awful subject: "But know this, that in the last days grievous times shall come. For men shall be lovers of self, lovers of money, boastful, haughty, railers, disobedient to parents, unthankful, unholy, without natural affection, implacable, slanderous, without self-control, fierce, no lovers of good, traitors, head-strong, puffed up, lovers of pleasure rather than lovers of God; holding a form of godliness, but having denied the power thereof: from these also turn away" (II Tim. 3: 1-5). The condition here depicted was as certain as important. Timothy was to have no doubt about it, and he was to be continually calling it to mind. The men of the last times were to be "lovers of self" and avaricious. Men had always been so in all ages; but the characteristic of the men in question was that they were to be "holding a form of godliness," but denying the power thereof.

But Paul is not the only one who comfirms the pre-

diction of the Lord.   The whole body of the apostles are at
one on this point.   James says: "Whence come wars and
whence comes fightings among you? come they not hence,
even of your pleasures that war in your members?   Ye
lust, and have not; ye kill, and covet, and can not obtain:
ye fight and war; ye have not, because ye ask not.   Ye ask
and receive not, because ye ask amiss, that ye may spend
it on your pleasures" (James 4: 1-3).   The wolfish work
had already begun; but it was little compared with what
was to follow, when the proud, money-loving priest would
find emperors and kings to arm in his quarrel.   Peter, too,
writes: "But there arose false prophets among the people,
as among you also there shall be false teachers, who shall
privily bring in destructive heresies, denying even the Master that bought them, bringing upon themselves swift destruction.   And many shall follow their lascivious doings;
by reason of whom the way of the truth shall be evil spoken
of" (II Peter 2: 1, 2).

Jude also gives warning against the apostates predicted
by Christ, and Paul, and Peter, and denounced by James.
He says: "For there are certain men crept in privily, even
who were of old written of beforehand unto this condem-
ation, ungodly men, turning the grace of God into lasciviousness, and denying our only Master, Jesus Christ" (Jude
4).   The self-styled vicar of Christ, with all his horde of
dignitaries, and all the multitude of corruptions in other
sectarian bodies, are sure that this can have no reference to
them, because they have never denied Christ; but on the
other hand have filled the world with their various creeds
and confessions of faith.   But it deserves consideration,
whether works are not always more weighty than words.
"Lord, Lord," is loathsome to him in the mouths of the
"workers of iniquity"; and Paul expressly declares that some
"profess that they know God; but by their works they deny
him, being abominable, and disobedient, and unto every
good work reprobate" (Titus 1: 16).

Coming down to John, the last of the apostles, and, in
point of time, nearest to the apostasy, we read: "Little
children, it is the last hour: and as ye heard that antichrist

cometh, even now have there risen many antichrists; whereby we know that it is the last hour. They went out from us, but they are not of us; for if they had been of us, they would have continued with us; but they went out, that they might be made manifest that they are not of us" (John 2: 18, 19). These antichrists were not open enemies, but wolves in the garb of sheep. Then we read: "Beloved, believe not every spirit, but prove the spirits, whether they are of God; because many false prophets are gone out into the world" (I John 4: 1). Not into the world as openly declaring their departure from the faith, but as destroyers thereof by false doctrine, while professing to be servants of Christ. Further: "For many deceivers are gone forth into the world, even they that confess not that Jesus Christ cometh in the flesh." This is the deceiver and the antichrist. They went forth into the world professedly as preachers of the Gospel of Christ, yet denying his true character. Again: "I wrote somewhat unto the church: but Diotrephes, who loveth to have the pre-eminence among them, receiveth us not. Therefore, if I come, I will bring to remembrance his works which he doeth, prating against us with wicked words: and not content therewith, neither doth he himself receive the brethren, and them that would he forbidden and casteth them out of the church" (III John 9: 10). Thus this bloated wolf had acquired such power in the church as to exclude those who held the truth as taught by the apostles. In the last message that God ever made to man, he said: "To the angel of the church in Ephesus write: These things saith he that holdeth the seven stars in his right hand, he that walketh in the midst of seven golden candlesticks: I know thy works, and thy toil and patience, and that thou canst not bear evil men, and didst try them that call themselves apostles, and they are not, and didst not find them false" (Rev. 2: 1, 2). Thus is appears that what Paul informed the elders of the church at Ephesus he knew would come to pass after his leaving them. The wolves in that case claimed to be the accepted apostles of Christ, but were found liars.

CHAPTER II.

THE FALLING AWAY

The origin of the Roman hierarchial system is obscured in pious frauds; but it is certain that it arose gradually. As we have already learned, the apostolic churches had a plurality of elders or bishops. At the first the elders of any particular congregation would select one of their number to preside at their meetings for the transaction of business, and in the course of time he came to be known as "The Bishop." Little by little he came to feel his importance till he was exalted above his fellow elders. This the presbyters would not concede. Divisions arose out of these troubles, and the authority of the bishops, closely united among themselves, came victorious over the presbyters, who opposed them singlehanded. The power and authority of these bishops were regulated by the prominence of the cities in which they presided. As Rome was the chief city of the world at that time, the bishops of cities of less importance regarded it an honor to themselves to concede to the bishop of Rome the pre-eminence in all things; and so he extended his authority from time to time, till almost the whole world bowed to his authority.

The changes which produced this condition are strikingly expressed by Lyman Coleman. He says:

1. In the college of equal and co-ordinate presbyters, some one would naturally act as moderator or presiding officer; age, talent, influence, or ordination by the apostles, might give one an accidental superiority over his fellows, and appropriate to him the standing office of president of the presbytery. To this office the title of bishop was assigned; and with the office and the title began to be associated the authority of a distinct order. Jerome alleges that the standing office and authority of a bishop were a necessary expedient to still the cravings and strife for preferrent which by the instigation of Satan, arose in process of time among the presbyters. Whatever may have been the cause, a distinction began to be made, in the course of the second century, between bishops and presbyters, which finally resulted, in the century following, in the establishment of the episcopal prerogatives.

2. Without reference to the causes which occasioned the distinction between the clergy and the laity, this is worthy of notice as another important change in the constitution of the Church, which gradually arose in connection with the rise of episcopal power. In opposition to the idea of universal priesthood, the people now became a distinct and inferior order. They and the clergy begin to feel the force of conflicting interests and claims, the distinction widens fast, and influence, authority and power centralize in the bishop, the head of the clerical order.

3. The clergy claim for themselves the prerogatives, relations and authority of the Jewish priesthood. Such claims, advanced in the third century by Cyprian, were a great departure from the original spirit and model of the Church derived from Christ and the apostles. It was falling back from the New to the Old Testament, and substituting the outward for the inward spirit. It presented the priesthood again as a mediating office between man and his God. It sought to invest the propitiating priest with awful sanctity, as the appointed medium by which grace is imparted to man. Hence the necessity of episcopal ordination, the apostolical succession, and the grace of the ordinances administered by consecrated hands. The clergy, by this assumption, were made independent of the people; their commission and office were from God; and, as a Mosaic priesthood, they soon began to claim an independent sovereignty over the laity. "God makes the priests" was the darling maxim of Cyprian, perpetually recurring in identical and varied phraseology. No change, perhaps, in the whole history of the changing forms of church government can be specified more destructive to the primitive constitution of the Church, or more disastrous to its spiritual interests. "This entire perversion of the original view of the Christian Church," says Neander, "was itself the origin of the whole system of the Roman Catholic religion—the germ from which sprang the popery of the Dark Ages."

4. Few and simple were the offices instituted in the Church by the apostles; but after the rise of episcopacy, ecclesiastical offices were multiplied with great rapidity. They arose, as may appear in the progress of this work, from different causes and at different times; many were the necessary results of changes in the Church and in society; but, generally, they will be found to have, as their ultimate effect and end, the aggrandizement of the episcopate. They are an integral, if not an essential, part of the ceremonial, the pomp and power of an outward religion, that carnal perversion of the true idea of the Christian Church, and the legitimate consequence of beginning in the spirit and seeking to be made perfect in the flesh. (Ancient Christianity Exemplified, pages 97-99.)

This testimony is confirmed by Neander, who says:

The changes which the constitution of the Christian Church underwent during this period related especially to the following particulars: (1) The distinction of bishops from presbyters, and the gradual development of the monarchico-episcopal church government; (2) The distinction of the clergy from the laity, and the formation of a sacerdotal caste, as opposed to the evangelical idea of the priesthood; (3) The multiplication of church offices. (Church History, Vol. I, page 259.)

Since it has been shown that episcopacy was the outgrowth of a wicked ambition for leadership and power that culminated in the papacy, I deem it important to give ample proof, since it is yet very popular in many of the denominations of this day. I now invite attention to the testimony of Mosheim. He says:

1. The form of church government which began to exist in the preceding century was in this century more industriously established and confirmed in all its parts. One president, or bishop, presided over each church. He was created by the common suffrage of the whole people. With presbyters for his council, whose number was not fixed, it was his business to watch over the interest of the whole Church, and to assign to each presbyter his station. Subject to the bishop and also to the presbyters were the servants or deacons, who were divided into certain classes, because all the duties which the interests of the Church required could not well be attended to by them all.

2. During a great portion of this century [second] all the churches continued to be, as at first, independent of each other, or were connected by no consociations or confederations. Each church was a kind of small, independent republic, governing itself by its own laws, enacted or at least sanctioned by the people. But in the process of time it became customary for all the Christian churches within the same province to unite and form a sort of larger society or commonwealth; and in the manner of confederated republics, to hold their conventions at stated times, and there deliberate for the common advantage of the whole confederation. This custom first arose among the Greeks, with whom a political confederation of cities, and the consequent convention of their several delegates, had been long known; but afterward, the utility of the thing being seen, the custom extended through all the countries where there were Christian churches. Such conventions of delegates from several churches assembled for deliberation were called by the Greeks synods and by the Latins councils; and the laws agreed upon in them were called canons, that is, rules.

3. These councils—of which no vestige appears before the middle of this century—changed nearly the whole form of the Church. For by them, in the first place, the ancient rights and

privileges of the people were very much abridged; and, on the other hand, the influence of the authority of the bishops were not a little augmented. At first the bishops did not deny that they were merely the representatives of their churches, and that they acted in the name of the people; but little by little they made high pretensions, and maintained that power was given them by Christ himself to dictate rules of faith and conduct to the people. In the next place, the perfect equality and parity of all bishops, which existed in the early times, these councils gradually subverted. For it was necessary that one of the confederated bishops of a province should in those conventions be intrusted with some authority and power over the others; and hence originated the prerogatives of metropolitans. And lastly, when the custom of holding these councils had extended over the Christian world and the universal Church had acquired the form of a vast republic composed of many lesser ones, certain head men were to be placed over it in different parts of the world as central points in their respective countries. Hence came the Patriarchs, and ultimately the Prince of Patriarchs, the Roman Pontiff. (Ecclesiastical History, Vol. I, pages 116, 117.)

Concerning this, I note the following facts:

1. That in the second century they digressed so far from apostolic practice as to have one bishop over each church, and that he had his elders under his control. He was the pastor of that church.

2. That there was a confederation of churches into councils.

3. These councils began to be held about the middle of the second century, and resulted in augmenting the power of the bishops and diminishing the privileges of the people. This power on the part of the clergy was not assumed all at once, but gradually assumed as the people would bear it. These councils soon began to enact laws, and claimed authority from Christ to thus dictate to the people.

4. That when the custom of holding these councils had extended over the Christian world, and the Church had acquired the form of a vast republic composed of many lesser ones, certain head men were placed over it in different parts of the world; hence came the patriarchs, and ultimately a prince of patriarchs, the Roman pontiff.

For centuries the struggle between the Church of Rome and the State raged furiously, so that when we reach the age of Hildebrand (A. D. 1073-1085) we find plots and counterplots the order of the day. It was the height of his ambition to subordinate the State to the Church, and subject the Church to the absolute authority of the Pope. The course pursued by Hildebrand and by aspiring pontiffs who succeeded him resulted in an open conflict between the papacy and the empire. In the persistent contest which followed the papacy gained a decided advantage. That the emperor was commissioned to preside over the temporal affairs of men, while it was left for the pope to guide and govern them in inspiritual things, was a rule too vague for defining the limits of spiritual and temporal jurisdiction. The co-ordination, the equilibrium of the two powers was a relation with which neither party would be content. It was a struggle on both sides for universal monarchy. The popes, by strategy and shrewd diplomacy, gained complete supremacy over Western Europe, and for many years the pope was everywhere acknowledged head of the Latin Church.

"It was during the progress of the struggle with the empire," says Professor Fisher, "that the papal power may be said to have culminated. In the eighteen years (1198-1216) in which Innocent III reigned the papal institution shone forth in full splendor. The enforcement of celibacy had placed the entire body of the clergy in closer relation to the sovereign pontiff. The vicar of Peter had become the vicar of God and of Christ. The idea of a theocracy on earth, in which the pope should rule in this character, fully possessed the mind of Innocent, who united to the courage, pertinacity and lofty conceptions of Gregory VII a broader range of statesmanlike capacity. In his view the two swords of temporal and ecclesiastical power had both been given to Peter and to his successors, so that the earthly sovereign derived his prerogative from the head of the Church. The king was to the pope as the moon to the sun; a lower luminary shining with borrowed light. Acting on this theory, he assumed the post of arbiter in the contention of nations, and claimed the right to dethrone kings at his pleasure." In the Church he assumed the character of universal bishop, under the theory that all episcopal power was originally deposited in Peter and his successors, and communicated through this source to bishops, who were thus only the vicars of the pope, and might be deposed at will. Being thus lifted up, he said: "Jesus Christ wills that the kingdom should be priestly, and the priesthood kingly. Over all he has set me as his vicar upon earth, so that as before Jesus 'every knee shall bow,' in like manner to his vicar all shall be obedient, and there shall be one fold and one shepherd." Moreover, he applied to himself the words of Jesus, "All authority hath been given unto me in heaven and on earth." And again, we hear one of them say: "For every human creature it is a condition of salvation to submit to the Roman pontiff." Not only did they assert the necessity of obedience to the pope, but they actually claimed the power to forgive sins and to bestow eternal life. This is a striking fulfillment of what Paul said to the Thessalonians: "He opposeth and exalteth himself against all that is called God or that is worshiped; so that he sitteth in the temple of God, setting himself forth as God" (II Thess. 2:4).

The corruption of the government of the Church naturally led to the corruption of everything connected with Christianity. A departure from the divine government in one thing opens the way for other departures. Such a course will soon cause men to lose sight of the Lord's directions and cause them to follow the doctrines and commandments of men. Prominent among the early departures from the divine order was the substitution of infant baptism for that of believers. This practice originated in the third century, and grew out of the doctrine of original sin. It was contended that baptism was regeneration in the sense of washing away original sin; that infants were depraved by original sin, and could not be saved without this washing away of that sin, and therefore they baptized infants that they might be saved. On this point Neander testifies:

But when now, on the one hand, the doctrine of corruption and guilt, cleaving to human nature in consequence of the first transgression, was reduced to a more precise and systematic form, and, on the other from duly distinguishing between what is outward and what inward in baptism (the baptism by water and the baptism by the Spirit), the error became more firmly established that without external baptism no one could be delivered from that inherent guilt, or could be saved from the everlasting punishment that threatened him, or raised to eternal life; and when the notion of a magical influence, a charm connected with the sacraments, continually gained ground, the theory was finally evolved of the unconditional necessity of infant baptism.   About the middle of the third century this theory was already generally admitted in the North African Church.   (Church History. Vol. I, pages 426, 427.)

To the same import is the testimony of Dr. Philip Schaff. He says:

The practice of infant baptism in the church, with the customary formula, "for the remission of sins," and such accompanying ceremonies as exorcism, presupposes the dominion of sin and of demoniacal powers even in infancy.   Since the child, before the awakening of self-consciousness, has committed no actual sin, the effect of baptism must relate to the forgiveness of original sin and guilt.   This was a very important point from the beginning of the controversy, and one to which Augustine frequently reverted. . . .   Constrained by the idea of original sin, and by the supposed necessity of baptism to salvation, he does not shrink from consigning unbaptized children to damnation itself. . . .   The Catholic doctrine of the necessity of outward baptism to regeneration and entrance into the kingdom of God, forbade him a more liberal view respecting the endless destiny of that half of the human race which die in childhood.   (History of the Christian Church, Vol. III, pages 835, 836.)

The departure from the practice of immersion, the original act performed in baptism, to affusion, was largely due to the idea of the magical effect of water to cleanse the polluted souls of men.   It was believed to contain the whole forgiving power of Father, Son and Holy Spirit.   On this account many put off baptism till death threatened them, that their iniquities might be removed as the King of terrors carried them into the land of spirits.   The first case of the kind on record is that of Novatian (A. D. 251), who was "baptized by affusion in the bed as he lay."   At first this practice caused a schism in the Church, but in the course of time that which was the exception became the rule.   On this radical change from apostolic practice the learned Roman Catholic bishop, Karl Joseph Hefele, says:

The Church has always been tender toward the sick; she has hastened to confer baptism upon them, because it is necessary to salvation; and for that reason she introduced clinical baptism.   (History of Church Councils, page 153.)

There were no serious controversies about the Lord's Supper until the early part of the ninth century, when one Paschasius Radbert, a monk of "great acuteness of mind," wrote a book in which he promulgated the doctrine of transsubstantiation. In this book he took the position that the wine in the Lord's Supper is "the very blood that ran out of the Saviour's side upon the cross, and for that reason water is mingled with the eucharistical wine;" and the bread "is the very flesh of our Saviour which was born of the Virgin." At first the doctrine was repugnant to the cultivated, but it was broached in a rude age, and the monks favored it; the materialistic character of European thought assisted it, and gradually it had a host of friends and was prepared to frown down all opposition. The controversy, however, continued with fury till A. D. 1215, when Pope Innocent III assembled a council in Rome, in the Lateran Church, consisting of 412 bishops, in whose hearing he read seventy canons which he had drawn up; among these was the famous canon which gave transubstantiation a legal place in the Catholic Church. The important part of the canon is:

There is one universal church of the faithful, out of which no one at all is saved; and in which Jesus Christ himself is at once priest and sacrifice; whose body and blood, in the sacrament of the altar, are truly constrained under the species of bread and wine, which, through the divine power, are transubstantiated, the bread into the body, and the wine into the blood; that for the fulfillment of the mystery of unity, we may receive of that which he received of ours.

Another step was taken about 350 years later, when the Council of Trent declared the host an atoning sacrifice:

And, since in the divine sacrifice which is performed in the mass, the same Christ is contained and offered in an unbloody manner, who, on the altar of the cross, offered himself, with blood, once for all; the holy synod teaches that that sacrifice is, and becomes of itself, truly propitiatory, so that if, with a true heart and a right faith, with fear and reverence, we approach to God, contrite and penitent, we may obtain mercy and find grace to help in time of need. The Lord, forsooth, being appeased by the offering of this, and granting grace and the gift of repentance, remit crimes and sins, even great ones; for it is one and the same host, the same person now offering by the ministry of the priests, who when offered himself upon the cross, only in a different manner of offering; and by this unbloody sacrifice, the fruit of that bloody one are abundantly received; only far be it that any dishonor should be done to that by this. Wherefore according to the tradition of the apostles, offering is duly made, not only for the sins, pains, and satisfactions, and other necessities of the faithful who are alive, but also for the dead in Christ, who are not yet wholly cleansed.

This same council further declared:

If any one shall deny that in the sacrament of the most holy eucharist, there is contained really, truly, and substantially, the body and the blood together with the soul and divinity, of our Lord Jesus Christ, and so whole Christ, but shall say he is only in it in sign, or figure, or power, let him be accursed.

Not content with this it declares that:

If any one shall say that in the holy sacrament of the eucharist, there remains the substance of the bread and wine, together with the body and blood of our Lord Jesus Christ, and shall deny that wonderful and remarkable conversion of the whole substance of the bread into the body, and of the whole substance of the wine into the blood, while only the appearance of bread and wine remain, which conversion the Catholic Church most appropriately names transubstantiation; let him be accursed.

The Council of Tridentine says there is a whole Christ in every particle of the Mass:

If any one shall deny that Christ entire is contained in the venerable sacrament of the eucharist, under each species, and, when they are divided, under every particle of each kind; let him be accursed.

The climax of blasphemy is reached when the Council of Trent asserts:

There is, therefore, no reason to doubt but that all Christ's faithful people, in their veneration, should render this most holy sacrament the same worship which is due to the true God, according to the custom which the Catholic Church has always received.

CHAPTER III.

THE CONFESSIONAL

As the mass is the aggregate of the Romish doctrine, the confessional is the chief of the papal system. By it the decrees of the "infallible Church" are applied and carried out with unequaled measure of minuteness and rigor.

That the New Testament requires the confession of sin is not denied; but such a thing as secret confession in the ear of a priest, to secure his absolution, was entirely unknown in the early churches. Even in Rome it was not till about the year 390 that there was a place appointed for the reception of penitents, when they stood mourning during the public service, from which they were excluded. They cast themselves upon the ground with groans and lamentations; the bishop who conducted the ceremony prostrated himself and wept; flooded with tears the people groaned aloud; then the bishop arose from his humble position and summoned up the people, and, after praying for the people, he dismissed them. This custom, with slight changes, was universal. For some sins men were required to do penance during the whole of their lives, and absolution was only granted them in death; but the common course of penance consigned men for ten, fifteen or twenty years to its various humiliating stages. After the long, distressing penance was completed, "the candidate for restoration knelt down between the knees of the bishop, or, in his absence, between those of the presbyter, who, laying his hand upon his head, solemnly blessed and absolved him. The people received him with transports of joy, as one escaped from the coils of the old serpent."

They were then received into communion with the imposition of hands, and the prayer of the whole church for them. The form of their prayer was:

O Lord Jesus Christ, Son of the living God, that takest away the sin of the world, remit, blot out and pardon their sins, both voluntary and involuntary, whatever they have done by transgression and disobedience. And whereinsoever thy servants have erred from thy commandments, in word or deed, or whatever curse or peculiar anathema they have fallen under, we pray and beseech thine ineffable goodness to absolve them with thy word, and remit their curse and anathema, according to thy mercy.   O Lord and Master, hear our prayer for thy servants and deliver them from eternal punishment.

Bingham informs us that the form, "I absolve you," was not known in the practice till the beginning of the thirteenth century.   Thomas Aquinas was one of the first men to write in defense of it.   In his day the expression excited much opposition.   Pope Innocent III, ambitious to establish a number of superstitions, called the fourth Council of the Lateran, A. D. 1215, which declared that "the church has always understood that an entire confession of sins was always appointed by the Lord, and that it is of divine requirement necessary to all who have lapsed after baptism. Because our Lord Jesus Christ, when about to ascend from earth to heaven, left his priests, his vicars, to be, as it were, the presidents and judges, to whom all mortal sins into which Christ's faithful people should fall should be brought, in order that, by the power of the keys, they might pronounce sentence of remission or retention.   For it is plain that the priest can not exercise this judgment without knowledge of the cause, nor can they observe equity in enjoining penalties if men declare their sins only generally, and not particularly and separately.   From this it is inferred that it is right that the penitent should recount in confession all the deadly sins of which, upon examination, their conscience accuses them, even though they be the most secret, and only against the last two commandments, which not unfrequently grievously wounds the soul and are more dangerous than those which are openly practiced."   This invests the priesthood with the prerogative of God himself, who is the searcher and discerner of "the thoughts and intents of the heart."   To this demand all the members of the Catholic Church, whether old or young, are required to bow, as is shown by the twenty-first canon of the Lateran Council, which is as follows:

Every one of the faithful of both sexes, after he shall have reached the years of discretion, shall, by himself alone, faithfully confess all his sins, at least once a year, to his own priest, and strive to perform according to his ability the penance imposed upon him, reverently partaking of the sacrament of the eucharist, at least at Easter; unless perhaps, by the advice of his priest, for some reasonable cause, he should judge that for a time he should abstain from partaking of it; otherwise, let the living be hindered from entering the church, and let the dead be deprived of Christian burial. On this account this salutary statute shall be frequently published in the churches that no one may pretend as an excuse the blindness of ignorance. But if any one should wish to confess his sins to a foreign priest, for proper reasons, he must first ask and obtain a license from his own priest, since otherwise he would not be able to bind or loose him.

The confessional as it exists today is chiefly the work of the Council of Trent, and those who lived in the age immediately after. In order to strike terror to the hearts of all who might refuse to accede to the demands of the priesthood, the Council of Trent published a number of canons on penance, pronouncing the most awful curses on those who refused obedience. I have not space to give the canons, but they teach that the form of the sacrament of penance in which its force especially lies is placed in the words, "I absolve thee," and that this absolution is not in words merely, but that "the ministers of God truly absolve." The priest is declared to represent Christ in the confessional, and therefore is invested with divine attributes and powers. The language used is: "Moreover, in the priest who sits a legitimate judge over him, he should venerate the person and power of Christ the Lord; for in administering the sacrament of penance, as in the other sacraments, the priest discharges the office of Christ." They further teach that the confession of sins to a priest is necessary to salvation; and that every mortal sin, even the most secret and infamous, must be confessed to a priest, otherwise there can be no pardon from God. Thus we see that they make the priest the judge of the soul, and that in the confessional he sits instead of Jesus Christ and that he can keep the sins of any man bound upon him, or loose them, according to his discretion.

In the confessional the penitent kneels beside the priest, makes the sign of the cross, saying: "In the name of the Father, and of the Son, and of the Holy Ghost. Amen." Then with her lips near the cheek of the priest she asks the priest's blessing in these words: "Pray, father, give me your blessing. I have sinned," after which the penitent repeats:

I confess to Almighty God, to blessed Mary, ever Virgin, to blessed Michael, the archangel, to blessed John the Baptist, to the holy Apostles, Peter and Paul, and to you, father, that I have sinned exceedingly, in thought, word and deed, through my fault, through my fault, through my most grievous fault!

Many of the questions of the confessional are too horrible to quote. Were I to do so I would lay myself liable to prosecution by the Government authorities. But every question put by the priest must be answered by the penitent on the peril of damnation; he sits instead of Christ, the penitent is confessing to God, the voice of the priest is Immanuel's; it is the Almighty that is addressing the trembling penitent. And for this reason the priest hears everything, however shocking, shameful, frightful; everything in thoughts, feelings, words, looks and deeds. That the modesty of women should be placed on the rack in the confessional by a bachelor priest, full of curiosity as well as sanctity, and torn and lacerated, under the awful sanctions of the Almighty, is indeed a dreadful thought.

"The confessional is the most odious espionage ever invented by cunning despots. It is the most flagitious outrage upon the rights of husbands and wives, parents and children, the sinning and the sinned against, that ever shocked modesty or ground trembling hearts under its fatal heel. It is strongly believed to be the greatest incitement to vice that a holy God ever permitted; frightful examples of which are on record. It turns priests into odious receptacles for the accumulated stench and nastiness of all the foul corruptions of thousands, making them the sons of the Man of Sin, ready bearers of the iniquities of whole communities." Yes, it is a withering curse, a cruel tyranny, without one redeeming quality, "which the Lord Jesus shall slay with the breath of his mouth, and bring to nought by the manifestation of his coming."

CHAPTER IV.

INDULGENCES

In order to make the absolution effective, the sacrament of confession comprises penances by which the wrongs done are paid. Originally the amount of satisfaction was measured by the time alone during which the state of penance should last. As we have already seen, this situation inflicted the greatest disgrace, and caused the greatest distress of mind. But gradually a change was wrought, and penitents who showed undoubted sorrow were relieved of their penance earlier than the old usage demanded. This abridgement of the long sentence was called an indulgence, and was really the beginning of that system which reached its infamous maturity under Leo X and in the preaching of the wicked Tetzel. In that age no one knew anything of purgatory or the treasury of merits acquired by the saints, and disposed by the Pope; or even of the supreme bishop at Rome, with authority over all the churches and clergy everywhere.

At first indulgences were limited exclusively to church penances, but in process of time they embraced all the temporary punishments due the soul on earth and in purgatory. Christ, it was said, had endured and removed the eternal penalties of sin; but the sufferings short of everlasting continuance must be borne in purgatory, pilgrimages, or be removed by indulgence. The earthly sufferings could be enduring by deputy—any amount of fasting, flagellation or pilgrimage work could be discharged by substitute—and throngs of monks in time of papal darkness were competitors for the repulsive service.

It was argued that when a man performs his allotted task for the day he deserves additional reward or credit for any further services he may render. Such labors are beyond what his agreement demands; they are works of supererogation. So when a Christian leading a blameless life is persecuted and killed, as his sins did not draw his sufferings, these pains were meritorious, they were higher than a man's deserts—these were works of supererogation.   It was claimed that millions of saints in heaven had left a legacy of such merits to the Church, and that in it she had a treasury of good deeds of immense value, incapable of exhaustion, no matter how many drafts, through indulgences, the Holy Mother might make upon it.   Sometimes it was said that that one drop of the Saviour's blood was sufficient for the sins of the whole world, and that all the rest went into the treasury, which the Church might give to souls in purgatory, or rich men on earth who had money to buy it, or to men not so wealthy who had some means.   This was the paid-up capital of the bank of indulgences.   The doctrine and practice of indulgence constitute the very center of the hierarchial system.

In the fifteenth century the disposal of indulgences became a common traffic, and public sale of them was generally preceded by some specious pretext.   Often the pretenses for selling them were in reality bloody, idolatrous and superstitious.   Pope John XXIII empowered his legates to absolve penitents from all sorts of crimes upon the payment of sums of money proportioned to their guilt.   D'Aubigné, in his "History of the Reformation," tells us that when such indulgences were to be published, the disposal of them was commonly farmed out; for the papal court could not always wait to have the money collected and conveyed from every country of Europe.   And there were rich merchants at Genoa, Milan, Venice and Augsburg who purchased the indulgences for a particular province, and paid to the papal chancery handsome sums for them.   Thus both parties were benefited.   The chancery came at once into large sums of money, and the farmers did not fail of a good bargain. They were careful to employ skillful men to sell the indulgences, persons whose boldness and impudence bore due proportion to the eloquence with which they imposed upon the simple people.   Yet, that this species of traffic might have a religious aspect, the Pope appointed the archbishops of the several provinces to be his commissaries, who in his name announced that indulgences were to be sold, and generally selected the men to sell them, and for this service shared the profits with the merchants who farmed them.   These papal hawkers enjoyed great privileges, and, however odious to the civil authorities, they were not molested. Complaints, indeed, were made against these contributions, levied by the popes upon all Europe. Kings and princes, clergy and laity, bishops, monasteries and confessors, all felt themselves aggrieved by them; the kings, that their countries were impoverished, under the pretext of crusades that were never undertaken, and of wars against heretics and Turks; and the bishops, that their letters of indulgence were rendered inefficient, and the people released from ecclsiastical discipline. But at Rome all were deaf to all these complaints, and it was not till the revolution produced by Luther that unhappy Europe obtained the desired relief.

JOHN TETZEL

Leo X, in order to carry on the expensive structure of St. Peter's Church in Rome, published indulgences, with a plenary remission to all such as should contribute toward erecting that magnificent building. The right of promulgating these indulgences in Germany, together with a share in the profits arising from the sale of them, was granted to John Tetzel, a Dominican friar, a licentious wretch, but an active and enterprising spirit, and remarkable for his noisy and popular eloquence. Assisted by the monks of his order, selected as his chief agent for retailing them in Saxony, he executed the commission with great zeal and success, but with no less indecency.

That my readers may have some idea of the course pursued, I give one of his harangues. After the cross had been erected and the arms of the Pope suspended from it, Tetzel went into the pulpit, and with a tone of assurance began to extol the value of indulgences in these words:

Indulgences are the most precious and most noble of God's gifts. This cross has as much efficacy as the very cross of Jesus Christ. Come and I will give you letters, all properly sealed, by which even the sins you intend to commit may be pardoned. I would not change my privileges for those of Saint Peter in heaven; for I have saved more souls by my indulgences than the apostle by his sermons. There is no sin so great that an indulgence can not remit; and even if one (which it doubtless is impossible) had offered violence to the Virgin Mary, Mother of God, let him pay—only let him pay

well, and all will be forgiven him.   Reflect then, that every
mortal sin you must, after confession and contrition, do penance for seven years, either in this life or in purgatory; now,
how many mortal sins are there not committed in a day, how
many in a week, how many in a month, how many in a year,
how many in a whole life!   Alas, these sins are almost infinite, and they entail an infinite penalty in the fires of purgatory.   And now, by means of these letters of indulgence, you
can once in your life, in every case except four, which are
reserved for the apostolic see, and afterward in the article of
death, obtain a plenary remission of all your penalties and all
your sins!

Do you know that if any one desires to visit Rome, or any
country where travelers incur danger, he sends his money to
the bank, and for every hundred florins that he wishes to have,
he gives five or six or ten more, that by means of the letters
of this bank he may be safely repaid his money at Rome or
elsewhere. . . . And you, for a quarter of a florin, will not
receive these letters of indulgence, by means of which you may
introduce into paradise not a vile metal, but a divine and im-
mortal soul, without its running any risk.

But more than this, indulgences avail not only for the
living, but for the dead.   For that repentance is not even
necessary.   Priests! nobles! merchant! wife! youth! maiden!
do you not hear your parents and your other friends who are
dead, and who cry from the bottom of the abyss: "We are
suffering horrible torments!   A trifling alms would deliver
us; you can give it, and you will not!"   At the very instant
that the money rattles in the bottom of the chest, the soul
escapes from purgatory, and flies liberated to heaven.   Oh,
stupid and brutish people, who do not understand the grace
so richly offered!   Now heaven is everywhere opened!   Do
you refuse to enter now?   When, then will you enter?   Now
you can ransom so many souls!   Stiff-necked and thoughtless
man! with twelve groats you can deliver your father from
purgatory, and you are ungrateful enough not to save him!   I
shall be justified in the day of judgment; but—you will be
punished so much the more severely for having neglected so
great salvation.   I declare to you, though you should have
but a single coat, you should strip it off and sell it, in order
to obtain this grace.   The Lord our God no longer reigns.   He
has resigned all power to the pope.

Do you know why our most Holy Lord distributes so rich
a grace?   It is to restore the ruined Church of Saint Peter
and Saint Paul, and those of a multitude of martyrs.   The
saintly bodies, through the present state of the building, are
now, alas, beaten upon, inundated, polluted, dishonored, reduced to rottenness, by the rain and the hail.   Alas, shall these
sacred ashes remain longer in the mire and in degradation?

"Blessed are the eyes which see the things that ye see:

for I tell you, that many prophets and kings have desired to see, and have not seen them; and to hear those things, which ye hear, and have not heard them!"

When Tetzel concluded his discourse he immediately left the pulpit, ran to the money box, and, in the sight of the people, dropped into it a coin, being very careful to make it rattle so that it could be heard by the excited people. This was the signal that "indulgence had established its throne in the place with due solemnity." Confessionals, decorated with the pope's arms, were arranged in convenient places. On "each of these confessionals were posted in large letters the names, the surnames and titles of the under commissaries and of the confessors. Men, women and children crowded around these confessionals, all with money in their hands. Even those who lived on alms found money to buy indulgences!"

After having privately explained to each individual the greatness of indulgence, the confessors addressed the following question to each penitent: "How much money can you conscientiously spare to obtain so complete a remission?" "The demand," said the instructions of the archbishop of Mentz to the commissaries, "should be made at this moment, in order that the penitents might be better disposed to contribute."

To all who should aid in building the cathedral of Saint Peter in Rome, the following graces were promised: (1) The full pardon for every sin; (2) the right of choosing a confessor, who, whenever the hour of death appeared at hand, should give absolution for all sin, even from the greatest crimes reserved for the apostolic see; (3) a participation in all the blessings, works and merits of the Catholic Church, prayers, fasts, alms, and the pilgrimages; and (4) redemption of the souls that are in purgatory. To obtain the first of these graces it was said to be necessary to "have contrition of heart and confession of mouth, or at least an intention of confessing. But as for the three others they might be obtained without contrition, without confession, simply by paying." The intention was to make it appear that whoever possessed money could, by using it in the purchase of indulgences, introduce souls into heaven. The indulgence mongers said:

> As for those who would deliver souls from purgatory and procure the pardon of all their offenses, let them put money into the chest; contrition of heart or confession of mouth is not necessary. Let them only hasten to bring their money; for thus they will perform a work most useful to the souls of the dead, and to the building of the Church of Saint Peter.

The confession over, there was a rush to the trafficker, who examined very closely the dress, manner, gait and appearance of the applicant. The sum required was measured by his judgment of the financial ability of the individual. If he made a mistake about the price set, he was empowered to make the best bargain possible, "and all was to be arranged according to the data of sound reason, and the generosity of the donor." For adultery, polygamy, sacrilege, perjury, murder, witchcraft, infanticide, and fratricide he had a particular tax. In fact, "there was no vein in the gold mine that they did not find the means of working." Tetzel executed the commission with great zeal and success, but with no less indecency. He assured the purchasers that their crimes, however enormous, would be forgiven; that the efficacy of indulgences was so great that the most heinous sins would be expiated and remitted by them, and the person freed both from punishment and guilt; and that this was the unspeakable gift of God to reconcile men to himself.

In order that my readers may understand more fully the frightful extent of the wickedness to which the traffic led, I give the usual form of the letters of absolution, which was as follows:

> May the Lord Jesus Christ have mercy upon thee, and absolve thee by the merits of his most holy passion. And I, by his authority, that of his apostles Peter and Paul, and of the most holy pope, granted and committed to me in these parts, do absolve thee, first, from all ecclesiastical censures, in whatever manner they may have been incurred; then from all thy sins, transgressions and excesses, how enormous soever they may be; even such as are reserved for the cognizance of our most holy father the pope and for the apostolic see. I remit to thee all punishment which thou deservest in purgatory on their account; and I restore thee to the holy sacraments of the Church, to the unity of the faithful, and to the innocence and purity which thou possessedst at baptism; so that when

thou diest the gates of punishment shall be shut, and the gates of the paradise of delights shall be opened; and if thou shall not die at present, this grace shall remain in full force when thou art at the point of death. In the name of the Father, and of the Son, and of the Holy Ghost. Friar John Tetzel, commissary, has signed with his own hand.

This abolished all guilt and fear of hell in the minds of the purchasers, and inasmuch as the sale of indulgences was universally prevalent, the Church of Rome was everywhere triumphant, darkness covered the earth, and gross darkness the people; the children of God were driven to caves and secret places of the earth, hunted by armed bands at the command of the apostate Church. The condition was appalling!

PART III

The Reformation in Europe

CHAPTER I.

JOHN WYCKLIFFE

The Roman Catholic Church, as we have already seen, had reached such a degree of corruption in doctrine and practice, so deep and widespread, that it would seem quite impossible for it to reach further degradation. The name of Christ was everywhere professed, but a devout believer was seldom found. The Christ was hidden that his pretended representatives might be all in all. Justification by faith was denounced in order to open up a trade in indulgences to enrich the papacy by the sale of salvation. The commands of God were openly made void by the doctrines and commandments of men. Apostolic order and ordinances had given place to those of the "man of sin." "The mystery of lawlessness" stood out in full proportions.

And yet, notwithstanding all this, there were forces at work, in different parts of Europe, moving on to conflict and reform that were destined to break the all but universal sway of the papacy. There can be no doubt that the invention of printing, the gradual revival of learning, and the enlarged acquaintance with the Scriptures, all made directly against the then existing conditions. The Reformation was effected and the names of its chief actors have come down to us with deserved honor, and yet how imperfect the work done and the spirit of the doers of it. Measuring both by the doctrine and practice of the apostles can not but compel the conclusion that the Reformation from the first onward needed immense reformation to bring it up to the measures of the divine standard. And still it may be that any nearer approach to a completely scriptural work and spirit would have been quite futile under the existing conditions.

John Wyckliffe, who flourished in the latter part of the fourteenth century, popularly called the "Morning Star of the Reformation," was the first to distinguish himself in fighting against the supremacy of the pope, the doctrine of transubstantiation, and the abuses of the hierarchy. As early as 1360 he became known as the opponent of the mendicant friars who infested England, interfering with school discipline, as well as domestic relations. He exposed the venality and superstition of the monkish orders with a vigor of reasoning and a keen satire. Efforts were made by a commission appointed by the king to have the evil abrograted, and such arrangements were finally made; but the pope soon violated the compact and Parliament again took action against the Roman usurpations. These developments fully opened the eyes of Wyckliffe to the intolerant corruption of the Roman See, and he began henceforth to argue and teach, preach and write, boldly and without reserve against the papal system.

TRANSLATES THE BIBLE INTO ENGLISH

But the greatest work of Wyckliffe for the enlightenment of the world was the translation of the Bible into the English language. But in order to appreciate the difficulties of his task, we should remember that Rome had not only utterly neglected and contemned the Sacred writings, but had interdicted their translation into any vernacular tongue. She claimed that it was not only unlawful, but injurious, for the people at large to read the Scriptures. Nor was this idea left to pass current merely as a received opinion, but it was a subject which was considered by councils, and canons were enacted against it. Not to mention other proofs of this, more than one hundred and fifty years before Wyckliffe had finished his translation of the Bible, in the year 1229, at the Council of Toulouse, forty-five canons were passed and issued for the extinction of heresy and the re-establishment of peace. One of these canons involved the first court of inquisition, and another, the first canon, forbade the Scriptures to the laity, or the translation of any portion of them into the common tongue. The latter was expressed in the following very pointed terms:

We also forbid the laity to possess any of the books of the Old or New Testament, except, perhaps, the Psalter or Breviary for the Divine Offices, or the Hours of the Blessed Virgin, which some, out of devotion, wish to have; but having any of these books translated into the vulgar tongue, we strictly forbid.

In the face of all this, and far more than I can now explain, Wyckliffe performed his arduous task of translation. Of this great work, a competent critic most appropriately remarks: "From an early period of his life he had devoted his various learning, and his powerful energies of mind, to effect this, and, at length, by intense application on his part, and from assistance from a few of the most learned of his followers, he had the glory to complete a book, which, alone, would have been sufficient (or at least ought) to have procured the veneration of his own age, and the commendation of posterity."

While engaged in this work, in the year 1379, he was taken violently ill, and the friars, imagining that his course was now near its end, contrived to visit him. Four of their ablest men had been selected, or a friar from each of the mendicant orders, and they were admitted to a patient hearing. After reminding him of the great injury he had done to their order, they exhorted him, as one near to death, that he would now, as a true penitent, bewail and revoke, in their presence, whatever he had said to their disparagement. As soon as they had done, Wyckliffe, calling for his servant, desired to be raised up on his pillow; and then collecting all his strength, with a severe and expressive countenance, and in a tone not to be misunderstood, exclaimed:

I shall not die, but live to declare the evil deeds of the friars.

Confounded at such a reply, they immediately left him; and he recovered, to finish in the next year his translation of the entire Bible.

As this was before the invention of printing, the translation could only be diffused by the laborious process of transcription; but transcribed it was most diligently, both entire and in parts, and as eagerly read. There were those who, at all hazards, sought wisdom from the Book of God, and their number could not be few. A contemporary writer, an enemy, and in the language of hatred and fear combined, with the wish to damage the cause, affirmed that "a man could not meet two people on the road, but one of them was a disciple of Wyckliffe." Certainly the opportunity was gladly received by the people; and while the word of the Lord did not have "free course," there can be no question that it was "glorified" in the reception given it by many. The same bitter opponent, in the tone of deep lamentation, makes the following remarkable admission about the wonderful progress made in the face of bitter persecution:

The soldiers, with the dukes and earls, are the chief adherents of this sect, its most powerful defenders, and its invincible protectors. This Master John Wyckliffe hath translated the Gospel out of Latin into English, which Christ had entrusted with the clergy and doctors of the Church, that they might minister it to the laity and weaker sort, according to the state of the times and the wants of men. So that by this means the Gospel is made vulgar, and laid more open to the laity, and even to women who can read, than it used to be to the most learned of the clergy and those of the best understanding! And what was before the chief gift of the clergy and doctors of the Church, is made forever common to the laity!

At about the same time another papal dupe, in the same spirit, most vehemently urged:

The prelates ought not to suffer that every one at his pleasure should read the Scriptures, translated even into Latin; because, as is plain from experience, this has been many ways the occasion of falling into heresies and errors. It is not, therefore, politic that any one, wheresoever and whensoever he will, should give himself to the frequent study of the Scriptures.

These men just quoted referred to the period between 1380 and 1400, and it was one, though but too short, which distinguished England from every other country in Europe. However transient, it was one that had much to do with wresting the world from the appalling darkness and ruin wrought by the papacy, and flooding the world with the glorious sunlight of eternal truth. It was all in vain that the bishops, with the primates of Canterbury at their head bellowed and remonstrated with the people, wrote letters to and received letters from Rome, made and executed fearful threats of punishment; the Bible had been translated, the people transcribed and read, and sent copies of it far and near.

In 1400 Parliament enacted a law that gave bishops the power to hand over obstinate or relapsed heretics to sheriffs and magistrates, who were enjoined to have them publicly burnt. In 1401 William Sawtre, a devout man, was burnt at Smithfield as a heretic. Of the many victims, I have only space to mention J. Badby, who was burnt in a barrel; and especially that generous friend of the Reformation, Sir John Oldcastle, who frequently sheltered preachers of reform in his castle, and devoutly did he adhere to these doctrines, since, as he himself attested his whole life through them had undergone a change. . Henry V had made vain efforts to induce him to change from his faith; but he refused to recant, and was condemned as a "pernicious heretic" in 1413. But during the respite granted him, he managed to escape into Wales, where he concealed himself till 1417, when he was captured and executed at St. Giles' Fields, amidst the most barbarous tortures, being roasted over a slow fire. The escape of Oldcastle and the rumors of a Lollard insurrection the following year were made the occasion for fresh measures of persecution. In 1414 it was ordered that all public officials should bind themselves by oath to aid in the extirpation of heresy, and that the lands and possessions of those convicted of heresy should be confiscated.

In 1416 a regular inquisition was instituted in every parish of the diocese of Canterbury. Among the common people, however, the desire for Biblical knowledge continued to spread; secret conventicles were held; and though the persecution, which lasted till 1431, may have crushed the "heresy," the principles lived and spread worldwide, and became the influence that led to reformation in other parts.

CHAPTER II.

WILLIAM TYNDALE

If I were to follow the strictly chronological order, I would here give a sketch of Luther and his work, but as I have given an account of the work of Wyckliffe, it is proper to give attention to the work of William Tyndale, because I am now seeking the basic principle of the return to apostolic purity and simplicity.

At the opening of the sixteenth century, a period of great interest to all the world, were four men—Le Fevre, in France; Zwingli, in Switezrland; Luther, in Germany, and Tyndale, in England—destined to make a great impression on the world for all time. But they were wholly unknown to each other. In France, Switzerland and Germany were the living voices throughout life, of the men raised up, calling upon their countrymen to hear and obey the truth; and so it was in England a century and a half before, in the case of Wyclif. But in the case of Tyndale, the procedure is entirely different, and out of the usual course pursued in other lands. He had, it is true, lifted up his voice with some effect, but he was driven from his native land, never to return. In the other cases the men lived and died at home. LeFevre when above one hundred years old wept because he had not felt and displayed the courage of a martyr; Zwingli, in battle for his country; and Luther, after his noble intrepidity, expired in his sick chamber; but Tyndale was strangled and his body burnt to ashes in a foreign land. Englishmen, Scotchmen and Germans were gathered together against him; yes, men of three nations at least concur to confer upon him the martyr's crown, so that among all his contemporaries, in several respects, but especially as a translator of the Scriptures, he stands alone.

The political and literary condition of England under Cardinal Wolsey did not afford the slightest indication that the Scriptures were about to be given to the people in their native tongue, but the reverse. In justice to that event it is necessary to observe, also, the nature of that connection which had existed for ages between Britain and Rome. Indeed, under Henry VIII it reached its climax. This connection sustained a peculiarly complicated character. There were no fewer than twelve distinct sources of revenue that went directly to Rome. These altogether were operating on the inhabitants without exception, and with as much regularity as the rising and setting of the sun. "It was a pecuniary connection of immense power, made to bear upon the general conscience, which knew no pause by day or night; falling, as it did, not merely on the living, but on the dying and the dead!"

In no other country throughout Europe was the papal system in all its oppressive and fearful integrity more fully maintained. Under the unscrupulous and imperative Henry VIII, who gloried in his knowledge of divinity and prided himself on his orthodoxy, with a prime minister so well known in every foreign court, and who himself yearned for the pontificate, England had become the mainstay of the system. In Worcester diocese above every other part of England was this power of Rome most intensely felt, yet here in about 1484 was William Tyndale born whose labors were destined to work the overthrow of its power in the realm.

ERASMUS ARRIVES IN ENGLAND

Erasmus arrived in England in 1498, and was delighted to find a taste for the study of Hebrew, Greek and Latin so pronounced, and he pursued his studies with great diligence and satisfaction. His zeal so inspired others that the influence of his residence there may be regarded as the opening of a new era in letters in that country. In 1516 the first edition of his Greek New Testament was published, accompanied by a new Latin translation, and spread far and wide. He received the hearty congratulations of his friends, but its appearance raised up a host of enemies.

Notwithstanding the opposition during the period during 1477 to 1526, fourteen editions of the Bible in Hebrew and Greek were published, and not one of the sacred originals had ever been restrained by any government. In fact, at this time, so far from such restraint being imposed in England, it was encouraged; as not a man in high authority seems to have foreseen that the cultivation of the knowledge of the original language would necessarily lead to a translation of the secred volume into the common tongue. Even Henry VII transmitted to the university a royal mandate "that study of the Scriptures in the original language should not only be permitted, but received as a branch of the academical institution." And this was at the period when Tyndale resided at Cambridge and Oxford. The advantages thus combined fully explain the source of the superior attainments in learning which he afterward turned to such wonderful account.

About 1504 Tyndale went to Oxford University, and took his degree of B.A., in 1508. One of the colleges at Oxford had forbidden the entrance of the Greek New Testament within its walls "by horse or by boat, by wheels or on foot." Possibly owing to this enmity Tyndale left Oxford for Cambridge, where Erasmus was teaching Greek and issuing his edition of the Greek New Testament. About the close of 1521 we find Tyndale as tutor in the family of Sir John Walsh, at Little Sudbury, in Gloucestershire, twelve miles north of Bristol. Walsh always kept a good table, and abbots, deans, archdeacons, and divers other doctors who were fond of discussion, were often invited to share his hospitality. In these discussions Tyndale always bore a conspicuous and decided part. He had an uncomfortable way of crushing his opponents by clinching his arguments with a "thus saith the Lord." His outspoken way caused Lady Walsh many an uneasy hour, and she often reminded him that bishops, abbots and others having an income of hundreds of pounds yearly held views the very opposite of his, "and were it reason that we should believe you before them?" Not being so skilled in the use of Scripture knowledge as some in these days of Gospel light and liberty, this was very embarrassing to him, a moneyless man, coming from such a source. In order to strengthen his position with his wavering hostess by the testimony of Erasmus, whose fame was resounding throughout Europe, he translated his "Christian Soldier" into English and presented it to Walsh and his wife. This won her, and they did not invite the clergy to their table any more. This change was attributed to Tyndale, and ever afterward they treasured a grudge against him. Of this opposition Fox says: "These blind and rude priests, flocking together to the alehouse, for that was their preaching place, raged and railed against him; affirming that his sayings were heresy, adding of their own heads moreover unto his sayings more than ever he spake."

TYNDALE RESOLVES TO TRANSLATE THE BIBLE INTO ENGLISH

Fortunately Tyndale has left on record his reflections at this period of his life. He says:

A thousand books had they lever [rather] to be put forth against their abominable doings and doctrines, than that the Scripture should come to light. For as long as they may keep that down, they will so darken the right way with the mist of their sophistry, and so tangle them that either rebuke or despite their abominations with arguments of philosophy, and with worldly and apparent reasons of natural wisdom, and with wresting the Scriptures to their own purpose, clean contrary unto the process, order, and meaning of the text; and so delude them in descanting upon it with allegories, and amaze them, expounding it in many senses, whose light the owls can not hide, that though thou feel in thy heart, and art sure, how that all is false that they saw, yet couldst thou not solve their subtle riddles. Which thing only moved me to translate the New Testament. Because I have proved by experience, how that it is impossible to establish the lay people in any truth, except the Scripture were plainly laid before their eyes in their mother tongue, that they might see the process, order and meaning of the text; for else, whatever truth is taught them, these enemies of all truth quench it again—partly with the smoke of their bottomless pit (Rev. 9), that is with apparent reasons of sophistry, and traditions of their own making; and partly in juggling with the text, expounding it in such a sense as it is impossible to gather of the text itself.

The Convocation of Canterbury had expressly forbidden any man to translate any part of the Scripture in English, or to read any such translation without authority of the bishop, an authority not likely to be granted. The study of the Bible was not even a part of the preparatory study of the religious teachers of the people. Writing against Alexander Alesius to James V of Scotland, Cochlæus, the notorious Roman Catholic theologian, writes about the Bible as follows:

The New Testament translated into the vulgar tongue, is in truth the food of death, the fuel of sin, the veil of malice, the pretext of false liberty, the protection of disobedience, the corruption of discipline, the depravity of morals, the termination of concord, the death of honesty, the well-spring of vice, the disease of virtues, the instigation of rebellion, the milk oı pride, the nourishment of contempt, the death of peace, the destruction of charity, the enemy of unity, the murderer of truth. (Demaus' Biography of William Tyndale, page 358.)

With such a sentiment prominent among the clergy, there is no surprise at the danger to which Tyndale subjected himself when in a warm discussion he revealed his intention. Of this incident Fox says:

Communing and disputing with a certain learned man in whose company he happened to be, he drove him to that issue, that the learned man said, "We were better to be without God's law than the pope's." Master Tyndale hearing that, answered him, "I defy the pope and all his laws; and if God spare my life many years, I will cause a boy that driveth the plow to know more of the Scripture than you do!"

After this, the murmurings of the priests increased to a fury. Such language flew over the country as on the wings of the wind. They branded him as a heretic, and hinted loudly of burning him.

It was now evident to Tyndale that a crisis had been reached, and he saw too clearly that it would be impossible for him to remain longer at Little Sudbury in the home of Walsh in peaceful prosecution of his great purpose. This purpose he was determined to prosecute whatever inconvenience or danger it might bring upon him; and it seemed to him quite possible that he might find that liberty in some other part of England. He resolved, therefore, to give up his position which he held in the family of Walsh. So with the good will of Walsh, he made his way to London, hoping to find in Cuthburt Tunstal, Bishop of London, a liberal patron under whose protection the work might be prosecuted. Tunstal accorded him an interview, acknowledged his scholarship, but said that his house was already full, and advised him to seek a place elsewhere. While in London Tyndale preached at St. Dunstan's-in-the West, and greatly impressed Humphrey Monmouth, a wealthy, educated, traveled cloth merchant, who took him into his house, where he remained six months diligently engaged in translating the New Testament. For this kindness Monmouth was imprisoned in the Tower.

While in London, Tyndale saw men around him led to prison and to death for having or reading the writings of Luther, which were finding their way into England, and he knew well that a Bible translation would be still a more dangerous book.   At last he "understood not only that there was no room in my lord of London's palace to translate the New Testament, but, also, that there was no place to do it in all England.   But Tyndale was not the man to put his hands to the plow and then turn back.   If only a life in exile could do the work, a life of exile he would gladly accept.   As Fox remarks: "To give the people bare text of Scriptures, he would offer his body to suffer what pain of torture, yea, what death His Grace (Henry VIII) would so that this be obtained."

GOES TO HAMBURG

Having now fully decided on going abroad, he sailed direct to Hamburg, about May, 1524, never to set foot on his native soil again.   Scarcely a year before, he entered London with bright anticipations of success, but all his anticipations had been cruelly disappointed, and now in sorrow and sadness he was sailing forth on the untried dangers of solitude and exile.   Had he been able to read the future that awaited him, and which he afterwards so patiently bewailed, "the poverty, the exile from his own native land, the bitter absence from his friends, the hunger, the thirst, the cold, the great danger wherewith he was everywhere compassed, the innumerable hard and sharp fightings which he had to endure," doubtless his loving soul would have been melted with the spectacle, and yet, no doubt, the stout and brave heart would have gone forward, "hoping with his labors to do honor to God, true service to his prince," and bestow unspeakable blessings upon his priest-ridden people.

In Hamburg he diligently applied his whole time to translating, but on being interrupted he moved to Cologne about the first of May, 1525, where he put his translation into the hands of the printer.   Not only was the entire sacred text then translated, but his prologue was composed before he began to print.   At this time John Cochlæus, dean of Frankfort, the watchdog of Romanism," was at Cologne, an exile from his own city on account of uprisings of the peasants against the clergy. He was occupied at Cologne printing a book. In consequence of this he became acquainted with the printers of Cologne, where he heard confidently boasting over their cups that whether the king and cardinal would or not all England in a short time would be furnished the New Testament in English. He heard that there was "an Englishman there, learned, skilled in languages, eloquent, whom, however, he never could see or converse with." Inviting, therefore, some printers to his lodging, and, after exciting them with wine, one of them disclosed to him that the New Testament had been translated into the English language; that it was then in the hands of the printers, who were then printing an edition of three thousand copies; and that the expenses were being met by English merchants, who were to convey it secretly to England and dispense it widely throughout the realm before the king or the cardinal could discover or prohibit it.

Though mentally distracted between fear and wonder, Cochlæus disguised his grief in a cheerful manner; and after having considered sadly the magnitude of the danger, he deliberated with himself how he might conveniently obstruct "these very wicked attempts." So he went to Herman Rinck, a Senator of Cologne, and a knight, well known both to the Emperor and the King of England, to whom he made known the whole affair. On hearing this Rinck went to the Senate of Cologne, and procured an order interdicting the printers from proceeding further with the work. Tyndale contrived, however, to procure the printed sheets, and sailed up the Rhine to Worms about October, 1525; but Rinck and Cochlæus wrote at once to the king and cardinal and the Bishop of Rochester to take the utmost precaution in all the seaports of England, lest that "most pernicious article of merchandise should be introduced." Apparently nothing could have been more complete than the triumph of Cochlæus. He had not only interrupted the printing of the New Testament at Cologne, but had disclosed the secret of Tyndale's intentions to those who were most able to take effectual steps to prevent the introduction of the work in England, if he should ever succeed in getting it printed at all.

This interruption, though felt most keenly at the time by Tyndale, only inflamed his zeal, and the remarkable result was that two editions were issued by him in the same period in which he had contemplated only one.   Thus the hostility of Cochlæus, which, as we have seen, threatened to arrest the progress of the work, only delayed its completion for a time and enabled Tyndale to issue six thousand copies of his translation instead of three thousand.   "Early in 1526 both editions were sent into England in cases, in barrels, iu bales of cloth, in sacks of flour, and in every other secret way that could be thought of."   The reception in England was remarkable.   They were eagerly bought and read to the inexpressible joy and comfort of thousands who had long walked in darkness, and as eagerly proscribed and sought out for destruction.   Sir Thomas More fiercely attacked the translation as ignorant, dishonest and heretical.   In the autumn Tunstal and Warham issued mandates for the collection and surrender of copies.   Tunstal attacked it in a sermon at St. Paul's, and professed to have found three thousand errors in it.   So the cardinal and all the bishops decided that the book should be burned, which was vigorously carried out.   But this was all in vain, for the tide was fairly flowing and it could not be checked.   A formidable organization was ready in England to welcome and circulate the books.   In proportion to the violence with which the clergy condemned the books was the esteem in which they were held by those in England to whom the light was breaking.

BISHOP OF LONDON SUPPLIES MONEY TO PRINT BIBLES

In 1529 Bishop Tunstal went to Antwerp to seize Tyndale's Testaments, and by a singular coincident Tyndale also was there and so it happened that one Parkington, who favored Tyndale, was at Antwerp at the same time.   On being informed by the bishop that he would be glad to buy the Testaments, Parkingham told him that, as he knew those who had them for sale, he could buy "every book of them that is imprinted and is here unsold."   The bargain was made, and as has been said by the quaint chronicler:

The bishop, thinking he had God by the toe, when indeed he had, as after he thought, the devil by the fist, said: "Gentle Mr. Parkington, do your diligence and get them; and with all my heart I will pay for them whatsoever they cost you, for the books are erroneous and nought, and I intend surely to destroy them all, and to burn them at Paul's Cross." Augustus Parkington came to William Tyndale, and said: "William, I know that thou art a poor man, and hast a heap of New Testaments and books by thee, for which thou hast both endangered thy friends and beggared thyself; and I have now gotten thee a merchant, which, with ready money, shall dispatch thee of all thou hast, if thou think it so profitable for yourself." "Who is this merchant?" said Tyndale. "The Bishop of London," said Parkington. "Oh, that is because he will burn them," said Tyndale. "Yea, marry," quoth Parkington. "I am the gladder," said Tyndale, "for these two benefits shall come thereof: I shall get money to bring myself out of debt, and the whole world will cry out against the burning of God's Word; and the overplus of the money that shall remain to me shall make me more studious to correct the New Testament, and so newly to imprint the same once again, and I trust the second will much better like you than ever did the first." And so went forward the bargain; the bishop had the books; Parkington had the thanks, and Tyndale had the money.

After this, Tyndale corrected the same New Testament, and caused them to be newly imprinted, so that they came thick and threefold over into England. When the bishop perceived that, he sent for Parkington, and said to him: "How cometh this, that there are so many New Testaments abroad? You promised me that you would buy them all." Then said Parkington: "Surely, I bought all that were to be had, but I perceive they have printed more since. I see it will never be better so long as they have letters and stamps; wherefore you were best to buy the stamps, too, and so you shall be sure." At which the bishop smiled and so the matter ended.

It so happened that shortly after this that George Constantine was apprehended by Sir Thomas More, suspected of certain heresies. During the time he was in custody, More said to him: "There are beyond the sea Tyndale, Joyce, and a great many of you, I know they can not live without help, and I pray thee tell me who they are that help them thus?" "My lord," quoth Constantine, "I will tell you truly, it is the Bishop of London that hath helped us, for he hath bestowed among us a great deal of money upon New Testaments to burn them; and that hath been, and yet is, our only succor and comfort." "Now my troth," quoth More, "I think even the same, for so much I told the bishop before he went about it."

BETRAYED AND MURDERED

Tyndale's enemies endeavored to decoy him into England, but he was too wary to be so easily entrapped, for he well knew what displeasure Henry VIII felt at his tract, called "The Practice of Prelates," and what penalty the royal indignation would speedily inflict. But his enemies in England, whose power had been shaken by the wide circulation of the English New Testament, were the more enraged against him, and conspired to seize him on the Continent, in the name of the Emperor, and through the treachery of one Henry Philips, a smooth, treacherous villian, in the employ of Stephen Gardiner, after having invited Tyndale to dine with him, had him arrested and had him put in the State prison of the Castle of Vivorde, twenty-three miles from Antwerp, May 23, 1535. The English merchants aggrieved by the loss of an esteemed friend, and by this treacherous assault of their rights and privileges, made every effort to secure his release, but all in vain. The neighboring University of Louvain thirsted for his blood. He was speedily condemned, and on Friday, October 6, 1536, he was strangled at the stake and his body then burned to ashes. At the stake, with a fervent zeal and a loud voice, he chied: "Lord, open the King of England's eyes."

As an apostle of liberty, Tyndale stands foremost among the writers of his day, whose heroic fortitude and invincible love of the truth were heard with a force superior to royal and ecclesiastical injunctions; and "the very flames to which fanaticism and tyranny consigned his writings burnt them into the very hearts of the people, and made them powerful instruments in attacking and converting multitudes to the principles of the Reformation. It is not exaggeration to say that the noble sentiments of William Tyndale, uttered in pure, strong, Saxon English, and steeped in the doctrines of the Gospel, gave shape to the views of the most conspicuous promoters of the great movement, who, like himself, sealed their convictions with their blood."

CHAPTER III.

MARTIN LUTHER

Notwithstanding th efact that the papacy had universal sway over Europe at the beginning of the sixteenth century, it must be noted that, from the beginning of the fourteenth century on, there were insurgents, however varied their cries and watchwords, who were persistent in their denunciation of the priesthood. The hatred arose from their intolerable extortions, which were a galling burden. While the tithing system was an intolerable yoke, the rapacity of the priests went far beyond tithes in their exactions. In speaking of this condition, Seebohm, a Spanish historian, says:

I see that we can scarcely get anything from Christ's ministers but for money; at baptism money, at marriage money, at bishoping money, for confession money—no, not extreme unction without money! They ring no bells without money, no burials in the Church without money; so that it seems that Paradise is shut up from them that have no money. The rich is buried in the church, the poor in the churchyard. The rich man may marry his nearest kin, but the poor not so, albeit he is ready to die for love of her. The rich may eat meat in Lent, but the poor may not, albeit fish be much dearer. The rich may readily get large indulgences, but the poor none, because he wanteth money to pay for them. ("The Era of the Protestant Revolution," pages 57, 58.)

All the efforts at reformation had always ignominiously failed, and the papacy with all its abuses had never been more powerful than at the time John Tetzel was trafficking in indulgences. Just thirty-four years before this time, Martin Luther was born. His parents were poor, but it was their desire to give him the best education possible. When he was fourteen years old they sent him to school at Magdeburg, where he relied upon the liberality of well-meaning citizens to supply his needs. The tuition was free at Magdeburg, but the students were required to provide their own lodgings and meals. The usual custom was for a company of poor boys to band themselves together and sing in the front of the house of the wealthy citizens. Sometimes they would be invited to a meal; at other times they would receive the remnants of a repast or at least some slices of bread.

After a year had gone by his father decided to send him to Eisenach, because he hoped that some of his relatives would take a kindly interest in him; but in this expectation he was mistaken, for as before he was compelled to beg and sing for his bread. Many times young Luther became so discouraged that he made up his mind to return to his home and become a miner like his father. But a very different life was awaiting him. When he had acquired the discipline resulting from the long struggle with poverty, a great change took place.

A FRIEND INDEED

One day, after having been harshly treated at three houses, he was preparing to return fasting to his lodgings; he stopped motionless in front of a house and reflected, "Must I for the want of food give up my studies and return with my father in the mines?" when suddenly a door opens and Madame Ursula Cotta, the wife of a wealthy merchant, stood on the threshold. She had heard the harsh words that had been addressed to him, and, seeing him standing thus sadly before her door, she came to his aid, beckoned to him to enter, and gave him food to satisfy his hunger. She and her husband took a liking to him, and offered him a place at their table and in their family, where he remained for three years. Thus were brought into his life the influences of gentleness and refinement.

A new life now opened to him. Free from care and anxiety as to his sustenance, he was able to devote his whole time to his studies. Here noble influences, very necessary for his future work, surrounded him, teaching him the fine and gentle traits of good breeding that elevated life above the struggle for mere existence and gave to it its peculiar charm. "The strength of his understanding, the liveliness of his imagination, the excellence of his memory, soon carried him beyond all his school fellows."

These years of his school period contributed much towards promoting that higher education which his father was so very anxious that he should obtain. Thus furnished, in the summer of 1501, in his eighteenth year, he entered the

University of Erfurt. Here he applied himself diligently and made rapid progress. He did not merely study to cultivate his intellect. He had serious thoughts about God, and fervently invoked the divine blessings to rest upon his labors. He passed all the time that he could possibly spare from his studies in the university library. Books were very scarce, and it was a great privilege for him to have access to the "great collection of books there brought together." After having been in the university for two years, one day, to his great surprise and delight, he found a copy of the Bible, the first that he had ever seen. His interest was greatly excited. "He was filled with astonishment at finding other matters than those fragments of the Gospels and Epistles that the Church had selected to be read to the people during public worship throughout the year. Until this day he had imagined that they composed the whole Word of God." And now he sees so much of which he had never thought! With eagerness and great emotion he turned its pages. The first passage on which he fixed his attention was the story of Hannah and Samuel, which gave him unbounded joy. He returned to his room with a full heart, saying, "Oh, that God would give me such a book for myself!" The copy of the Bible that had filled him with so much joy was in Latin. After this he returned to the library again and again to pore over this wonderful treasure, and thus the glimmerings of new truth were beginning to dawn upon his mind. "In that Bible the Reformation lay hid."

BECOMES A MONK

Luther's father required him to study law. At considerable expense the necessary books had been purchased, and he had begun to attend lectures on jurisprudence; but for the calling he had no love; and yet, from a sense of obedience to his father, he felt it his duty to follow the path he had prescribed. He was, however, frequently disturbed by the thought of the endangered spiritual condition of those who followed the legal profession. This conflict quickened within him the sense of his relation to the higher law, on which his obedience to his father was based. The sudden death of a friend followed shortly afterward by a narrow escape from death by lightning, in a forest on the way between Erfurt and Eisleben, determined him to obey what he then regarded as the commands of higher law. Terrified by the violence of the storm that was raging around him, and especially by the bolts of lightning that were crashing through the trees, addressing one of the patron saints of his childhood, he cried out: "Help me, dear Saint Anna, I will be a monk!"

The vow thus made was faithfully performed. ' Two weeks later, July 16, 1505, he invited his most intimate friends to a cheerful but frugal supper. For the last time he determined to enjoy music and song. The decision once made all sadness was gone. His intention was to tell no one of his decision, but at the very moment his guests were giving way to their gayety, he could no longer control the serious thoughts that filled his mind. They endeavored to dissuade him from his purpose, but all in vain. Sorrowfully they accompanied him the next morning to the Augustinian cloister located in the town, where he knocked for admission. As they opened, he entered. When the heavy portals of the monastery closed behind him, and the bars were fastened again, he had no idea but that he was separated from the world forever. The great struggle was at an end. Was his soul satisfied? Had he found that for which he was looking—the "peace that passeth all understanding"? We shall see in our next.

Luther was received among the novices of the monastery with sacred hymns, prayers and other solemnities. After this he was given over to the care of the master of the novices, whose duty it was to initiate them into the practices of the monastic sanctity, to observe their actual conduct, and to watch over their souls. Above all things, the will of the novices were to be entirely broken. They were to learn that everything enjoined upon them was to be performed without the least resistance, and even to be the more willing to render obedience the more it was against their own disposition and taste. Inclination to pride was to be overcome by imposing upon them the meanest services. So at the very beginning of Luther's monastic life he was compelled to perform the most degrading work in sweeping and scrubbing, and it afforded those envious of him peculiar pleasure when he, the hitherto proud young master, was ordered, with a sack upon his shoulders, to beg through the town in company with a more experienced brother. He did not shirk from these services; but even desired to perform self-mortifying duties, so that he might the more de· serve God's favors. Of these days Luther says:

I chose for myself twenty-one saints, read mass every day, calling on three of them each day, so as to complete the circuit every week; especially did I invoke the Holy Virgin, as her womanly heart was more easily touched, that she might appease her Son. I verily thought that by invoking three saints daily, and by letting my body waste away with fastings and watchings, I should satisfy the law, and shield my conscience against the goad; but it all availed me nothing: the further I went on in this way the more I was terrified.

From this we see that Luther subjected himself to every possible form of discipline and mortification. He was a model of monkish piety. He says, "If ever a monk got to heaven by monkery, I would have gotten there." No one could surpass him in prayers by day and night, in fasting, in vigils, self-discipline and self-mortification, and yet—had he found what his soul was looking for? There is no mistake. He is as far from peace of conscience as ever. He read the Bible, but a veil was before his eyes. Christ was still to his mind a merciless judge. The righteousness of God, which, according to Paul, was revealed in the Gospel, he took to mean the righteousness which metes out just punishment.

Finally, John Staupitz, the vicar-general of the Augustinian order, a man of sympathetic nature, and one who possessed in a singular degree the power to discern and appreciate the needs of whomsoever applied to him for aid, came to his rescue. Looking into the haggard face of Luther, he said: "Brother, you must obey God and believe in forgiveness." "You have altogether a wrong idea of Christ. Christ does not terrify; his office is to comfort." "You must make up your mind that you are a very sinner, and that Christ is a very Savior." These were starting points for new currents of thought. They shed light upon many passages of scripture. For days and weeks Luther pondered over these words: "The Gospel is the power of God unto

salvation to every one that believeth; . . . For therein
is revealed a righteousness of God from faith unto faith:
as it is written, But the righteous shall live by faith" (Rom.
1: 16, 17). Many years after receiving this help, Luther
wrote:

If Dr. Staupitz, or, rather, God, through Dr. Staupitz, had
not aided me in this, I would have been long since in hell.

Luther now devoted himself earnestly to the study of
theology. Among other writings, he read those of Augustine more frequently and fixed them more thoroughly in
his memory than any others. In 1508 his scholarship received acknowledgement by a call to the chair of philosophy
in the newly-founded University of Wittenburg. As a
professor he made rapid progress, and soon reached a position of great responsibility and influence.

MAKES A PILGRIMAGE TO ROME

"To make a pilgrimage to Rome; to confess in the Holy
City all his sins committed from early youth; to visit the
many sacred places, sacred to the memory of saints and
martyrs; to avail himself of the rich influences offered there;
to read mass in Rome—had been a long-cherished hope of
the young monk. Hardly had he dared to look for its
realization." But all of a sudden he was sent by Staupitz
to Rome to assist in the settlement of some difficulties which
had arisen in the management of the monastic order. On
foot, from monastery to monastery, he and his companion
went across the Alps, and by the picturesque plain of Lom-
bardy passed into Italy. Everywhere his eyes were opened,
and important lessons for the future were learned.

The first sight of Rome inspired him with great enthusiasm. It was a great moment to him. He fell upon the
ground, and, with outstretched hands, exclaimed, "Hail, thou
Holy City!" The visit continued four weeks, giving him
ample time to see the ruins of the Colosseum, tne Baths of
Dioclesian, the Pantheon, and other remains   ast glory.
He visited also the catacombs and other places made sacred
by the sufferings of martyrs, and, above all, those churches
and shrines where "special grace" could be obtained.

The chief attraction, however, was not that of sight-seeing, but the spiritual blessings that he hoped to receive. It was his purpose to make while there an unreserved confession of all the sins that he had ever committed. Although he had made such confession twice before at Erfurt, he expected an especial blessing from the same confession, if made in the "Holy City." Mass he celebrated a number of times, and actually wished that his parents were dead, because, by such services at Rome, he thought that he could have been able to deliver them from purgatory.

But in all this he found no satisfaction for his mind; on the contrary, there was aroused in him a consciousness of another way to salvation which had previously taken root in his heart. While he was painfully climbing on his knees in devout prayer the steps of the identical staircase, as was superstitiously believed, which formerly led up to the palace of Pilate in Jerusalem—in order to receive the rich blessings promised by several popes upon all who would perform this meritorious deed—again and again as he struggled up the stairway, the words of Paul—"the just shall live by faith" —came to him as though uttered in tones of thunder. But Luther never became sensible of any blessing.

Even Rome did not give to his soul the peace for which he longed. On the contrary, his sojourn in the "Holy City," brief though it was, sufficed to convince him that Rome could never supply the needs of his spiritual nature. The high ideals of the sanctity of the worship of the saintly life of the pope and the other ecclesiastical dignitaries, which filled his own soul with aspirations and stimulated him to like endeavors, were rudely shattered. What he saw and heard in Rome was the very opposite of what he had expected. Instead of piety he found levity; instead of holiness he met lasciviousness; instead of seeing pure spirituality, he beheld nothing but carnal-mindedness, greed and self-seeking. Religion was but the cloak which covered up the shame and vice. The white garments of the Church were polluted with the stains of the most disgraceful and carnal manner of living. Wherever he turned he saw hypocrisy and sin. Everything that was to him an object of holy adoration was made the butt of blasphemous jests. Of the impressions made on his mind he wrote:

Nobody can form an idea of the licentiousness, vice and shame that is in vogue in Rome. Nobody would believe it unless he could see it with his own eyes and hear it with his own ears. Rome was once the holiest city, now it is the vilest. It is true what has been said, "If there be a hell, Rome must be built over it."

Yet in spite of all he saw and heard, he "loved the grand old Church" with all his heart. He did not return from Rome an enemy of the Church, nor even intending to reform it. But if ever a man left the "Holy City" thrust down from the heights of zeal and enthusiasm to the very depths of despair, wounded and crushed in spirit, it was the plain, honest Luther. This experience, however, was but another step in his preparation, for he says:

I would not take a thousand florins for missing that visit to Rome. I would constantly fear that I had wronged the pope. But now I can speak of what I have seen myself.

PROFESSOR OF THEOLOGY AT WITTENBURG

When Luther returned from Rome to Wittenburg in the early summer of 1512, Staupitz sent him to Erfurt to complete his training for the doctorate in theology. His advancement was so rapid that by the time he reached his twenty-ninth year he found himself not only installed in a professorship of Theology at Wittenburg, but also with the main responsibility resting upon him for all instruction that was to be given. From that time the presence of Staupitz was not frequent. In this position he did not hesitate to break through all traditional modes of theological instruction.

Luther was still a genuine monk, with no doubt of his vocation. He became the sub-prior of the Wittenburg Monastery in 1512, and was made district vicar over eleven monasteries in 1515. These administrative duties occasioned frequent interruptions of his professional and literary labors. It was his duty, by means of visitations and frequent correspondence, to learn the condition and decide concerning the necessities of each monastery and its inmates. The already thoroughly occupied professor was thus called to a truly pastoral care of an extensive and difficult field. To every one in doubts and perplexities, like those which agitated him, he sought to give the full benefit of his experience.

So far as the record shows, Luther first heard of Tetzel in 1516, just as he was beginning his visitation of the churches. It was reported to him that Tetzel was making a great noise, and some of his extravagant sentiments, which I have already quoted, were related to him, and when he heard this he indignantly exclaimed, "If God permit, I will make a hole in his drum!" Shortly after this he gave warning, not against indulgences, but what he regarded their abuse. "What should be regarded with all reverence," said he, "has become a horrid means of pampering avarice, since it is not the salvation of souls, but solely pecuniary profit that is in view."

He justified the intentions of the pope, but charged that Tetzel had misinterpreted and misapplied them. In a sermon delivered February 24, 1517, he grows in severity. "Indulgences," he declared, "are teaching the people to dread the punishment of sin, instead of sin itself. If it were not to escape the punishment for sin, no one would care about indulgences, even if offered gratitously."

As Tetzel drew near to Wittenburg, attracting larger crowds to his preaching, and as some over whom Luther had spiritual jurisdiction sought to excuse themselves from worshiping of relict and of engaging in revolting sins by producing letters of indulgence obtained from Tetzel, he could not, by silence, connive at what would have carried with it the violation of his fidelity as a spiritual guide. Still it was only after much hesitation, after many of his friends had urged him to interfere, and in deep distress of mind, that he resolved to protest. When he had detremined to do something he went about the matter with a mixture of caution and courage.

THE NINETY-FIVE THESES

The Church of All-Saints in Wittenburg had always been intimately connected with the university; its doors were used as boards on which to publish important academic documents; and notices of public "disputations," common enough at the time, had frequently appeared there. The day of the year which drew the largest concourse of townsmen and strangers to the church was All-Saints Day, so on the day before, October 31, 1517, Luther nailed the Ninety-five Theses protesting against what he regarded as the abuse of indulgences, to the door of the church. Crowds of eager students gathered for hours before the door of the church, intent upon reading and copying the sensational document. The first effect upon those nearest Luther was stunning. Whatever their abhorrence of the methods of Tetzel, and their dissatisfaction of the whole system which admitted of such manifest abuses, the impression was that he had spoken inadvisedly. His colleagues were apprehensive of the results for the university. The Augustinian monks saw the stake in the foreground, and dreaded the disgrace which Luther's presence among them would cast upon their order. For the moment, Luther stood alone at Wittenburg, but copies of the Latin original and translations of it into German were sent to the university printing house and the presses could not print them fast enough to meet the demand which came from all parts of Germany, and "in four weeks they were diffused throughout all Christendom, as though the angels were the postmen." The result was unexpected and startling to Luther.

Many approved Luther's course, saying that the man who was to break the tyranny of the papacy had arisen. In the meantime the opposition was industriously gathering its forces, but the controversy increased the popularity of the theses. Luther was summoned to Rome to answer for his attack on the Indulgence system. To have disobeyed would have meant death. This peremptory summons was construed as an affront to the University of Wittenburg. The officials of the university interfered, with the result that the summons to Rome was canceled and it was arranged that the matter was to be left in the hands of the Papal Legate Cajetan in Germany, and Luther was ordered to present himself before the official at Augsburg. The interview was not satisfactory. The cardinal demanded that Luther should recant his heresies without any argument. When pressed to say what the heresies were, he named the statement in fifty-eighth thesis that the merits of Christ work effectually without the intervention of the pope, and that which said that the sacraments are not efficacious apart from faith in the recipient. There was some discussion, notwithstanding the cardinal's declaration; but in the end Luther was ordered to recant or depart. Luther appealed to a general council and returned to Wittenburg.

On returning to Wittenburg Luther's first task was to prepare for the press an account of his interview with Cardinal Cajetan, the pope's representative at Augsburg. He was careful to take the people of Germany into his confidence, and published an account of every important interview he had; thus the people were able to follow him step by step, and he was never so far in advance that they were unable to see his footprints. The immediate effect of the report was an immense outburst of sympathy for him.

Soon after the interview at Augsburg, the papal court reached the conclusion that it would be to their interest to win him by compromise and kindness. Miltitz, a papal chamberlain, was sent to Germany. On reaching there he found that "the state of matters was undreamt of at the papal court." He saw that Cajetan had never perceived that he had not only to deal with Luther, but with the slow movement of the German nation. He found that three out of five of the people stood with Luther. He wisely resolved that he would see both Luther and Tetzel privately before producing his credentials. Tetzel he could not see, for it was dangerous for him to stir from his convent, so greatly was he in danger from violence of the people. On meeting Luther, he at once disowned the speeches of Tetzel; showed that he was not pleased with Cajetan's methods of action; and so prevailed on Luther that he promised to write a submissive letter to the pope, to advise the people to reverence the Roman Church, and to say that indulgences were useful in the remission of canonical penances.

The letter was actually written and the language is replete with expressions of condescension, and it exalts the Roman Church above everything but Christ himself. He also promised to discontinue the controversy if his opponents would do the same. But Miltitz was not supported by the Roman court, and he had also to reckon with John Eck, who was burning with a desire to vanquish Luther in a public discussion.

The time between his interview at Augsburg and the discussion with the vainglorious John Eck was spent by Luther in hard and disquieting studies. His opponents had confronted him with the pope's absolute supremacy in all ecclesiastical matters, and this was one of his oldest inherited beliefs. The Roman Church had been for him "the pope's house," in which the pope was the house-father, to whom all obedience was due. It was hard for him to think otherwise. He re-examined his convictions about justifying and attempted to trace clearly their consequences, and whether they did lead to his declarations about the efficacy of indulgences. He came to no other conclusion. He also investigated the evidence for the papal claim of absolute authority, and found that it rested on the strength of a collection of decretals many of which were plainly forgeries. Under the combined influence of historical study, of the opinions of the early "church fathers," and of the Holy Scriptures, one of his oldest landmarks crumbled to pieces. His mind was in a whirl of doubt. He was half-exultant and half-terrified at the result of his studies; and his correspondence shows how his mind changed from week to week. "It was while he was thus 'on the swither,' tremulously on the balance, that John Eck challenged him to dispute at Leipzig on the primacy and supremacy of the Roman pontiff." Luther accepted the challenge, thinking that the discussion might clear the air, and might enable him to see more clearly where he stood.

DEBATES WITH JOHN ECK AND BURNS THE PAPAL BULL

The discussion began June 27th and closed July 15, 1519. This is the first time Luther ever met a controversialist of European fame. Eck came to Leipzig from his triumphs at the great debates at Vienna and Bologna, and was and felt himself to be the hero of the occasion. Eck's intention was to force his opponent to make some declaration which would justify him in charging Luther with being a partisan of the medieval heretics, and especially of the Hussites. He continually led the debate away to the Waldenses, the Wycliffites, and the Bohemians. The audience was swayed with a wave of excitement when Luther was gradually forced to admit that "the Hussite doctrines are not all wrong." Throughout the debate Eck's deportment was that of a man striving to overcome his opponent rather than one striving to win a victory for the truth. There was as much sophistry as good reasoning in his arguments; he continually misquoted Luther's words or gave them a meaning they were not intended to convey.

"Triumphant, lauded by his friends, and recompensed with favor and honor by Duke George, Eck departed from the debate." He had done what he had meant to do. He had made Luther declare himself. In his estimation, all that was needed was a papal bull against Luther, and the world would be rid of another pestilent heretic. He had made him the central figure around which all the smoldering discontent could gather. As for Luther, he returned to Wittenberg, disgusted and full of melancholy foreboding. This did not prevent him preparing and publishing for his people an account of the discussion, which was eagerly read and gained for him great favor. In some respects the Leipzig debate was the most important point in the career of Luther. It made him see for the first time what lay in his opposition to indulgences. It made the people see it, too. His attack was no criticism, as he had at first thought, of a mere excresence on the medieval ecclestiastical system. He had struck at its center: at its ideas of priestly mediation which denied the right of every believer to immediate entrance into the very presence of God.

Great men now came to the support of Luther, including Philip Melanchthon, one of the greatest scholars of the age. The conflict between Rome and Luther became one of life and death. In September, 1520, Eck again appeared in Germany with a papal bull against Luther, dated June 15th. It condemned as heresies forty-one propositions extracted from his writings, ordered his works to be burned wherever they were found, and summoned him on pain of excommunication, to confess and retract his errors within sixty days, and to throw himself upon the mercy of the pope. This bull fight brought Luther to a step decisive beyond recall. He met this threat of violence with unshakable courage. He at once "carried the war into the heart of the enemy's territory.   In the presence of a vast multitude of all ranks and orders, he burned the papal bull, and with it the decree, the decretals, the Clementines, and extravagants, the entire code of Romish canon law, as the root of all the evil, December 10, 1520."

When the news spread that a poor monk had burnt the pope's bull, a thrill went through Germany, and, indeed, throughout all Europe. Papal bulls had been burnt before Luther's day, but the actors had for the most part been powerful monarchs. This time it was done by a monk with nothing but his faith and courage to back him.

Rome had now done its utmost to get rid of Luther by ecclesiastical measures, and had failed. If he was to be overthrown, if the new religious movement and the national uprising which indorsed it were to be stifled, this could only be done by the aid of the supreme secular authority. The Roman court now turned attention to the emperor.

Emperor Maximilian died January 12, 1519, and after some months of papal intriguing, his grandson, Charles, the King of Spain, was chosen to be his successor. Troubles in Spain prevented his leaving that country at once to take possession of his new dignities. He was finally crowned on October 20, 1520, and opened his first German diet, at Worms, January 22, 1521.

After the coronation, and especially after the burning of the pope's bull, every step was toward Worms. The decision of the Roman court had not settled the case as to Luther; the bull was slow in getting itself executed; very many thought it were better not executed. Men's minds were not at rest—they wished for some other tribunal to which the case might be referred; in the absence of a general council, the highest authority in the Roman Church, they thought of the emperor and the diet, the highest authority in the State. But if Luther were to appear before the diet, it was not at all clear what the diet was to demand of him or to do with him. There was no need that judgment should be passed upon him; the pope had already condemned him. It was not necessary that the diet should order his execution; the bull made it the duty of any prince to do that without any order. He might be required to retract his teaching, but that had already been done by the bull If the diet should undertake to hear his cause, that would be a virtual denial of the pope's supremacy, and an acknowledgment of the justice of Luther's complaint that he had been condemned unheard. Both parties felt that for the diet to do anything was a reflection on the pope; and yet it was evidently necessary for the diet to do something.

The emperor, too, felt the difficulty. He was a politician from his youth, and his conduct toward the pope, even from the first, was affected by political considerations; but apart from these things, there was sufficient reason for his hesitation and vacillation. He was influenced now by one party now by the other or, as is likely, now by his own independent judgment and now by what seemed to be required of him by his position as the civil head of the Church. On November 28, 1520, he wrote to the Elector of Saxony, directing him to bring Luther to Worms, "in order to give him there a full hearing before the learned and competent persons," and promising that no harm should come to him; in the meantime, the elector was to require of Luther to write nothing against the pope. The emperor was acting on the suggestion of the elector, but between the time of this suggestion and the time of the elector's receiving the letter things had been changed—by the burning of his books he had been treated as a condemned heretic. This offended the elector, and he wrote the emperor declining to require Luther's presence at the diet. The emperor, too, had changed; he had begun to realize that Luther was under the papal ban, and that any place in which he might be was declared under the interdict. Luther, therefore, could not be permitted to come to Worms. If he would not retract what he had said against the papacy he was to stay at home until the emperor should have opportunity to confer with the elector personally.

BEFORE THE DIET OF WORMS

The diet met on January 22, 1521, and on February 10th there came a brief from Rome making final Luther's excommunication, urging his condemnation by the diet and emperor. But there was evident reluctance to proceed against him; something might be accomplished by negotiations. The pope had selected Marino Carraccioli and Jerome Aleander to wait on the young emporer and to represent his case before the diet. Aleander was a clearsighted, courageous and indefatigable diplomatist, a pure worldling, a man of indifferent morals, who believed that every man had his price, and that law and selfish motives were alone to be reckoned with. The defeat of the papacy at Worms was not due to any lack of thoroughness of his work. He had spies everywhere—in the households of the emperor and of the leading princes, and among the population of Worms. He did not hesitate to lie when he thought it useful to the Roman Church. The Roman court had put upon him the difficult task of putting Luther under the ban of the empire at once and unheard.

His speech before the diet was long and eloquent, but weakened by his bitterness and vehemence. He said he spoke in defense of the papal throne, which was so dear to them all. He enumerated the heresies taught in Luther's works. Luther was obstinate, disobedient to the pope's summons, refused to be instructed; the pope had condemned him, and it was the emperor's duty to enforce the condemnation; the laity had nothing to do with such questions except to carry out the pope's decrees; ruin would follow if Luther was not condemned; a decree from the diet and the emperor would restore quiet, and preserve the Church and empire. Such were the considerations urged by Aleander. He sat down amid murmurs of approbation, but he had made no new points, given no fresh reasons.

A few days afterward a representative German, Duke George of Saxony, already Luther's enemy, presented the case of Germany against the pope. There were many things of which he complained, exactions and usurpations, the growth and accumulation of years. A committee of the diet was appointed to draft the grievances, and brought in a long list. With so many grievances against the pope already the diet was in no hurry to take the pope's part against a popular German; the condemnation of Luther, and especially the manner of condemnation, was itself another grievance.

The law required the execution of the pope's bull, and was against granting to a condemned heretic a new hearing before a secular tribunal. It was a case in which the law demanded one thing and expediency and justice another. After a long discussion in the diet it was "held stoutly that no countryman of theirs should be placed under the ban of the empire without being heard in his defense, and that they and not the pope of Rome were to be the judges in the matter."

There was open opposition between the emperor and the diet, and abundant secret intrigue—"an edict proposed against Luther, which the diet refused to accept; an edict proposed to order the burning of Luther's books, which the diet also objected to; this edict revised and limited to seizure of Luther's writings, which was also found fault with by the diet; and, finally, the emperor issuing this revised edict of his own authority and without the consent of the diet."

The command to appear before the diet on April 16, 1521, and the safe conduct were delivered to Luther on March 26th. He was to face in a practical way the question of going to the diet, and for him and his friends the crisis had come. Many of Luther's associates at Wittenberg endeavored to dissuade him from obeying the emperor's mandate. Well it was for his fame, work and cause that he refused to heed their advice. These good-intentioned, but faint-hearted, colleagues were advising him to take a fatal step, one that would have been more damaging to his work than all the machinations of his foes; that would, in fact, have been playing his enemies' game, and bringing the Reformation in Germany to a sudden close. A crisis had been reached where a failure in moral courage in Luther would have ruined everything. He rose to the occasion, and his moral stature was disclosed to the whole world.

The journey seemed to the indignant papists like a royal progress; crowds came to bless the man who had stood for the people against the pope, and they believed he was going to his death for his courage. The nearer he came to Worms, the fiercer became the disputes there. Friends and foes found that his presence would prove oil thrown into the flames. The emperor regretted having sent the summons.

Messengers were dispatched secretly to endeavor to prevent his coming.   Just as he was approaching the city a messenger from one of his best friends in great alarm said: "Do not enter Worms!"   But Luther, undismayed, turned to him and said: "Go and tell your master that even should there be as many devils in Worms as tiles on the housetops, still I would enter it."

On the morning of April 16th Luther entered the city, accompanied by fully two thousand persons.   The citizens eagerly pressed forward to see him, and every moment the crowd was increasing.   It was much greater than the public entry of the emperor.   The news of his arrival filled both friend and foe with great alarm.   On the next morning the "marshal of the empire cited him to appear at four o'clock before his imperial majesty and the states of the empire." Luther received this summons with profound respect.   Thus everything was arranged.   At four o'clock the marshal appeared, and Luther set out with him.   He was agitated at the thoughts of the solemn congress before which he was about to appear.   The streets were so densely crowded that they advanced with great difficulty.   At length they reached the doors of the hall, which were opened to them.   Luther went in, and with him entered many persons who formed no portion of the diet.   And now was enacted "the most splendid scene in history."   As has been aptly said:

Never had man appeared before so imposing an assembly. The Emperor Charles V, whose sovereignty extended over a great part of the old and new world; his brother, Archduke Ferdinand; six electors of the empire, most of whose descendants now wear the kingly crown; twenty-four dukes, the majority of whom were independent sovereigns over countries more or less extensive, and among whom were some whose names afterward became formidable to the Reformation—the Duke of Alva and his two 'sons; eight margraves, thirty archbishops. bishops, and abbots; seven ambassadors, including those from the kings of France and England; the deputies of ten free cities; a great number of princes, counts, and sovereign barons; the papal nuncios—in all two hundred and four persons.   Such was the imposing court before which appeared Martin Luther. The appearance was of itself a signal victory over the papacy. The pope had condemned the man, and yet there he stood before a tribunal which by this very act, set itself above the pope.   The pope had laid him under an interdict, and cut him off from all human society; and yet he was summoned in respectful language, and received before the most august assembly in the world. The pope had condemned him to perpetual silence, and yet he was now about to speak before thousands of attentive hearers drawn together from the farthest parts of Christendom. An immense revolution had thus been effected by Luther's instrumentality. Rome was already descending from her throne, and it was the voice of a monk that caused this humiliation. (D'Aubigne's History of the Reformation, p. 240.)

Into the presence of this august body Luther was led, and the sight of this great assemblage of dignitaries almost paralyzed him. The marshal commanded him not to speak unless he was spoken to, and to answer promptly and truly all questions put to him. The court was conducted with great pomp, but all its solemn apparatus was an empty pageant; for however Luther might defend himself, the sentence had been already arranged with Rome. Aleander had arranged the procedure. After a moment of solemn silence John Eck rose and said in a loud and clear voice:

Martin Luther, his sacred and invincible imperial majesty has cited you before his throne, in accordance with the advice and counsel of the States of the holy Roman empire, to require you to answer two questions: (1) Do you acknowledge these books to have been written by you? [At the same time pointing to twenty books on a table directly in front of Luther.] (2) Are you prepared to retract these books, and their contents, or do you persist in the opinions you have advanced in them?

It was then requested that the titles of the books be read, which was done, and Luther acknowledged them to be his. He was again asked, "Will you retract the doctrines therein?" Then Luther, after having briefly and precisely repeated the questions put to him, said:

I can not deny that the books named are mine, and I will never deny any of them; they are all my offspring. But as to what follows, whether I shall reaffirm in the same terms all, or shall retract what I may have uttered beyond the authority of Scripture—because the matter involves a question of faith and of the salvation of souls, and because it concerns the Word of God, which is the highest thing in heaven and on earth, and which we all must reverence—it would be dangerous and rash in me to make any unpremeditated declaration, because in unpremeditated speech I might say something less than the facts and something more than the truth; besides, I remember the saying of Christ when he declared, "Whosoever shall deny me before men, him will I also deny before my Father which is in heaven, and before his holy angels." For these reasons I beg, with all respect, that your Imperial Majesty give me time to deliberate, that I may answer the question without injury to the Word of God and without peril to my own soul.

Luther made his answer in such a low voice that those who were sitting near him could scarcely hear him. Many present inferred that Luther's low voice indicated that his spirit was broken, and that he was greatly alarmed. But from what followed it is evident that Luther's whole procedure on this first appearance before the diet was intended to defeat the intrigues of Aleander, which had for their aim to prevent Luther addressing the diet in a long speech; and in this he succeeded.

The emperor expressed the opinion that the question was one for which Luther ought to be prepared to make immediate answer; but after much delay and consultation with his advisers he granted Luther's request for a postponement until the next day at the same hour. Then he was required to present himself before the diet on April 18th. After he had been called on the following day, Eck began by reproving him for asking for further time for consideration, and then proceeded to put a second question, somewhat modified and more in conformity to the ideals of the States: "Will you defend all the books that you have acknowledged as your own, or recant some of them?"

Luther had now freed himself from the web of intrigue that Aleander had so skillfully woven around him to compel him to silence, and stood forth a free German to plead his cause before the most illustrious audience Germany could offer to any of her sons, before which he made a deliberate reply in a firm and decided tone. He divided his books into three classes. The first were written for the edification of believers, and his adversaries admitted them to be harmless, and even useful. He could not retract these. Were he to do it, he would be the only man doing so. In other books he had attacked pernicious laws and doctrines of the papacy, which, as no one could deny, tortured the consciences of Christians and also tyrannically devoured the property of the German nation; if he should recant these he would be but adding to the force of the Roman tyranny, and opening, not merely the windows, but the doors, to great impiety, and make himself a disgraceful abettor of wickedness and oppression. In the third place, he had written against persons who defend and sanction this tyranny, and aiming at annihilating these pious teachings; against them he said he had possibly been more severe than he should have been, and that he did not claim that his conduct had always been faultless. "But the question," said he, "is not concerning my conduct, but concerning the doctrine of Christ; and therefore I could not recant these writings, for Rome would make use of such disavowal to extend her oppression. I demand the evidence against me, and a fair trial. I stand here ready, if any one can prove me to have written falsely, to recant my errors, and to throw my books into the fire with my own hands." In conclusion he uttered an earnest admonition to the emperor, and the empire, that instead of securing peace and quiet by a condemnation of the divine Word, they would, on the other hand, open the floodgate of untold miseries and evils that can not be conceived. He did not mean to say that his distinguished hearers required this admonition, but that he could not refrain from discharging this duty in behalf of his beloved Germany.

"It was a brave speech, a strong speech, delivered with self-possession and in a clear voice that could be heard by the whole assembly—a striking contrast in every way to his manner of the previous day." When Luther had finished, Eck addressed him in a threatening manner, and told him that he had not answered the question; that this was not an occasion for general discussion, but to ascertain from him whether he would retract his errors. "In some of your books you deny the decision of councils and that they have often erred and contradicted the Holy Scriptures. Will you recant or reaffirm what you have said about them? The emperor demands a plain answer."

To which Luther replied:

Well then, since His Imperial Majesty wants a plain answer, I will give him one without horns or teeth. Unless I am convinced of error by the testimony of Scriptures or clear arguments—for I believe neither the pope nor the councils alone, which have erred and contradicted each other often—I am convinced by the passages of Scripture which I have cited, and my conscience is bound by the Word of God. I can not and will not recant anything, for it is neither safe nor right to act against one's conscience. Such is my profession of faith, and expect no other from me. Here I stand, I can not do otherwise. God help me, Amen!

In astonishment, the emperor suggested the question whether Luther actually was of the opinion that councils could err, and he was promptly answered by Luther:

Of course; because they have often erred. For, since the council of Constance decided in many points against the clear text of Holy Scripture, Holy Scripture forces me to say that councils have erred.

Eck declared that it could not be proved that general councils had erred. Luther said he could prove they had. The disputation that they said they would avoid was beginning. The emperor, seeing this, arose, and all the assembly with him. Eck cried out in a loud, clear voice: "The diet will meet again to-morrow to hear the emperor's opinion." It was night; each man retired to his home in darkness. Two imperial officers escorted Luther. Some supposed that his fate was decided and that they were leading him to prison, whence he would never return till he was brought out to be burned at the stake. A great tumult arose. Some cried out, "Are they taking him to prison?" "No," replied Luther, "they are only accompanying me to my hotel." At these words the excitement subsided.

UNDER IMPERIAL BAN

Luther had produced a profound impression on the chiefs of the empire, and many lords and princes were won to his cause. On the next morning the emperor submitted to the estates of the empire the proposition to immediately dismiss Luther, and then on the expiration of his self-conduct, to proceed against him as a heretic. On May 26th, after a majority of the diet had departed from Worms, an imperial edict against Luther was passed, and published as the "unanimous act of the Electors of the States." In order to make it appear that the emperor's signature was affixed when all the members of the diet were assembled, it was dated May 8th. It decreed against Luther the imperial ban; after applying to him the usual severe expressions of the papal bulls, it said:

Under the pain of incurring the penalties due to the crime of high treason, we forbid you to harbor the said Luther after the appointed term shall be expired, to conceal him, to give him food or drink, or to furnish him, by word or by deed, publicly or secretly, with any kind of succor whatever.   We enjoin you, moreover, to seize him, or cause him to be seized, wherever you may find him, to bring him before us without any delay, or to keep him safe in custody, until you have learned from us in what manner you are to act toward him, and have received the reward due to your labors in so holy a work.

Thus the diet of Worms added to the pope's excommunication the ban of the emperor.   The bold stand of the poor monk, in the face of the combined civil and ecclesiastical powers of the age, is one of the sublimest scenes in history, and marks an epoch in the progress of freedom.   The disaffections with the various abuses of Rome and the desire for free preaching of the Gosped were so extensive that the Reformation, both in its negative and positive features, spread in spite of the pope's bull and the emperor's ban, and gained a foothold before 1530 in the greater part of Northern Germany.

Among the principal causes of this rapid progress were the writings of the reformers, Luther's German Bible, and the evangelical hymns, which introduced the new ideas into public worship and the hearts of the people.

On leaving Worms, after having gone some distance, Luther dismissed the imperial herald and proceeded leisurely, attended by only two friends.   Toward night on May 4th, as he was in a lonely part of the wood, a band of armed horsemen suddenly appeared and surrounded the carriage. His friends supposed themselves attacked by bandits; one of them fled for his life, the other, Amisdorf, went on to Wittenberg with the news that Luther was violently dragged away and his fate was unknown.   As the weeks passed and nothing was heard of him, the people were filled with anxiety.   Even his enemies rejoiced with trembling when they heard that he had disappeared, for things were in such a state that "Luther dead might well be more troublesome to them than Luther living."

Luther has left no record of his feelings when he was dragged from his carriage, mounted on a horse and spirited away.   If he at first supposed himself to be a real captive he was soon informed that he was in the hands of friends. He was taken in the darkness and silence of the night to the castle at Wartburg, eight miles distant, by the order of the Elector Frederick, as a means of protecting him, where he spent the next ten months.   He doffed his monk's gown, put on the garb of a country gentleman, let his beard grow, and was known as "Junker George."   His time was spent in meditation, translating the New Testament into German and writing.

At Wartburg he began that course of interference with political administration and ecclesiastical organization which made his later years as a reformer so different from his earlier, and in the end led him to the practical denial of nearly every principle that he had affirmed.   His own protection by the Elector Frederick against the combined power of pope and emperor made clear to him, he thought, the method by which a reformation might be attempted.   While at Wartburg he thought out and wrote what he entitled, "Warning to all Christians to Abstain from Rebellion and Sedition," in which he maintained the principle from which he never thereafter departed, that the civil Rulers had both the right and the duty to undertake the reformation of the church, and that any other principle was impracticable and dangerous.   That there be no mistaking his meaning I give his words:

> Therefore have regard to the rulers.   So long as they undertake nothing and give no command, keep quiet with hand, mouth and heart, and undertake nothing.   If you can persuade rulers to undertake and command, you may do it.   If they will not you should not.   But if you proceed, you are wrong and much worse than the other party.

This no doubt was called forth by the news of the proceedings at Wittenberg.   For even with Luther away, Wittenberg, with its growing, aggressive university, was the center of the Reformation.   New thoughts had been put into men's minds, new aspirations, new purposes had come into their hearts.   Luther had long before preached that the mass was wrong, but had gone right along celebrating it, and so had he taught about other things, but continued to practice them.   His teaching had taken deep root, and Zwilling, chaplain of the Augustinian convent, a bold, zealous and eloquent man, who had the confidence of the people, declared that the mass ought to be abolished and that it was a sin to celebrate it. "The members of the convnt, the prior excepted, agreed with him. The prior asserted his authority; the monks rebelled; the elector interfered and referred the case to the university. The university decided in favor of Zwilling and the monks, Melanchthon writing the opinion." He attacked earnestly and bitterly monastic vows, celibacy, clerical garb, the use of images and pictures in the churches. His teaching strongly implied that liberty could not be attained till all these things were swept away.

The movement to put these exhortations into practice began first among the clergy. Two priests in parishes near Wittenberg married; several monks left their cloisters and donned the garments of the common people; Melanchthon and several of his students "communicated in both kinds in the church," and his example was followed by others. Images were condemned and cast out of the churches. No one knew what would next be done, and disturbing rumors were being circulated. Carlstadt now took the lead and announced that on the first day of the new year he would "celebrate the Lord's Supper after the ancient manner in both kinds. When opposition threatened he anticipated the time and held the service on Christmas day. A beginning was made; opposition was silenced and Carlstadt had his way."

Things were going too fast for the Elector Frederick, too fast for Luther. In his quiet retreat in Wartburg he wrote against the mass and monkish vows, "but how great a step there is between condemning old customs in our hearts and changing them with our hands—between the thoughts and the act!" On being informed of the reformatory movements in Wittenberg, Luther resented it, and most sharply reproved them for practicing what he had preached. In a letter written to the Wittenbergers in December, 1521, he said:

They have introduced changes in the mass and images, attacked the sacrament and other things that are of no account, and have let love and faith go; just as though all the world hereabouts had great understanding in these matters, which is not the fact; and so many have brought it about that many pious people have been stirred up to do what is really the devil's work. It would, indeed, be a good thing to begin such changes,

if we could all together have the needful faith; and if they
suited the church in such measure that no one could take offense
at them.   But this can never be.   We can not all be as Carlstadt.   Therefore we must yield to the weak; otherwise those
who are strong will run far, and the weak who can not follow
them at like pace will be run down.

It was not by Luther, but by men of a different type, that
this practical work was begun.   There was sore need for a
Zwilling and a Carlstadt.   This was an occasion when those
who were called fanatics did a real service for mankind.
They were strong in their convictions, saw only one thing,
reckless of all consequences, and brave where other men are
appalled, and with no misgivings kindled a fire that wrapped
the world in flame.   Had it not been for what they did,
"Luther's writing and preaching might have ended in preaching and writing.   They saw that something must be done,
and they did it!"   While this was needful in precipitating
the conflict, it was equally necessary that others should
direct it.

The excitement at Wittenberg soon reached an alarming
height, and was intensified by the arrival of the Zwickan
prophets, who claimed to be the first to have properly received the divine Spirit, and to have been called to carry
on God's work.   They boasted of prophetic visions, dreams
and direct communications with God.   They also rejected
infant baptism, saying that there was no such thing taught
in the Scriptures.   The people, losing their hold on the
old, were ready to take up with anything that came with a
plausible face.   Even the most prudent were afraid to condemn anything that might have truth in it, and especially
were they unwilling to reject anything that seemed to be
taught in the Scripture.   Melanchthon was greatly troubled
and disturbed.   It was not so much the visions of the
Zwickan prophets that disturbed him as their teaching on
baptism, and instead of settling the matter by an appeal to
the Word of God, he referred it to the Elector Frederick,
who advised him not to discuss the subject with them, but
wait for Luther, for they quoted Saint Augustine to prove
that nothing could be brought in favor of infant baptism
except ecclesiastical custom.

RETAINS THAT WHICH THE SCRIPTURES DO NOT EXPRESSLY FORBID

Luther returned from Wartburg to Wittenberg in the early part of 1522, when efforts were made to get him to drop infant baptism and make the Reformation thorough. But while translating the Bible, at Wartburg, he had determined to retain whatever practices it did not forbid. At first he had no little struggle on the subject of infant baptism. On other subjects he had been forced, against his will, step by step, to abandon the fathers, the councils, and Catholic tradition, being driven to it by the Scriptures. But when he found no authority in the Bible for infant baptism he assumed a new attitude. At that point he had a fiery contest with himself as to the true key of Biblical interpretation, and he deliberately chose the negative turn. That is, he determined to abide by what the Scriptures did not forbid, instead of by what they enjoined. He saw at a glance where his rule of interpretation on other subjects must inevitably lead him on this point. And he dared not venture one step further in free thought, for fear of invoking a complete revolution. To take one step more was to let infant baptism go and the State church with it. But this was not the kind of a church Luther wanted, so he dismissed the whole matter as a very inopportune question. Thus it appears that he was willing to do as a positive duty to God whatever the Scriptures did not prohibit, as in the Supper, when asked, "What scripture have you for elevating the cup?" to which he indignantly replied, "What is there against it?" By the same answer he might have justified the offering of masses for the dead, auricular confession, purgatory, infallibility of popes, and any other unauthorized thing practiced by the Catholics, but which the Scriptures had not positively forbidden.

The imperial edict against Luther at the diet of Worms could scarcely have been stronger than it was, and yet it was wholly ineffective, for after Luther returned from his hiding place to Wittenberg he went on tours of numerous places, preaching to thousands, encouraging them in reformation, and never felt any ill effects of the ban placed upon him.

The papal court made determined efforts to bring to nought the efforts of Luther at the diet of Nurnberg, 1522-

1523, but with no success, for they were compelled to say that "among a thousand men scarcely one could be found untainted by Lutheran teaching."

It is generally agreed that the real separation into two opposite camps really began at the diet of Spires in 1524, although the real parting of the ways actually occurred after the Peasants' War. When Germany emerged from the social revolution which perpetrated this war, it soon became apparent that the religious question was still unsettled and was dividing the country into two parties, and' that both held as strongly as ever to their distinctive principles. The reason for the increased strain was the conduct of many of the Romanist princes in suppressing the rebellion; and on the other hand those princes who favored Luther's teaching had a mutual understanding to defend one another against the attack upon their faith.

ORIGIN OF PROTESTANTISM

When the diet met at Spires in 1526 it was apparent that the national hostility to Rome had not abated. The grievances of Germany against the Roman court were again revived, and it was alleged, as it was in fact, that the chief causes of the Peasants' War were the merciless exactions of clerical landholders. In the absence of Charles V, who was at war with France, Ferdinand of Austria presided over the diet. "He demanded the enforcement of the edict of Worms and a decree of the diet to forbid all innovations in worship and in doctrine," but the diet was not inclined to adopt the suggestions. Luther's followers were in the majority, and the delegates from the cities insisted that it was impossible to enforce the edict. The Committee of Princes proposed to settle the religious question by a compromise which was almost wholly favorable to Luther's teaching. It was decided that "the marriage of priests, giving the cup to the laity, the use of the German as well as the Latin in the baptismal and communion services, should be recognized; that all private masses should be abolished; that the number of ecclesiastical holy days should be largely reduced; and that in the exposition of Holy Writ the rule ought to be that scripture should be interpreted by scripture"; and that each

State should so live as it hoped to answer for its conduct to God and the emperor.

This was interpreted by those States favorable to the Reformation that they had a legal right to organize territorial churches and to make such changes in public worship as would bring it into harmony with their beliefs. This gave new life to the Reformation. Almost the whole North Germany adopted the principles of the Reformation. Various political intrigues caused division and discredit among the reform party. When the diet again met at Spires in 1529, the Roman Catholic party was largely in the majority. The emperor at the outset declared:

> By my imperial and absolute authority I abolish the clause in the ordinance of 1526 on which the Lutherans relied when they founded their territorial churches; it has been the cause of much ill counsel and misunderstanding.

The majority of the diet upheld the emperor's decision, and the practical effect of the ordinance was to rescind that of 1526; re-establish Roman Catholic rule everywhere, and with it the right of the bishops to direct all preachers in their dioceses. This ordinance called forth the celebrated "Protest," which was read before the diet April 19, 1529, when all concessions to the reformers had been refused. The legal position taken was that the unanimous decision of the diet in 1526 could not be rescinded by a majority. The "protesters" declared that they intended to abide by the decision of 1526, and not by that of 1529. They also declared their readiness to obey the emperor and the diet in all "dutiful and possible matters, but any order considered by them repugnant to God and his holy Word, to their soul's salvation, and their good conscience," they appealed to the emperor, to the free council, and to all impartial Christian judges. The essential principles involved in the protest against this decree and in the arguments on which it was grounded were:

> We protest publicly before God, our only Creator, Preserver, Redeemer and Savior, who, as the only Searcher of all our hearts, judgeth righteously, and we also protest before all the world, that both for ourselves and for our connections and subjects, we do not consent or agree with any resolutions or acts contained in the last degree of Spires above referred to, which, in the great concern of religion, are contrary to God

and to his holy word, injurious to our soul's salvation, and also in direct opposition to the dictates of our conscience, as well as to the degree issued by an imperial diet at Spires; and we hereby solemnly declare that, from reasons already assigned, and from other weighty considerations, we regard all such resolutions or acts as null and void.

Thus in the presence of the diet spoke those courageous men. This is the origin of the name "Protestant."

So critical was the situation that the Protestants immediately entered into an armed alliance for mutual defense. But as the only object now was to secure mutual defense in the right to have the same Gospel, the contest in progress was not one in which all wrongs were to be righted, but one in which they felt themselves justified in resistance only when the emperor attacked that which they all were convinced was of God.

An effort was made to perfect a union between the Protestants in Germany, but without success, and a divided Germany awaited the coming of the emperor. Charles V was now at the zenith of his power, and was determined to visit Germany and by his personal presence and influence end the religious difficulty which was distracting that portion of his vast dominions. He meant to use every persuasion possible, to make what compromises his conscience permitted, to effect a peaceful settlement. But if these failed he was determined to crush the Reformers by force.

He summoned the diet to meet at Augsburg on April 8, 1530, but it was not formally opened till June 20th. In his speech Charles V. announced that the assembly would be invited to discuss armament against the Turk, and that his majesty was anxious "by fair and gentle means" to end the religious differences which were distracting Germany. The Protestants were invited to give in writing their opinions and difficulties which compelled them to forsake the Church of Rome. It was resolved to take the religious question first. By June 24th the Lutherans were ready with the "statement of their grievances and opinions relating to the faith." On the following day it was read before the diet by the Saxon Chancellor, Dr. Christian Bayer, in such a clear voice that it was heard not only by those assembled within the chamber, but by the crowd that thronged the court outside.

They were reviewed before the Protestant princes, and it being deemed desirable that they should be extended and enlarged, the work was assigned to Melanchthon; thus was completed the famous Confession of Augsburg, the standard of faith of all the Lutheran churches. When read before the diet it produced a profound impression. It was signed by four princes of the empire, by the imperial cities of Nuremberg and Reutlingen, and by the Elector of Saxony. Faber, Eckins and Cochlaeus, who represented the Roman court at the diet, drew up a refutation which was publicly read before the diet, the emperor demanding the acquiescence of the Protestants; for he was now determined to insist on their submission, and to close the dispute. This they absolutely refused. The emperor again took counsel with the pope, and the result was an imperial edict commanding the princes, States and cities which had thrown off the papal yoke to return to their duty, on pain of incurring the displeasure of the emperor as a patron and defender of the Holy See.

The emperor published the decision on November 19th, and the Protestants had to arrange some common plan for facing the situation. They met, princes and delegates of cities, in the town of Smalkald, December 22d to 31st, when they formed a religious alliance, to which they invited England, Denmark and other States in which the Reformation had now dawned, to join them. In 1532 the peace at Nuremberg composed for a tmie the differences between the emperor and the reformers; the Lutherans were permitted the free exercise of their worship until a general council or another diet should finally determine the faith of "Continental Christendom." In 1535 the pope, Paul III, proposed to summon a general council at Mantau. The Protestants of Germany, well satisfied that no advantages would result from such a synod, assembled at Smalkald in 1537, and published a solemn protest against the constitution of the council as partial and corrupt. To this they added a summary of their doctrine, drawn up by Luther, in order to present it to the council, if the pope should persist in calling it together. This summary, which was distinguished by the title of the "Articles of Smalkald," is generally joined with the creeds and confessions of the Lutheran Church. The pope, however, died and the council at Mantau was postponed. New projects were raised, with the vain hope of setting at rest the spirit of religious freedom by which all Germany was now disturbed. The emperor summoned a conference at Worms in 1541, and Melanchthon disputed three days with Eckins on the points at issue. A diet followed at Ratisbon, another at Spires in 1542, and a third was held at Worms in 1545; the emperor vainly attempting to intimidate the Protestants, or to induce their leaders to consent to a general council to be summoned by the pope. But their resolution was fixed: they denied the pope's right to call a general council; they regarded the proposal as a snare, and treated it with scorn.

The Council of Trent met in 1546, but the Protestant representatives appeared. It thundered its decrees, and the Protestant princes of Germany bade it defiance. The emperor, exasperated by their resistance and stimulated by the pope, assembled his forces, resolved to crush the spirit he could not otherwise subdue. All Germany was arming in defense of Protestantism or in submission to the emperor, and the storm darkened on every side. Such was the state of Germany when Luther died, February 18, 1546.

A religious war now broke out. The emperor was victorious and the Interim followed. This was an imperial edict, issued in 1547, guaranteeing certain concessions more specious than really important, to the Protestants, until the decisions of a general council should be given. It satisfied neither party, and the war soon raged anew. The emperor was defeated by the German confederate, under Maurice of Saxony, in 1552, and the pacification of Passau followed. At last, in 1555, the diet of Augsburg met, peace was restored, and the Protestant States of Germany secured their independence. It was decreed that the Protestants who embraced the Confession of Augsburg should be entirely exempt from the jurisdiction of the pope of Rome, and from the authority and interference of his bishops. They were free to enact laws for the regulation of their own religion in every point, whether of discipline or doctrine. Every subject of the German empire was allowed the right of private judgment, and might unite himself with the church he preferred; and those who should prosecute others under the pretext of religion were declared enemies of the common peace.

The "Religious Peace of Augsburg" has been claimed, and justly so, as a victory for religious liberty. The victory lay in this, that the first blow had been struck to free mankind from the fetters of Rome; that the first faltering step had been taken on the road to religious liberty; and the first is valuable not for what it is in itself, but for what it represents and for what comes after it. It is always the first step that counts.

The German Reformation was a vast stride from Rome, but it fell far short of a return to Jerusalem. About the best that can be said is that the Reformation was a change of masters; a voluntary one, no doubt, in those who had any choice; and in this sense an exercise, for the time, of their personal judgment. But as soon as the Augsburg Confession of Faith was written no one was at liberty to modify or change it, and those who did not conform to it were no less heretics than Luther had been when he failed to conform to the behests of Rome.

CHAPTER IV.

THE REFORMATION IN SWITZERLAND

Hulerreich Zwingli, the Reformer of German Switzerland, was born at Wildenhaus, January 1, 1484. In school he made rapid progress and was soon recognized as a youth of much promise. His bright mind, love of truth, and devotion to the Scriptures soon brought him prominently before the public. On discovering the corruptions of the clergy, and learning of the dogmas and traditions, not found in the Bible, such as indulgencies, the worship of the "Virgin" Mary and of images, he attempted to reform the Roman Catholic Church. This soon caused charges of heresy to be brought against him, for his influence was subversive of the established order of things.

In a discussion held in the Town Hall at Zurich, January 29, 1523, in the presence of more than six hundred persons, the entire clergy of the canton and large numbers of the laity, Zwingli presented reformatory doctrines he had preached in sixty articles, and defended them so successfully that "the council at Zurich charged all the preachers to preach the pure gospel in the same manner." Soon after Zwingli received an efficient co-laborer in his reformatory efforts by the appointment of Leo Pudea, as Lent priest in Zurich. Several events signalized at this time the cause of the Reformation. The council allowed nuns to leave their convents, several of the clergy married without hindrance, a German baptismal service was introduced, and the cathedral chapter, at its own request, received new and suitable ordinances.

The council decided that the time was ripe for a second public discussion, to be held October 26, 27, 1523. More than eight hundred and fifty persons were present, of whom more than three hundred and fifty were clergymen. On the first day, Zwingli set forth his views on the presence of images in churches, and appealed to the council to forbid their use. No champion for their use was found, and the council decided that the images and pictures should be removed from the churches, but without disturbance. On the second day the following proposition was discussed: "The mass is no sacrifice, and hitherto has been celebrated with many abuses, quite different from its original institution by Christ." As no champion for images and mass was found, the Council of Zurich concluded to promote the reformation of the canton by diffusing the proper instruction in the country districts, for which purpose Zwingli drew up and published his "Christian Introduction," which explained to the people the meaning of the Reformation. Soon after this the council remodeled the public worship according to the views set forth by Zwingli. While Luther favored the retention of everything in the practice of the church of Rome not forbidden by the Scriptures, Zwingli contended that nothing should be practiced that was not expressly commanded by the Scriptures. On this difference between Luther and Zwingli, D'Aubigne says:

The Swiss Reformation here presents under an aspect somewhat different from that of the German Reformation. Luther had risen up against the excesses of those who had broken the images in the churches of Wittenberg; and in Zwingli's presence the idols fell in the temples of Zurich. This difference is explained by the different lights in which the two reformers viewed the same object. Luther desired to retain in the church all that was not expressly contrary to the Scriptures, and Zwingli to abolish all that was opposed to the Word of God. The Zurich reformer passed over those ages, returned to the apostolic times, and carrying out an entire transformation of the church, endeavored to restore it to its primitive condition. (History of the Reformation, p. 401.)

Thus Zwingli reduced the church service "to extreme simplicity; pictures and statues were removed from the churches, on the assumption that their presence was contrary to the Ten Commandments; organs were banished, and sacred music disparaged as interfering with spirituality."

From Zurich the Reformation spread, and soon Zwingli was joined by Œcolampadius, who was a great leader and counselor. The majority of the cantons were, however, still opposed to the Reformation, and the act of Lucerne (January, 1525) endeavored to satisfy the longing for a reformation without rending the church. Its decrees did not, however go into effect; and the Catholic cantons, in accordance with the advice of Dr. Eck, arranged a new religious discussion at Baden, which began May 10, 1526. Œcolampadius was the spokesman in behalf of the Reformation. Though both sides claimed the victory, the Reformation continued to make progress. As the most zealous of the Catholic cantons resorted to forcible measures for the suppression of the Reformation, Zurich and Constance formed, December 25, 1527, a defensive alliance under the name of "Burgher Rights." Later on this alliance was joined by eight other cantons. In the meanwhile five Catholic cantons had concluded to league with King Ferdinand for the maintainance of the Catholic faith. A war declared by Zurich in 1529 against the five cantons was of short duration, and the peace was favorable to the Reformation. In 1531 the war was renewed. Zurich had lost somewhat of its earlier evangelical purity, while the neighboring cantons were conspiring for its ruin.

In the awful immergency, when the public mind was alarmed, Zwingli maintained tranquility. The war began, but Zurich was dilatory, and far from being prepared; but the horn of the enemy echoed among the hills, and Zwingli bade farewell to his wife and children, mounted his horse and went forth as a warrior to share the common danger. The reformers were defeated with great slaughter, October 11, 1531. Zwingli was found after the battle, lying on his back, and his eyes upturned to heaven, with his helmet on his head, and his battle-ax in his hand. He had been struck near the commencement of the engagement, and then, as he reeled and fell, he was several times pierced with a lance. He was living when discovered in the evening, but the infuriated fanatics soon dispatched him. Next day his body was barbarously quartered and burned. The Protestants had provoked a contest for which they were not prepared, and the blow given at Cappel checked for a time the general progress of the Reformation in Switzerland.

In French Switzerland, the reformatory movement began in 1526, in Berne and Biel, where William Farel preached. In 1530 he established the Reformation in Neufchatel. In Geneva a beginning was made as early as 1528; in 1534, after a religious conference held at the suggestion of the reformers at Berne, in which Farel defended the Reformation, public worship was allowed to the reformers. Rapid progress was made through the zeal of Farel, Fromdnt, and Viret; and in 1535, after another discussion, the papacy was abolished by the council and the principles of the Reformation adopted.

In 1536 John Calvin arrived at Geneva and was induced by Farel to remain in the city and to aid hi min his struggle against a party of free-thinkers. On July 20, 1539, the citizens renounced the papacy and professed Protestantism. Prior to this a reaction of the popish and conservative elements in the State led to such dissentions and opposition that Calvin and Farel were banished; but the earnest petition of the citizens and rulers at Geneva at last induced them to return in 1541. On his return Calvin set about modeling the policy of the reformers in Geneva on the principles of Presbyterianism, the theory which he had wrought out, and commenced the dissemination of that theological system which bears his name. Both his theology and church polity became dominant throughout Switzerland.

The theological academy of Geneva, founded in 1588, supplied the churches of many foreign countries, especially France, trained in the spirit of Calvin. When Calvin died, in 1564, the continuation of his work devolved upon Theodore Beza. Calvin disagreed in many points with Zwingli, whose views gradually lost ground as those of Calvin advanced. The second Helvetic Confession, the most important among the symbolic books of the Reformed Church, which was compiled by Bullinger in Zurich, published in 1566, and recognized in all reformed countries, completed the supremacy of Calvin's principles over those of Zwingli.

Although the majority of German Protestant Churches remained in connection with the Lutheran Reformation, a German Reformed Church, which bore a moderately Calvinistic aspect, sprang up in several parts of Germany. In 1650 the Elector Frederick II, of the Palatine, embraced the reformed creed, and organized the church of his dominions according to reformed principles. By his authority the Heidelberg Catechism, which soon came to be regarded not only as a standard symbolical book of the German Reformed Church, but was highly esteemed throughout the reformed world, was written.

CHAPTER V.

THE REFORMATION IN ENGLAND

To say that the Reformation in England was brought about by the desire of Henry VIII to be divorced from Catharine of Aragon is to ignore the well-established facts of history. No king, however despotic, could have forced on such a revolution unless there was much in the life of the people that reconciled them to the change, and evidence of this is abundant.

There was much that wa scalled "heresy" in England long before Luther raised his voice against Catholicism in Germany. Wycliffe's writings and translations of the Scriptures into English had a tremendous influence on the people in England and for many years the fires of martyrdom were kept burning in the mad endeavor to stop the spread of the "heresy," and so great was the exasperation that forty years after the death of Wycliffe Romanists dug up his bones and burned them, and still the "heresy" spread. As I have already shown in a former article, the work of Tyndale, "who won a martyr's crown," had a wonderful influence over the English people.

In the Dictionary of National Biography, Dr. Rashdall says:

> It is certain that the Reformation had virtually broken out in the secret Bible readings of the Cambridge reformers before either the trumpet call of Luther or the exigencies of Henry VIII's personal and political position set men free once more to talk openly against the pope and the monks, and to teach a simpler and more spiritual gospel than the system against which Wycliffe had striven. (Wycliffe, Vol. 63, p. 218.)

The Parliaments showed themselves anti-clerical long before Henry threw off his allegiance to Rome; and Englishmen could find no better term of insult to throw at the Scots than to call them "Pope's men." These, and many other things that might be mentioned, indicate a certain preparedness in England for the Reformation, and that there was a strong national force behind Henry, when he at last decided to defy the Pope of Rome. The possibility of England breaking away from papal authority and erecting itself into a separate church under the archbishop of Canterbury had been thought probable before the divorce precipitated the quarrel between Henry and the pope.

Henry clung strenuously to the conception of papal supremacy, and advocated it in a manner only done hitherto by canonists of the Roman court. It is evident that the validity of his marriage and the legitimacy of his children by Catharine of Aragon depended on the pope being in possession of the very fullest powers of dispensation. Henry had been married to Catharine under very peculiar circumstances, which suggested doubts about the validity of the marriage ceremony.

To make the alliance stronger between England and Spain the pope had a marriage arranged between Arthur, Prince of Wales, and Catharine, the daughter of Ferdinand and Isabella of Spain. The wedding took place in St. Paul's, November 14, 1501, but Arthur died April 2, 1502, and it was proposed from the side of Spain that the young widow should marry Henry, her brother-in-law, now Prince of Wales. Ferdinand insisted that if this was not done Catharine should be sent back to Spain and her dowry returned. Pope Julius II was then besieged to grant a dispensation for the marriage. At first he refused to give his consent. Such a marriage had been branded as a sin by canonical law, and the pope himself had grave doubts whether it was competent for him to grant a dispensation in such a case; but he finally yielded to the pressure and granted the dispensation. The archbishop of Canterbury, who doubted whether the pope could grant dispensation for what was a mortal sin in his eyes, was silenced. The marriage took place June 11, 1509.

The first four children were either stillborn or died soon after birth; and it was rumored in Rome as early as 1514 that Henry might ask to be divorced in order to save England from a disputed succession. Mary was born in 1516 and survived, but all the children who came afterwards were either stillborn or died soon after birth. There is no doubt that the lack of a male heir troubled Henry greatly. There seems to be no reason for questioning the sincerity of his doubts about the legitimacy of his marriage with Catharine, or that he actually looked on the repeated destruction of his hopes of a male heir as a divine punishment for the sin of that contract. Questions of national policy and impulses of passion quickened marvelously his conscientious convictions. In the perplexities of his position the shortest way out seemed to be to ask the pope to declare that he had never been legally married to Catharine. He fully expected the pope to grant his request; but the pope was at the time practically in the power of Charles V, to whom his aunt, the injured Catharine, had appealed, and who had promised her his protection. From the protracted proceedings in the divorce case, Henry learned that he could not depend on the pope giving him what he wanted; and although his agents fought the case in Rome, he at once began preparing for the separation from papal jurisdiction. In the meantime, Henry had taken measures to summon a parliament; and in the interval between summons and assembly it had been suggested that Cranmer was of the opinion that the best way to deal with the divorce was to take it out of the hands of the pope and lay it before the canonists of the various universities of Europe. Through Cranmer this was so successfully done that the universities of England, France and Italy decided that the marriage was null and void. The king separated from Catharine, married Anne Boleyn, and fell under the papal ban.

Parliament sundered the connection between England and Rome, and passed an act declaring that the king was "their singular protector and only supreme lord, and, as far as that is permitted by the law of Christ, the Supreme Head of the Church and of clergy." The king's desire was to destroy the influence of the pope over the Church of England, to which, in other respects, he wished to preserve the continuity of its Catholic character; but it was impossible, however, for the Church of England to maintain exactly the same place which it had occupied. There was too much stirring of reformation life in the land. "The cloisters were subjected to visitation in 1535, and totally abolished in 1536; and the Bible was diffused in English in 1538 as the only source of doctrine; but the statute of 1530 imposed distinct limits upon the Reformation, and in particular confirmed transubstantiation, priestly celibacy, masses for the dead, and auricular confession."

When Henry died in 1547 the English Church was Roman in appearance. Excepting the litany in English, he left the ritual very much as he found it, as he did nearly the whole framework of religious belief. He was, however, the instrument whereby three great barriers to improvement— the papacy, monasticism, and Biblical ignorance—were broken down. The course of national events during Henry's latter years prepared the country for that reformation which it subsequently embraced.

A remarkable thing connected with the issuing of the Bible, in English, is that Tyndale's New Testament, which had been publicly condemned in England at the council called by his majesty in May, 1530, and copies of it had been burned in St. Paul's churchyard, while Tyndale himself had been tracked like a wild beast by the emissaries of the English Government in the Netherlands, was published in 1538, by the king's command, to be "sold and read by every person without danger of any act, proclamation, or ordinance heretofore granted to the contrary." Copies of it were placed in the churches for the people to read, and portions of it were read from the pulpit every Sunday.

When Henry died the situation was difficult for those who came after him. A religious revolution had been half accomplished; a social revolution was in progress, creating popular ferment; evicted tenants and uncloistered monks formed raw material for revolt; the treasury was empty, the kingdom in debt, and the coinage debased.

CHANGES MADE BY EDWARD VI.

Edward VI, "a child in years, but, mature in wisdom, intelligence and virtue," was crowned king, February 20, 1547. He collected learned men around him from every quarter, and ordered the kingdom to be purged entirely of popish fictions, and a better religion to be publicly taught. On July 31st the council began the changes. A series of injunctions was issued to the clergy, ordering them to preach against "the bishops of Rome's usurped power and jurisdiction ; to see that all images which had been objects of pilgrimages should be destroyed ; to read the Gospel and Epistles in English during the service, and to see that the litany was no longer recited or sung in processions, but said devoutly kneeling." The council were evidently anxious that the whole service should be conducted in English, and that a sermon should always be a part of the service.

The first Parliament of Edward VI made great changes in the laws of England affecting treason, which had the effect of sweeping away the edifice of absolute government which had been so carefully erected by Henry VIII. The kingly supremacy in matters of religion was maintained, but all heresy acts were repealed, giving the people an unwonted amount of freedom. An act was passed ordaining that "the most blessed sacrament be hereafter commonly administered unto the people . . . under both kinds, that is to say, of bread and wine, except necessity otherwise require." An act was also passed permitting the marriage of the clergy. The next important addition to the progress of the Reformation was the preparation of a Service Book, commonly called "The First Prayer-Book of King Edward VI." It was introduced by an "Act of Uniformity," which, after relating how there had been for a long time in England "divers forms of common prayer . . . and that diversity of use caused many inconveniences," ordains the universal use of this one form, and enacts penalties on those who make use of any other.

The changes made in the laws of England—the repeal of the "bloody statute" and of the treason laws—induced many of the English refugees who had gone to Germany and Switzerland to return to their native land. These, with other learned Protestants, who were invited to come to England, were appointed as teachers in the English universities. Thus the "New Learning" made great strides, leavening all the more cultured classes, leading to the discredit of the old theology, and gave a strong impulse to the Reformation movement. The feeling of the populace changed rapidly, for instead of resenting the destruction of images, they were rather inspired by too much iconoclastic zeal.

In 1552, the "Second Prayer-Book of King Edward VI,"

was issued. which was enforced by the second "Act of Uniformity," containing penalties against laymen as well as clergymen—against "a great number of people in divers parts of the realm, who did willfully refuse to come to their parish churches." Soon after there followed a new creed or statement of the fundamental doctrines received by the Church of England. This is interesting because they form the basis of the "Thirty-nine Articles," the creed of the Anglican Church of today.

It was during the reign of Edward VI that Puritanism, which became so prominent in the time of Elizabeth, first manifested itself. Its two principal spokesmen were Bishops Hooper and Ridley. Hooper was an ardent follower of Zwingli, and was esteemed to be the leader of the party. While the Reformation was being pushed forward at a speed too great for the majority of the people, Edward died (July 6, 1553), and the collapse of the Reformation afterwards showed the uncertainty of the foundation on which it had been built.

"BLOODY MARY"

Mary, the daughter of Henry VIII and Catharine of Aragon, was crowned with great ceremony October 1, 1553, and her first Parliament met four days later. It reversed a decision of the former Parliament, and declared that Henry's marriage with Catharine had been valid, and that Mary was the legitimate heir to the throne; and it repealed all the religious legislation under Edward VI. On taking the throne Mary promised to force no one's religion, but as soon as she dared she began to restore Romanism with a zeal that delighted the pope.

Mary was married to Philip of Spain January 1, 1554; but the alliance was very unpopular from the first. Immediately after the marriage "the bloody acts of the tragedy were begun." Care was taken to elect to Parliament members "of a wise, grave and Catholic sort." This body obtained the pope's absolution of the nation for its guilt of schism and abolished all acts which made the sovereign the supreme head of the Church. The Latin service was restored. Fully half of the clergy were thrust out of their

offices.   Bishop Gardner secured the passage of the terrible
edicts and laws, and Bishop Bonner so applied them as to
gain the title of "the bloody."   The fires of Smithfield and
the ax at the Tower were in such active service during four
years that some four hundred "martyrs left their record of
faith and triumph as one of painful glories of the English
Reformation."

Among those burned were Latimer and Ridley.   Bound
to the stake with his friend, Latimer said, when the lighted
fagot was applied: "Be of good comfort, Master Ridley,
and play the man; we shall this day, by God's grace, light
such a candle in England as, I trust, shall never be put out."

Cranmer had been the decisive ag nt in the divorce
against Catharine, thus branding the birt._' her daughter,
Mary, as illegitimate.   This Mary never forgave.   But
there were other motives.   "To burn the Primate of the
English Church for heresy was to shut out meaner victims
from all hope of escape."   He was more than any other man
the representative of the religious revolution which had
passed over the land.   In an hour of weakness, and under
the entreaties of his friends, he recanted.   But in the end
he redeemed his momentary weakness by a last act of heroism.   He knew that his recantations had been published, and
that any further declaration made would probably be sup-
pressed by his unscrupulous antagonists.   He resolved by
a single action to defeat their calculations and stamp his
sincerity on the memories of his countrymen.   His dying
speech was silenced, as he might well have expected; but he
had made up his mind to something that could not be stifled.
In his speech he said:

And now I come to the great thing that so troubleth my
conscience, more than any other thing that I said or did in my
life: and that is my setting abroad of writings contrary to the
truth, which here now I renounce and refuse as things written
with my hand contrary to the truth which I thought in my
heart, and written for fear of death, and to save my life, if it
might be; and that is all such bills which I have written or
signed with mine own hand since my degradation; wherein I
have written many things untrue.   And forasmuch as my hand
offended in writing contrary to my heart, it shall be first burned.
And as for the pope, I refuse him as Christ's enemy and antichrist, with all his false doctrine and as for the sacrament—

He got no further; his foes had been dumb with amazement, but now their pent-up feelings broke loose. "Stop the heretic's mouth!" cried one; "Take him away!" cried another; "Remember your recantations and do not dissemble!" cried Lord Williams. "Alas, my lord," replied Cranmer, "I have been a man that all my life loved plainness, and never dissembled till now against the truth; for which I am sorry;" and he seized the occasion to add that as for the sacrament, he believed that it should be administered in "both kinds." The tumult redoubled. Cranmer was dragged from the stage and led to the place where Ridley and Latimer had been burned.

The friars ceased not to ply him with exhortations: "Die not in desperation," cried one; "Thou shalt drag innumerable souls to hell," cried another. On reaching the appointed place he was bound to the stake with a steel band, and fire was set to the fagots of wood which made his funeral pyre. As the flames leaped up, he stretched up his right hand, saying with a loud voice, "This hand hath offended," and held it firmly in the fire till it was consumed. No cry escaped his lips and no movement betrayed his pain. If the martyrdom of Ridley and Latimer lighted the torch, Cranmer's spread the conflagration which in the end burnt up the Roman Catholic reaction and made England a Protestant nation.

The death of Cranmer was followed by a long succession of martyrdoms. Mary tried most desperately to restore Romanism in its fullness, but failed, and died November 17, 1558, "the unhappiest of queens, and wives, and women." The people who had welcomed her when she was crowned, called her "Bloody Mary"—a name which was, after all, so well deserved that it will always remain. "Each disappointment she took as a warning from heaven that atonement had not yet been paid for England's crimes, and the fires of persecution were kept burning to appease the God of Roman Catholicism."

ELIZABETH, THE PROTESTANT QUEEN

The people of England were coming to the conclusion that Elizabeth must be queen, or civil war would result. It seemed also assumed that she would be a Protestant. Many things contributed to create such expectations. The young intellectual life of England was slowly becoming Protestant. "This was especially the case among the young ladies of the upper classes, who were becoming students learned in Latin, Greek and Italian, and at the same time devout Protestants, with a distinct leaning to what afterwards became Puritanism." The common people had been showing their hatred of Roman Catholicism, and "images and religious persons were treated disrespectfully." It was observed that Elizabeth "was very much wedded to the people and thinks as they do," and that "her attitude was much more gracious to the common people than to others." The burning of Protestants, and especially the execution of Cranmer, had stirred the indignation of the populace of London and the south countries against Romanism, and the feelings were spreading throughout the country.

The accession of Elizabeth, the daughter of Henry VIII and Anne Boleyn, to the throne, gave new life to the Reformation. As soon as it was known beyond the sea, most of the exiles returned home, and those who had hid themselves in the houses of their friends began to appear; but the public religious service continued for a time the same as Mary left it—the popish priests still celebrated mass and kept their livings. None of the Protestant clergy who had been ejected in the last reign were restored; and orders were given against all innovations without public authority. The only thing Elizabeth did before the meeting of Parliament was to prevent pulpit disputes.

Elizabeth was crowned on January 15, 1559. The bishops swore fealty to the new queen, but took no part in the coronation of "one so plainly a heretic." Her first Parliament passed a new act of supremacy in which the queen was declared to be "the only supreme governor of this realm, as well in spiritual or ecclesiastical things or causes as temporal." While not proclaimed as "Supreme Head of the Church," all the drastic powers claimed by Henry VIII were given to her. It may even be said that the ecclesiastical jurisdiction bestowed upon her was more extensive than that given to her father, for *schisms* were added to the list of matters subject to the queen's correction, and she was empowered to delegate her authority to commissioners, thus enabling her to exercise her supreme governorship in a way to be felt in every corner of the land.

The same Parliament passed the "Act of Uniformity," which threatened all non-conformists with fines and imprisonment, and their ministers with deposition and banishment. When the provisions of the act began to be enforced, a number of the non-conformist ministers who demanded a greater purity of the church (hence the name Puritan), a simple, spiritual form of worship, a strict church discipline, and a Presbyterian form of government, organized separate congregations in connection with presbyteries, "and a considerable portion of the clergy and laity of the Established Church sympathized with them. The rupture was widened in 1592 by an act of Parliament that all who obstinately refused to attend public worship, or led others to do so, should be imprisoned and submit, or after three months be banished, and again in 1595 when the Presbyterians applied the Mosaic Sabbath laws to the Lord's day, and when Calvin's doctrines of predestination excited animated disputes."

In our study of the Reformation we have found that the pretentions of Roman Catholic infallibility were replaced by a not less uncompromising and intolerant dogmatism, availing itself, like the other, of the secular power, and arrogating to itself, like the other, the assistance of the Spirit of God. The mischief from this early abandonment of the right of free inquiry is as evident as its inconsistency with the principles upon which the reformers had acted for themselves

Hence under the Protestant banner there arose sectarian churches, professing to take the Bible alone as their rule of faith and practice, when assailing the claims of Rome, and yet binding by creeds, unknown to the Bible, all embraced within their folds; till Protestantism becomes as creed-bound as Romanism. Taking into view the larger results of this inconsistency, they bring under notice the Lutheran Church, the State churches of England and Scotland, as well as non-conformist churches which have arisen from them.

Bible interpretation by the dogmatic and mystic methods even before the death of Luther, but more intensely afterward, made the Lutheran churches a very Babeldom. Then

came "Forms of Concord," made obligatory, each one resulting in further discord.   Lutherans acknowledge the
head of the State as the supreme visible ruler of the Church.
The supreme direction of ecclesiastical affairs is vested in
the councils or boards, generally appointed by the sovereign,
termed "consistories," consisting of both laymen and ministers.   The Lutheran established churches are so inter-
woven with the State as to be usually dependent on it.   They
are almost destitute of discipline, and, in some places, exclude dissent.   Dr. Schaff says:

> The congregations remained almost as passive as the
> Roman Church.   They have, in Europe, not even the right of
> electing their pastor.   They are exclusively ruled by their
> ministers, as they are ruled by the provincial consistories, al-
> ways presided over by a layman, the provincial consistory by
> a central consistory, and this again by the minister of worship
> and public instruction, who is the immediate organ of the
> ecclesiastical supremacy of the crown.

Add to this infant baptism and infant membership, and
then you have the world in the Church, and a state of things,
if not so bad as that of Rome, yet as completely unlike the
apostolic churches, and as wide a departure from what must
result from surrender to the Bible alone and submission to
Christ and his apostles as it were possible to reach.

The Reformation in England was fraught with immense
blessings to the world at large, the advantage of which the
English people now enjoy.   But in England's so-called
Protestant Church there is no trace of the three fundamental
principles enunciated by the reformers:

(1) The Bible the only rule of faith and practice.
(2) The duty of every man to judge the Bible for himself.
(3) The priesthood of every member of the Church.

Instead of "the Bible only as the rule of faith and practice," they have creeds and Parliamentary control of church
services; in place of "the duty of every man to interpret the
Bible for himself," this same State Church has burned and

hung Roman Catholics and Dissenters, the one for holding too much Romanism, and the other for not holding as much as the king and the clergy were pleased to demand. Then, in lieu of "the priesthood of every member," there is a limited priesthood, differing but little from that of Rome; with infant baptism, infant membership, and numerous other human inventions "making void the commandments of God."

CHAPTER VI.

THE REFORMATION IN SCOTLAND

Had I the time and space I would be glad to give a history of the Reformation in Scotland under John Knox and others. After all the prolonged suffering and conflict, it has precious little more of Protestantism than is common in the English State Church. There we also find the reigning monarch represented in the General Assembly by a nobleman, as Lord High Commissioner, who, on some occasions, has taken upon himself to dissolve the Assembly without the consent of its members. In 1843 a conflict between the ecclesiastical and civil courts brought about a great disruption, giving rise to the Free Church of Scotland, so that there is also the "General Assembly of the Free Church." But these two General Assemblies are not on equal footing—in the very nature of the case could not be. In the one, the proceedings of the Assembly carry with them the sanction of the law, backed by the civil power; while those of the other have no such sanction, and are only binding upon willing adherents, who, by tacit agreement, are under moral obligation. The one is a corporate body in the eye of the law; the other entirely voluntary. But both bodies hold that the acts of their respective assemblies are binding upon their churches. Consequently those churches are in subjection to a rule of which the apostolic churches knew nothing, and, therefore, are not in faith and practice in subjection to the Bible alone. The "Confession of Faith" is the standard of appeal. Infant baptism, infant membership, and numerous other departures from apostolic Christianity stand out to refute any claims that these churches of Scotland might put in. They may protest against Rome or Episcopacy, but what matters that, as the Bible protests all of them?

THE INDEPENDENTS

But it is not to be supposed, even though the multitudes settled down in violation of their professed principles, that all would refrain from a fuller application of them. Hence the multiplication of distinct parties, each claiming to be the church, or a nearer approach to the church as ordained by Christ. Coming out in this way from the English State Church we find the Independents, who sacrificed property, liberty and life. They were glad to escape to Holland or to this country. Others suffered on and aided largely to win against a persecuting State Church the liberties the people now enjoy. Belknap's "Life of Robinson" gives the following principles as underlying their church organization:

(1) That no church ought to consist of more members than can meet in one place for worship and discipline

(2) That a church of Christ is to consist only of such as appear to believe in and obey him.

(3) That any competent number of such have a right, when conscience obliges them, to form themselves into a distinct church.

(4) That, being thus incorporated, they have a right to choose their own officers.

(5) That these officers are teaching elders, ruling elders, and deacons.

(6) That elders being chosen and ordained have no power to rule the church, but by consent of the brethren.

(7) That all elders and all churches are equal in respect to power and privileges.

(8) That the Lord's Supper is to be received sitting at the table. (When in Holland they observed it every Lord's day.)

(9) That ecclesiastical censures are wholly spiritual, and not to be accompanied with temporal penalties.

They admitted no holy days but the "Christian Sabbath," though they had occasional days of fasting and thanksgiving; and finally they had renounced all human inventions or impositions on religious matters.

In Scotland we find Congregational principles as far back as the Commonwealth. Independency had obtained much hold in England among all classes. The soldiers of Cromwell carried their principles with them, and are said to have formed a Congregational church in Edinburgh. But that church was not permanent, and we find nothing of churches of like order in Scotland till 1726, when John Glass, an eloquent and able minister, with avowed convictions in harmony with those of the English Independents, withdrew from the Church of Scotland and formed churches in most of the large towns of Scotland. These churches were called "Glassite." Mr. Glass and his adherents taught:

(1) That national establishments of religion are unlawful and 'inconsistent with the true nature of the Church of Christ. That the church being spiritual, ought to consist only of true spiritual men.

(2) That a congregation of Jesus Christ, with its elders, is in its discipline subject to no jurisdiction under heaven, save that of Christ and his apostles.

(3) That each church should have a plurality of elders or bishops, chosen by the church, according to instruction given to Timothy and Titus, without regard to previous education for the office, continuous engagement in secular employment being no disqualification.

(4) That the churches observe the Lord's Supper on the first day of every week; and that love feasts be held, after the example of the primitive Christians.

(5) That mutual exhortations be practiced on the Lord's day, any member able to edify being at liberty to address the church.

(6) That a weekly collection be made in connection with the Lord's Supper in aid of the poor, and for necessary expenses.

Mr. Glass was largely eclipsed by Robert Sandeman, whose activity wielded a wide influence. Those who adhered to his teachings were called "Sandemanians." Sandeman prominently repudiated that mischievous mysticism which views "saving faith" as an inspiration directly from the Holy Spirit. His teaching has been thus summarized:

"One thing is needful," which he called the sole requisite to justification, or acceptance with God. By the sole requisite to justification, he understood the work finished by Christ in his death, proved by his resurrection to be all sufficient to justify the guilty; that the whole benefit of this is conveyed to men only by the apostolic report concerning it; that every one who understands this report to be true, or is persuaded that the events actually happened, as testified by the apostles, is justified, and finds relief to his guilty conscience; that he is relieved not by finding any favorable symptom about his heart, but by finding their report to be true; that the event itself, which is reported, becomes his relief so soon as it stands true in his mind, and accordingly becomes his faith; that all the divine power which operates in the minds of men, either to give the first relief to their consciences, or to influence them in every part of their obedience to the Gospel, is persuasive power, or the forcible conviction of truth.

From this we see that he saw with some degree of clearness the nature of faith, but not that the divine economy provides that faith shall be perfected by surrender to an ordinance of the Lord's own appointment. On some other points in regard to faith he was more or less confused. He advocated the weekly observance of the Lord's Supper; love feasts; weekly contribution for the poor; mutual exhortation of members; plurality of elders; conditional community of goods; and approved of theaters and public and private diversions, when not connected with circumstances really sinful. His influence extended to the north of Ireland, but the people there did not adopt all his views. They attended weekly to the Lord's Supper, contributions, etc., but were opposed to going to theaters or such places of amusement; to the doctrine of the community of goods; feet washing, etc., as advocated by Sandeman. Sandeman's influence extended also to England and to this country.

HALDANE AND AIKMAN

At the close of the eighteenth century spiritual religion in Scotland was at a very low ebb. Then village preaching and extensive itineraries were entered upon by James A. Haldane and John Aikman. They were members of the Established Church of Scotland. They took in hand preaching tours unauthorized by the clergy. They were "laymen," and preaching by such men was then a strange thing in Scotland. Their labors were so far successful that a revival of spiritual life set in at many places and a spirit of inquiry was aroused. They made successive tours throughout all Scotland, as far as the Orkney Islands. Then Robert Haldane turned his attention to the spiritual needs of his native land, and determined to devote his large fortune to spreading the Gospel through its benighted districts. This led to the formation of a society for the dissemination of religious knowledge, and to the employment of young men of known piety to plant and superintend evening schools for the instruction of the young in religious truths. This movement grew to considerable proportions. But it met with determined opposition, both from Presbyterian Dissenters and the Established clergy. The decrees were fulminated by entire bodies, as the Relief Synod, obviously leveled against the devout and ardent itinerants. In like spirit the Antiburger Synod decreed.

> That as lay preaching has no warrant in the Word of God, and as the Synod has always considered it their duty to testify against promiscuous communion, no person under the inspection of the Synod can, consistently with these principles, attend upon or give countenance to public preaching by any who are not of our community; and if any do so they ought to be dealt with by the judicatories of the Church, to bring them to a sense of their offensive conduct.

Going beyond this, the General Assembly of 1799 accused the itinerant preachers of "being artful and designing men, disaffected to the evil constitution of the country, holding secret meetings, and abusing the name of liberty as a cover for a secret democracy and anarchy." In the midst of this opposition a church was formed of some fourteen persons in a private house on George Street, Edinburgh, which was the beginning of the Tabernacle Church Leith Walk, in which James Haldane eventually became minister, in which capacity he exercised, without any emolument, all the public and private duties with unbroken fidelity and zeal for a period of fifty years. For some time this church was content with monthly communion, but in 1802 it resolved to spread the Lord's table on the first day of every week. By the close of 1807 some eighty-five Independent churches had been established. Out of this movement a further advance took place, and thence arose Baptist churches in Scotland.

THE SCOTCH BAPTISTS

Churches holding the immersion of believers as the only authorized baptism have, possibly, stood out against the apostasy (not as Baptists), even from the days of the apostles, though frequently driven into hiding places by the force of persecution and for the preservation of their faith and order and also of their lives.

Concerning the origin of the Baptists in England I shall not dwell; though their early history is very interesting, and far more in accord with the apostolic style than the present day Baptists. Passing at once to Scotland, I find no trace of Baptist churches till the latter part of the eighteenth century, excepting one of short duration formed by soldiers of Cromwell's army. The earliest Scotch Baptist Church is said to have been formed in Edinburgh in 1765 under the efforts of Robert Carmichael, who had been a minister in the Antiburger Church at Coupar-Augus; but later became minister of an Independent Church ("Glassite") in Edinburgh, of which Archibald McLean was a member. Early in life a strong impression had been made on the mind of McLean by the preaching of George Whitfield. In 1762 he withdrew from the Established Church of Scotland and united with this Independent Church. But it was not long till some trouble arose over a case of discipline which resulted in the withdrawal of both Carmichael and McLean from the church. While thus standing aloof from church membership they directed their attention to baptism. McLean, not having read a line upon the subject, went carefully through the whole of the New Testament with the inquiry before him, "What is baptism?" This led him to the firm conviction that only those capable of believing in Christ are its subjects and that it must be performed by immersion of the whole body in water. A year later Carmichael reached the same conclusion. He then went to London where he was immersed by Dr. Gill at Barbican, October 9, 1765. On returning to Edinburgh, he baptized McLean and six others, and formed a Baptist church. In 1769, Carmichael moved to Dundee, and McLean became minister of the newly-formed church. Other churches of immersed believers were soon planted in Glasgow, Dundee, Montrose and other places, and the sentiment in favor of returning to the scriptural act of baptizing grew among the people. The marked piety and noble disinterestedness of Archibald McLean stand out as worthy of all admiration. His labors were immense and given gratuitous, as he persisted in continuing in employment as overseer of a printing establishment.

As Scotch Baptist churches multiplied there arose a disturbing element. McLean and others held the necessity of an ordained elders to the proper observance of the Lord's Supper; consequently, notwithstanding that they taught the importance of observing the Lord's Supper on the first day of every week, it had to be omitted when an ordained elder could not be present. But ere long others among them saw more light and insisted that elders were not essential to the being of a church, that the church existed before its elder-ship, and that where the church is the Lord's table should be spread on the first day of every week, irrespective of the presence of an ordained elder. This led to contention, and, indeed, to separation. But truth will not down. We may go with it any distance we please, but when we say, "Thus far and no farther," truth struggles to remove the hindrances thrown across its path, and in the end starts on afresh to complete the journey.

As leaven will permeate so truth must influence more or less the mass into which it is cast. From Scotland the principles associated with the names of the Haldanes, Car-michael and McLean found receptive hearts in Wales. Even in Ireland, also, there was in men's minds the struggling of truth and error, the partial expulsion of the false by the true, the consequent advance to apostolic faith and order, and falling short of a complete return thereto, notwithstanding progress calling for thankful recognition.

THE SEPARATISTS

About the year 1802 there were a few persons in Dublin, most of them connected with the religious establishments of the country. The most noted among them were John Walker, G. Carr and Dr. Darby, all of whom organized re-ligious bodies, differing in minor points from one another. Their attention was directed to Christian fellowship, as they perceived it to have existed among the disciples in apostolic times. They concluded from the study of the New Testa-ment that all the first Christians in any place were connected together in the closest brotherhood; and that as their con-nection was grounded on the one apostolic gospel which they believed, so it was altogether regulated by the precepts de-livered to them by the apostles, as the divinely commissioned ambassadors of Christ. They were convinced that every departure of professing Christians from this course must have originated in a withdrawing of their allegiance from the King of Zion, and in the turning away from the instruction of the inspired apostles; that the authority of their word, being divine, was unchangeable, and that it can not have been annulled by or weakened by the lapse of ages, by the varying customs of different nations, or by the enactments of earthly legislators.

With such views in their minds they set out in the attempt to return fully to the course marked out in the Scriptures; persuaded that they were not called to make any laws or regulations for their union, but simply to learn and adhere to the law recorded in the divine Word. Their number soon increased; and for some time they did not see that the union which they maintained with each other, on the principles of scripture, was at all inconsistent with the continuance of their connection with the various religious bodies round them. But after a time they were convinced that these two things were utterly incompatible; and that the same divine rule which regulated their fellowship with each other forbade them to maintain any religious fellowship with others. From this view, and the practice consequent upon it, they were called "Separatists."

They held that even two or three disciples in any one place, united together in the faith of the apostolic gospel, and in obedience to the apostolic precepts, constitute the Church of Christ in that place.

They held that the only good and sure hope toward God for any sinner is by the belief of this testimony concerning the great things of God and his salvation. And as they understood by faith, with which justification and eternal life were connected, nothing else but belief of the things declared to all alike in the Scriptures, so by repentance they understood nothing else but the new mind which that belief produces. Everything called repentance, but antecedent to the belief of the Word of God, or unconnected with it, they considered spurious and evil.

They considered the idea of any successors to the apostles or of any change of Christ's laws as utterly unchristian, and did not tolerate any men of the clerical type among them. They believed that the Scriptures taught the community of goods. They held that there is no sanction in the New Testament for the observance of the first day of the week as the Sabbath; and that the Jewish Sabbath was one of the shadows of good things to come, which passed away on the completion of the work of Jesus on the cross. They believed themselves bound to meet together on the first day of the week, the memorial day of Christ's resurrection, to show his death, in partaking of bread and wine, as the symbols of his body and his blood shed for the remission of sins.

In their assembly they joined together in the various exercises of praise and prayer, reading the Scriptures, exhorting and admonishing one another as brethren according to their several gifts and ability; contributed of their means and saluted each other with "an holy kiss." In the same assemblies they attended, as occasion required, to the discipline appointed by the apostles, for removing any evil that might appear in the body.

When any brethren appeared among them possessing all the qualifications of the office of elders or overseers, which are marked in the apostolic writings, they thought themselves called upon to acknowledge them as brethren in that office, as the gifts of the Lord to his church. They held themselves bound to live as peaceable and quiet subjects of any government under which the providence of God placed them; to implicitly obey all human ordinances which did not interfere with their subjection to their heavenly King.

The baptism of believers was cast aside as anti-Christian, except in the case of the heathen, who on conversion had made no previous confession of faith. Their mistake lay in the belief that baptism was intended to mark the mere profession of Christian faith. They failed to see that it was commanded by the Lord himself to follow upon a real believing with the heart, and a confession with the mouth. Any act called baptism prior to that is not the ordinance of Christ, and stands for nothing. The time for baptism is so soon as that believing confession and heart trust exists as a fact. So long as it remains unperformed after that there is a cessation in that particular of compliance with the divine command, which should be terminated by obedience so soon as possible.

While these people were scriptural in a number of things, in others they fell far short of returning to apostolic Christianity. So we must continue our search.

As we have already seen, there was a great struggle in Europe to escape from the direful effects of departure from apostolic simplicity. These efforts brought forth many sects, and each sect fought desperately to secure the Bible within its own party by the spiritual fetters of partisan interpretation. The clergy of each denomination, arrogating to themselves the claim of being its divinely-authorized expounders, caused it to speak only in the interest of their sect, and thus the Bible was made to speak in defense of each particular creed. Detached sentences, relating to matters wholly distinct and irrelevant, were placed in imposing array in support of positions assumed by human leaders; the people, on the other hand, seemed to have quietly surrendered into the hands of the clergy all power of discrimination and all independence in religious matters. It seemed vain that the Bible had been put into the hands of the people in their mother tongue, since the "clergy" had succeeded in imposing upon it a seal which the "laity" dared not break, so that while Protestants were delighted that they were in possession of the Bible, it was, in fact, little else than an empty boast, so long as they could be persuaded that they were wholly unable to understand it.

The Bible thus trammeled had, nevertheless, set free from spiritual bondage individuals here and there, who were more or less successful in their pleadings for reform. But among them all, however, there was no one who took hold of the leading errors with sufficient clearness and grasp as to liberate it from the thraldom of human tradition and restore the Gospel to the people in its primitive simplicity and power.

PART IV

The Restoration Movement in America

CHAPTER I

SPIRITUAL UNREST IN MANY PLACES

The close of the eighteenth and the beginning of the nineteenth century were characterized by efforts to get entirely on apostolic ground, originating almost simultaneously inwidely-separated localities and amidst different and antagonistic sects. But, as the greatest of these efforts developed in our own country, we now turn our attention to them.

One of these originated among the Methodists at the time of the establishment of the American colonies, and the subject of church government became a matter of discussion among them. Thomas Coke, Francis Asbury and others labored to establish prelacy, regarding themselves as superintendents or bishops. Against this movement, James O'Kelley, of North Carolina, and some others of that State and of Virginia, with a number of members, pleaded for a congregational system, and that the New Testament be the only creed and discipline. Those contending for the episcopal form of government were largely in the majority, and the reformers were unable to accomplish their wishes. Led by James O'Kelley, they finally seceded at Mankintown, N. C., Dec. 25, 1793. McTiere says: "The spirit of division prevailed chiefly in the southern part of Virginia, and in the border counties of North Carolina, in all of which region the personal influence of O'Kelley has been seen. It extended also beyond these limits. We find the first two missionaries in Kentucky—Ogden and Haw—drawn away into his scheme. And in other places he had adherents" (History of Methodism, page 411). At first they took the name "Republican Methodists," but in 1801 "resolved to be known as Christians only, to acknowledge no head over the Church but Christ, and to have no creed or discipline but the Bible." In respect to increase of numbers, this movement was not great, and in the course of time was weakened by changes and removals, but its principles spread into other States.

About the same time Abner Jones, a physician, of Hartland, Vt., then a member of the Baptist Church, became "greatly dissatisfied with sectarian names and creeds, began to preach that all these should be abolished, and that true piety should be made the ground of Christian fellowship. In September, 1800, he succeeded by persevering zeal in establishing a church of twenty-five members at Lyndon, Vt., and subsequently one in Bradford and one in Piermont, N. H., in March, 1803." Elias Smith, a Baptist preacher, who was about this time laboring with much success in Plymouth, N. H., adopted Jones' view and carried the whole congregation with him. Several other preachers, both from the Regular and Freewill Baptists, soon followed, and with many other zealous preachers, who were raised up in the newly-organized churches, traveled extensively over the New England States, New York, Pennsylvania, Ohio and into Canada, and made many converts. Those in this movement also called themselves Christians only, and adopted the Bible as their only rule of faith and practice.

Dr. Chester Bullard was the pioneer in the cause of primitive Christianity in all Southwest Virginia. He separated himself from the Methodist Church and most earnestly desired to be immersed, but would not receive it at the hands of the Baptists, as he was not sufficiently in harmony with their tenets to unite with them. About this time Landon Duncan, the assessor of the county, happened to call in the discharge of his official duties. Engaging in a religious conversation with him, Dr. Bullard freely expressed to him his feelings and his desires, and though he freely expressed his dissent from some of the views held by Duncan, the latter agreed to baptize him.

In early life Duncan had united with the Baptists and was ordained by them, but after a time adopted the views of the "Christians," chiefly through the teaching of Joseph Thomas, who was in some respects a remarkable man. He was born in North Carolina, whence he removed with his father to Giles County, Virginia, where he became deeply imbued with religious fervor, and began while quite a young man to urge his neighbors to the importance of devoting themselves to the service of God. Associating with O'Kelley in North Carolina, he desired to be immersed, when O'Kelley persuaded him that pouring was more scriptural, to which he submitted after stipulating that a tubful of water should be poured upon him. But afterward he became fully convinced that immersion alone is baptism, and was immersed by Elder Plumer. This brought him into intimate association with Abner Jones, Elias Smith and others of the "Christians." He now devoted his life wholly to preaching and became noted for the extent of his travels throughout the United States. He traveled on foot dressed in a long, white robe, hence he was called the "White Pilgrim," and frequently, in imitation of the Master, retired to lonely places for fasting and prayer. He made a strong impression on the people, and finally died of smallpox amidst his itinerant labors in New Jersey.

Dr. Bullard, after his baptism by Duncan, at once began preaching, delivering his first discourse the evening following his baptism. Avoiding those speculation points with which Duncan and those associated with him were so much occupied, he presented simple views of the Gospel and the freeness of the salvation through Christ, and showed that faith comes by hearing the Word of God, and that "he that believeth and is baptized shall be saved." It was a considerable time, however, before he convinced enough people of the scripturalness of the doctrine to form a church. By degrees, most of those associated with Duncan were convinced by Dr. Bullard, and through the assistance of James Redpath and others joining him in the ministry of the Word, a number of churches were established in that part of Virginia. About 1839 Dr. Bullard incidentally came into possession of a copy of Alexander Campbell's "Extra on Remission of Sins." On reading it he was so surprised and delighted with the new views therein set forth that he obtained all the numbers of the Christian Baptist and Millennial Harbinger, and was filled with great joy to find how clear and consistent were Campbell's views, and how different from the slanderous misrepresentations which had been so persistently circulated through the press and from the pulpit.   He immediately began to circulate Campbell's writings, preaching with great success the ancient Gospel, and overjoyed in finding himself unexpectedly associated with so many fellow laborers in the effort to restore primitive Christianity.   He endured hardships as a good soldier of Jesus Christ and pushed forward against great odds.   He traveled all over Virginia, from the mountains to the seashore, and baptized thousands. In his prime he was one of the most powerful exhorters that could be found, and his sermons were exceedingly clear, scriptural and persuasive.

On a notable occasion the Methodists, who had become greatly stirred by Dr. Bullard's preaching, chose one of their preachers, T. J. Stone, to represent them in a debate with Dr. Bullard on the "Act of Baptism."   The debate was to be held in a grove at a place some distance from Dr. Bullard's home, and he had to start the day before in order to reach the place in time.   Late in the afternoon of the first day's journey he fell in with the preacher who was to be his opponent in the debate.   Stone had been studying the Campbell and Rice Debate in search of arguments to sustain his side of the question.   As they rode along together their conversation turned on the debate, and Dr. Bullard noticed rather a lack of confidence in the language of his opponent.   The doctor turned the conversation so that he might learn the cause of this, and soon reached the conclusion that his opponent had little relish for the debate, and, in short, in his research his confidence in affusion had been overturned.   Dr. Bullard finally said: "You had better let me baptize you to-morrow instead of debating."   Stone replied: "If it were not for two or three things in the way, I would."

That night they spent at Stone's home, and the doctor soon perceived that one of the greatest things in the way was Stone's wife.   Accordingly he gave her much attention, and the three searched the Scriptures the greater part of the night.   A large crowd assembled the next day to hear the discussion.   Dr. Bullard announced that there would be no debate, but that he would preach that morning and

Stone in the afternoon; also that there would be an immersion immediately after the morning discourse.   Much to the surprise of all, both Mr. and Mrs. Stone presented themselves for baptism when the invitation was given.

CHAPTER II.

BARTON W. STONE

We have already learned that efforts were being made to return to apostolic Christianity in different places in the East, and I mentioned these efforts first because as emigration is most usually westward, the influences thus exerted spread far and wide. This is one of the reasons why the plea to return to the original practice of the apostolic churches has been more effective in the West than in the East.

I now give attention to a great movement that was inaugurated in what was then called the "West," through the untiring labors of Barton W. Stone and others. Stone was born in Maryland, December 24, 1772. His father died and the mother, being left with a large family of children, moved to Pittsylvania County, Va., in 1779, where the manners and customs of the people were very simple, and contentment seemed to be the lot of all, and happiness dwelt in every breast amidst the abundance of home stores, acquired by honest industry. His first teacher was a tryant, who seemed to take pleasure in whipping and abusing his pupils for every trifling offense. When called upon to recite, he was so affected with fear, and so confused in mind, that he could say nothing, and remained in that school only a few days. He was then sent to another teacher, who was patient and kind, and he advanced so rapidly that after five years' training his teacher "pronounced him a finished scholar." This fired him with ambition and spurred his efforts to rise to eminence in learning.

CONFRONTED BY MANY DIFFICULTIES

About this time some Baptist preachers came into the neighborhood and began preaching to the people, and great excitement followed. Multitudes attended their ministrations, and many were immersed. Immersion was so novel that people traveled long distances to see the ordinance administered.   Young Stone was constant in his attendance, and was particularly interested in hearing the converts relate their experiences.   Of their conviction and great distress they were very particular in giving an account, and how and when they obtained deliverance from their burdens.   Some were delivered by a dream, a vision, or some uncommon appearance of light; others by a voice spoken to them—"Thy sins are forgiven thee"; and others by seeing the Savior with their natural eyes.   Such experiences were considered good by the Church, and those relating such were baptized and received into full fellowship.   The preachers had an art of affecting their hearers by a tuneful voice in preaching. Not knowing any better, he considered all this a work of God, and the way of salvation.

After these came Methodist preachers who were bitterly opposed by the Baptists and Episcopalians, who publicly declared them to be the locusts of Revelation, and warned the people against receiving them.   Stone's mind was much agitated, and vacillated between the two parties.   For some time he had been in the habit of retiring in secret, morning and evening, for prayer, with an earnest desire for religion; but being ignorant of what he ought to do, he became discouraged and quit praying, and turned away from religion.

When he was about sixteen he came into possession of his portion of his father's estate.   This absorbed his mind day and night endeavoring to devise some plan as to how to use it to the best advantage.   At last he decided to acquire a liberal education, and thus qualify himself for the practice of law.   Having reached this decision he began immediately to arrange his affairs to put his purpose into execution. Accordingly he bade farewell to his mother, and made his way to the noted academy at Guilford, N. C.   Here he applied himself with great diligence to acquire an education or die in the attempt.   He divested himself of every hindrance for the course.   With such application he made rapid progress.

Just before he entered the academy the students had been greatly stirred by James McGready, a Presbyterian preacher, and Stone was not a little surprised to find many of the students assembled every morning in a private room before the hour for recitation to engage in singing and prayer. This was a source of uneasiness to him, and frequently brought him to serious reflections. He labored diligently to banish these serious thoughts, thinking that religion would impede his progress in learning, thwart the object he had in view, and expose him to the ridicule of his relatives and companions. He therefore associated with those students who made light of such things, and joined them in the ridicule of the pious. For this his conscience severely condemned him when alone and made him so very unhappy that he could neither enjoy the company of the pious nor that of the impious. This caused him to decide to go to Hampden-Sidney College, Virginia, that he might be away from the constant sight of religion. He determined to leave at once, but was prevented by a violent storm. He remained in his room all day and reached the decision to pursue his studies there and to attend to his own business, and let others do the same.

Having made this resolution, he was settled till his roommate asked him to accompany him to hear Mr. McGready preach. Of the deep impression made on him by the discourse he heard on that occasion he says:

His coarse, tremulous voice excited in me the idea of something unearthly. His gestures were the very reverse of elegance. Everything appeard by him forgotten but the salvation of souls. Such earnestness, such zeal, such powerful persuasion, enforced by the joys of heaven and miseries of hell, I had never witnessed before. My mind was chained by him, and followed him closely in his rounds of heaven, earth and hell, with feelings indescribable. His concluding remarks were addressed to the sinners to flee the wrath to come without delay. Never before had I comparatively felt the force of truth. Such was my excitement that had I been standing I should have probably sunk to the floor under the impression.

When the meeting was over he returned to his room, and when night came he walked out into a field and seriously reasoned with himself on the all-important subject of religion. He asked himself: "What shall I do? Shall I embrace religion, or not?" He weighed the subject and counted the cost. He concluded that if he embraced religion he would then incur the displeasure of his relatives and lose the favor and company of his companions: become the object of their scorn and ridicule; relinquish all his plans and schemes for worldly honor, wealth and preferment, and bid adieu to all the pleasures in which he had lived. He asked himself, "Are you willing to make this sacrifice?" His heart answered, "No, no." Then there loomed before him a certain alternative, "You must be damned." This thought was so terrible to him that he could not endure the thought, and, after due deliberation, he resolved from that hour to seek religion at the sacrifice of every earthly good, and immediately prostrated himself before God in supplication for mercy.

In accordance with the popular belief, and the experience of the pious in those days, he anticipated a long and painful struggle before he should be prepared to come to Christ, or, in the language of that day, before he should "get religion." This anticipation was fully realized. For a year he was tossed about on the waves of uncertainty, laboring, praying and striving for "saving faith," sometimes desponding and almost despairing of ever getting it. He wrestled with this condition until he heard a sermon on "God is love," which so impressed his mind that he retired to the woods alone with his Bible. There he read and prayed with various feelings, between hope and fear, till the great truth of the love of God so triumphed over him that he afterward said:

I yielded and sunk at his feet, a willing subject. I loved him, I adored him, I praised him aloud in the silent night, in the echoing groves around. I confessed to the Lord my sin and folly in disbelieving his word so long, and in following so long the devices of men. I now saw that a poor sinner was as much authorized to believe in Jesus at first as last; that now was the accepted time and the day of salvation.

From that time he looked forward to preaching, and in the spring of 1796 applied to the Presbytery of Orange, N. C., for license to preach. In describing the proceedings of the presbytery, he says: "Never shall I forget the impression made on my mind when a venerable old father addressed the candidates, standing up together before the presbytery. After the address he presented to each of the candidates the Bible (not the Confession of Faith), with this solemn charge, 'Go ye unto all the world, and preach the Gospel to every creature.'" He was assigned to a certain district, but soon became much discouraged, and contemplated seeking regions where he was not known and turning his attention to some other calling in life.

In the midst of much doubt and perplexity, he turned westward and finally reached Caneridge. Bourbon County, Ky., where he remained for a few months, then returned to Virginia.

ORDAINED TO THE MINISTRY

In the fall of 1798 he received a call from the united congregations of Caneridge and Concord, through the Transylvania Presbytery. He accepted, and a day was appointed for his ordination to the ministry. Knowing that at his ordination he would be required to adopt the Westminster Confession of Faith, as the system of doctrine taught in the Bible, he determined to give it a very careful examination. This was to him almost the beginning of sorrows. He stumbled at the doctrine of the Trinity as therein taught, and could not conscientiously subscribe to it. Doubts, too, arose in his mind on the doctrines of election, reprobation and predestination, as then taught. He had before this time learned from those higher up in the ecclesiastical world the way of divesting those doctrines of their hard, repulsive features, and admitted them as true, yet unfathomable mysteries. Viewing them as such, he let them alone in his public discourses and confined himself to the practical part of religion, and to subjects within his depth. But in re-examining these doctrines he found the covering put over them could not hide them from a discerning eye with close inspection. Indeed, he saw that they were necessary to the system, without any covering.

He was in this state of mind when the day for his ordination came. He determined to tell the presbytery honestly his state of mind, and to request them to defer his ordination until he should be better informed and settled. When the day came a large congregation assembled, but before the presbytery convened he took aside the two pillars—James

Blythe and Robert Marshall—and made known to them his difficulties and that he had determined to decline ordination at that time. They labored, but in vain, to remove his difficulties and objections. They asked him how far he was willing to receive the Confession of Faith. To this he replied, "As far as I see it is consistent with the Word of God." They concluded that that was sufficient. The presbytery then convened, and when the question, "Do you receive and adopt the Confession of Faith as containing the system of doctrine taught in the Bible?" he answered aloud, so that the whole assembly could hear, "I do, so far as I see it consistent with the Word of God." No objection being raised to this answer he was ordained.

The reception of his ordination papers neither ended his intellectual misgivings nor his difficulties with his strictly orthodox ministerial associates in the presbytery. His mind, from this time until he finally broke the fetters of religious bondage, "was continually tossed on the waves of speculative divinity," the all-engrossing theme of the religious community at that time. Clashing, controversial theories were urged by the different sects with much zeal and bad feeling. At that time he believed and taught that mankind were so depraved that they could do nothing acceptable to God until his Spirit, by some physical, almighty and mysterious power had quickened, enlightened and regenerated the heart, and thus preprared the sinner to believe in Jesus for salvation. He began to see that if God did not perform this regenerating work in all, it was because he chose to do it for some and not for others, and that this depended upon his own sovereign will and pleasure. He then saw that the doctrine was inseparably linked with unconditional election and reprobation, as taught in the Westminster Confession of Faith; that they are virtually one, and that was the reason why he admitted the decrees of election and reprobation, having admitted the doctrine of total depravity. Scores of objections continually crossed his mind against the system. These he imputed to blasphemous suggestions of Satan, and labored to repel them as satanic temptations and not honestly to meet them with Scripture arguments. Often, when addressing the multitudes on the doctrine of total depravity, on their inability to believe and on the physical power of God to produce faith, and then persuading the helpless to "repent and believe" the Gospel, his zeal would in a moment be chilled by such questions as: "How can they believe?" "How can they repent?" "How can they do impossibilities?" "How can they be guilty in not doing them?" Such thoughts .almost stifled his ability to speak, and were as great weights pressing him down to the shades of death. The pulpits were continually ringing with this doctrine; but to his mind it ceased to be a relief; for whatever name it was called, he could see that the inability was in the sinner, and therefore he could not believe nor repent, but must be damned. Wearied with the works and doctrines of men and distrustful of their influence, he made the Bible his constant companion. He honestly, earnestly and prayerfully sought for the truth, determined to buy it at the sacrifice of everything else.

He was relieved from this state of perplexity by this resolve. By reading and meditating upon the Word of God, he became convinced that God did love the whole world, and that the only reason why he did not save all was because of their unbelief, and that the reason why they believed not was because they neglected and received not his testimony concerning his Son, for the Scripture says: "These are written, that ye may believe that Jesus is the Christ, the Son of God; and that believing ye may have life in his name." From this he saw that the requirement to believe in the Son of God was reasonable, because the testimony given is sufficient to produce faith in the sinner, and the invitation and encouragement of the Gospel are sufficient, if believed, to lead him to the Savior for the promised salvation and eternal life. From that moment of new light and joy he began to part company with Calvinism, declaring it to be the heaviest clog on Christianity in the world, a dark mountain between heaven and earth, shutting out the love of God from the sinner's heart.

In the joy of this new-found liberty he received such power that made him one of God's choicest instruments in awakening religious society out of its apathy, and in preparing the way for the great religious movement with which the last century was ushered in.   Born with his new convictions of God's all-abounding love, was an intense yearning to bring his fellow men to the joy of such a salvation.   While the fire was kindling in his soul, he heard of a great religious excitement which had already begun in Logan County, Kentucky, under the labors of certain Presbyterian preachers, among whom was the same James McGready whose preaching had so strongly affected Stone, while a youth, in North Carolina.   In the spring of 1801 he attended one of these camp meetings, and for the first time witnessed those strange agitations and cataleptic attacks, which baffled description. He describes them thus:

> The scene to me was new, and passing strange. It baffled description.   Many, very very many, fell down as men slain in battle, and continued for hours together in an apparently breathless and motionless state; sometimes for a few moments reviving and exhibiting symptoms of life by a deep groan or a piercing shriek, or by a prayer for mercy most fervently uttered. After lying thus for hours they obtained deliverance.   The gloomy cloud which had covered their faces seemed gradually and visibly to disappear, and hope in smiles brightened into joy; they would rise shouting deliverance, and then would address the surrounding multitude in language truly eloquent. (Biography of Stone, page 34.)

REMARKABLE MEETING AT CANE RIDGE

Returning from these strange scenes, he entered the pulpit at Caneridge with heart aglow with spiritual fervor.   No longer shackled by the doctrine of election and reprobation, he took for his text the inspiring message of the great commission: "Go ye into all the world and preach the Gospel to the whole creation.   He that believeth and is baptized shall be saved; but he that disbelieveth shall be condemned." Old as was the text, it came like a new evangel to this people, who had known nothing but the hard terms of a Calvinistic creed.   The audience was visibly affected, and he left them promising to return in a few days.   This was the beginning of one of the greatest revivals in history.   On his return a vast multitude awaited him, and he had scarcely begun to picture before them the great salvation when scores fell to the ground as if smitten by some unseen hand. It is well to let Mr. Stone describe the scene in his own language:

> Some attmepted to fly from the scene panic-stricken, but they either fell or returned immediately to the crowd, as unable to get away. In the midst of this exercise an intelligent deist in the neighborhood stepped up to me and said, "Mr. Stone, I always thought before that you were an honest man, but now I am convinced that you are deceiving the people." I viewed him with pity, and mildly spoke a few words to him; immediately he fell as a dead man, and arose no more until he had confessed the Savior. (Biography, pages 36, 37.)

The report of this remarkable meeting soon spread through the country, and shortly afterward he held a protracted meeting at Concord. The whole country was aroused and multitu·s of all denominations attended. Party spirit shrank away and all joined heartily in the meeting, which continued five days and nights without a break, and great numbers abandoned sin.

On July 2, 1801, Barton W. Stone was married to Miss Elizabeth Campbell, of Muhlenberg County, Kentucky. Soon after marriage they hurried on to Caneridge for the memorable meeting which began on Friday before the third Sunday in August. The news concerning the remarkable meeting at Concord had spread far and wide, and when the time came to begin the meeting at Caneridge the roads were literally crowded with wagons, carriages, horsemen and footmen, moving to the camp grounds. The crowd was estimated at thirty thousand. During the meeting four or five preachers were frequently speaking at the same time, in different parts of the encampment, without confusion. All denominations joined in the conduct of the meeting. Party spirit for the time had disappeared, and all united in the great work. Multitudes abandoned sin and entered the profession and practice of religion. The meeting continued six or seven days and nights, and would have continued longer but food for the multitude could not be found.

This meeting was attended by many from Ohio and other distant parts, who returned to their homes and spread the same spirit in their neighborhoods, and the same results followed, and it can not be denied that great good resulted. Nor were its effects by any means transient, but were felt for years in the rapid growth of the churches in general and in a great degree of religious fervor.

From the beginning of this great excitement Mr. Stone had been employed almost day and night in preaching, singing, visiting, and praying with and for the distressed, till his lungs failed and became inflamed, attended with a violent cough, and it was believed that he had tuberculosis. His strength failed and he believed that his end was near. Notwithstanding this he had an intense desire to attend a camp-meeting a few miles distant from Caneridge. His physician had strictly forbidden him to preach any more till his disease should be removed.

This meeting was held in a grove near Paris. Here for the first time a Presbyterian preacher opposed the work and the doctrine by which the zeal among them had its existence and life. He labored hard to bring the people under the yoke of Calvin and to regulate them according to his standard. He wished to leave the camp at night and repair to the town, nearly a mile away, and hold the meeting in a house that would not hold half the people. This could not be done without leaving their tent and other things exposed. The consequence was, the meeting was divided and the work greatly hindered. Infidels and formalists were greatly elated over this supposed victory and passed great encomiums on the preacher; but the hearts of the revivalists were filled with sorrow. Stone went to the meeting in town. A preacher was put forward who had always been hostile to the work and seldom mingled with the revivalists. He addressed the assembly in "iceberg style," and its influence was very depressing. Stone had decided to lead the congregation in prayer just as soon as the preacher closed. When he finally closed, Stone arose and said, "Let us pray." At that very moment another preacher of the same cast with the former rose in the pulpit to preach another sermon; but Stone proceeded to pray, feeling a tender concern for the people. While he was praying the people became much affected and the house was filled with distress. Some of the preachers jumped out of the window back of the pulpit and fled. Stone then pushed his way through the crowd to those in distress, pointed them to the way of salvation, and administered to them the comforts of the Gospel. The physician who was attending him being present, pressed his way through the crowd and found Stone wet with perspiration. He ordered him to his home, lecturing him severely for violating his orders. He put on dry clothes and retired at once, slept sounding, and arose next morning perfectly relieved from his affliction. He soon regained his strength and joyfully resumed his ministerial duties. This incident brought the campmeeting to a sudden close.

"A TIME OF DISTRESS"

There were at this time several other preachers in the Presbyterian Church who coincided in religious views with Stone. These were Richard McNemara, John Thompson, John Dunlavy, Robert Marshall and David Purviance. The three former lived in Ohio, and the three latter lived in Kentucky. They all boldly preached the sufficiency of the Gospel to save men, and that the testimony of God was designed and able to produce faith, and that sinners were capable of understanding and believing this testimony, and of acting upon it by coming to the Savior and from him obtaining salvation and the Holy Spirit. When they first began to preach these things, "the people appeared as just awakened from the sleep of ages. They seemed to see for the first time that they were responsible beings, and that a refusal to use the means appointed was a damning sin."

This departure from the doctrine of the Westminster Confession of Faith soon occasioned a virulent opposition on the part of those who adhered to it. "At first they were pleased to see the Methodists and Baptists so cordially uniting with us in the worship; but as soon as they saw these sects drawing away disciples after them, they raised the tocsin of alarm—The Confession of Faith is in danger, 'To your tents, O Israel!' "

These partisans began to preach boldly the doctrines of their Confession of Faith and used the most potent arguments in their defense. "A fire was now kindled that threatened to ruin the great fervor among the people. It revived the dying spirit of partyism and gave strength to trembling infidels and lifeless professors. The sects were aroused. The Methodists and Baptists, who had so long lived in peace and harmony with the Presbyterians and with one another, now girded on their armor and marched into the deathly field of controversy and war. These were times of distress. The spirit of partyism soon expelled the spirit of love and union—peace fled before discord and strife and religion was stifled and banished in the unhallowed struggle for pre-eminence. Who shall be the greatest seemed to be the spirit of the contest. The salvation of the world was no longer the burden, and the spirit of mourning in prayer took its flight from the breasts of many preachers and people. Yet there were some of all the sects who deplored this unhappy state of things; but their entreating voice was drowned in the din of battle."

The Presbytery of Springfield, Ohio, arraigned Mc-Nemara on the charge of heresy, and the case came before the synod at Lexington, Ky. Foreseeing their fate before that body, Stone, McNemara, Thompson, Dunlavy and Marshall drew up a protest, declaring their independence and withdrawal from the jurisdiction of the synod. The synod then suspended them and declared their congregations vacant. This act produced great commotion and division among the churches and confirmed the seceding ministers in their opposition to creeds and authoritative ecclesiastical systems. But as yet they had no thought of ceasing to hold the Presbyterian faith, and that they might continue in the service of the Church organized themselves into an independent presbytery, called the "Springfield Presbytery," but soon finding this position an impossible one and the whole system out of harmony with their views, they now took another step in their work of reform. Renouncing their allegiance to all authority but that of their divine Master, they resolved to be governed by the Bible as their only rule of faith and practice. This called for the tracts and sermons from the opposition, and the views thus canvassed became widely disseminated.

Soon after his separation, Stone called the churches at Caneridge and Concord together and informed them that he could no longer preach to support Presbyterianism, but that his labors should henceforth be directed to advance the kingdom of God, irrespective of party, releasing them from all pecuniary obligations to him. Thus for the cause of truth he sacrificed the friendship of two large churches and an abundant salary for his support. He preferred the truth to the friendship and kindness of his associates in the Presbyterian ministry, who were dear to him, and tenderly united in the bonds of love. Having now no support from the congregations, and having emancipated his slaves, he turned his attention cheerfully to labor on his farm. Though fatigued in body, his spirit was happy and calm. He did not relax his ministerial labors, preaching almost every night and often in the daytime to those who were anxious to hear the Word. He had no money to hire laborers, and often on his return home he had to labor at night while others were asleep to redeem his lost time.

Co-operating with his associates in the Springfield Presbytery in preaching and planting churches, a year had scarcely passed until such an organization was perceived to be unscriptural, and was by common consent renounced, all agreeing to take the name "Christian," which they believed to be the only proper title for Christ's followers, and believed it to have been given by divine appointment to the disciples at Antioch. Having divested themselves of all party creeds and party names, and trusting alone in God and the word of his grace, they became a byword and laughing stock to the whole family of the sects; all of whom prophesied their speedy annihilation. Through much tribulation and strenuous opposition they advanced, and churches and preachers were multiplied.

As their renouncing their allegiance to all authority in religious matters but that of the Lord Jesus Christ aroused much interest and no little opposition at the time, it will, no doubt, be interesting to my readers to have this remarkable production in full, together with the witnesses' address in full, which is as follows:

THE LAST WILL AND TESTAMENT OF THE SPRINGFIELD
PRESBYTERY

The Presbytery of Springfield, sitting at Caneridge, in
the county of Bourbon, being, through a gracious Providence,
in more than ordinary bodily health, growing in strength and
size daily; and in perfect soundness and composure of mind;
but knowing that it is appointed for all delegated bodies once
to die; and considering that the life of every such body is
very uncertain, do make and ordain this our last will and
testament, in manner and form following, viz:

Imprimis. We *will*, that this body die, be dissolved, and sink into union with the body of Christ at
large; for there is but one body and one spirit, even
as we are called in one hope of our calling.

Item. We *will*, that our name of distinction, with
its *Reverend title*, be forgotten, that there be but one
Lord over God's heritage, and his name one.

Item. We *will*, that our power of making laws for
the government of the Church, and executing them by
delegated authority, forever cease; that the people
may have free course to the Bible, and adopt the *law
of the spirit of life in Jesus Christ.*

Item. We *will*, that candidates for the gospel ministry henceforth study the Holy Scriptures, with fervent prayer, and obtain license from God to preach the
simple Gospel, *with the Holy Spirit sent down from
heaven*, without any mixture of philosophy, vain de-
ceit, traditions of men, or the rudiments of the world.
And let none take *this honor to himself, but he that is
called of God, as was Aaron.*

Item. We *will*, that the Church of Christ resume
her native right of internal government, try her candidates for the ministry, as to their soundness in the
faith, acquaintance with experimental religion, gravity
and aptness to teach; and admit no other proof of their
authority but Christ speaking in them. We will that
the Church of Christ look up to the Lord of the harvest to send forth laborers into the harvest; and that
she resume her primitive right of trying those *who
say they are apostles and are not.*

Item. We *will*, that each particular church as a
body, actuated by the same spirit, choose her own
preacher and support him by a free-will offering, without a written *call* or *subscription*, admit members, remove offenses; and never henceforth *delegate* her right
of government to any man or set of men whatever.

Item. We *will*, that the people henceforth take the Bible as the only sure guide to heaven; and as many as are offended with other books, which stand in competition with it, may cast them into the fire if they choose; for it is better to enter into the life having one book than having many to be cast into hell.

Item. We *will*, that preachers and people cultivate a spirit of mutual forbearance; pray more and dispute less; and while they behold the signs of the times, look up, and confidently expect that redemption draweth nigh.

Item. We *will*, that our weak brethren who may have been wishing to make the Presbytery of Springfield their king, and wot not what is now become of it, betake themselves to the Rock of Ages, and follow Jesus for the future.

Item. We *will*, that the Synod of Kentucky examine every member who may be suspected of having departed from the Confession of Faith, and suspend every such heretic immediately, in order that the oppressed may go free, and taste the sweets of gospel liberty.

Item. We *will*, that Ja—— ———, the author of two letters lately published in Lexington, be encouraged in his zeal to destroy *partyism*. We will, moreover, that our past conduct be examined into by all who may have correct information; but let foreigners beware of speaking evil of things which they know not.

Item. Finally, we *will*, that all our *sister bodies* read their Bibles carefully, that they may see their fate there determined, and prepare for death before it is too late.

SPRINGFIELD PRESBYTERY.

June 28, 1804. (L. S.)

Robert Marshall, John Dunlavy, Richard McNemar, B. W. Stone, John Thompson, David Purviance,
Witnesses.

THE WITNESSES' ADDRESS

We, the above-named witnesses of the Last Will and Testament of the Springfield Presbytery, knowing that there will be many conjectures respecting the causes which have occasioned the dissolution of that body, think proper to testify that from its first existence it was knit together in love, lived in peace and concord, and died a voluntary and happy death. Their reasons for dissolving that body were the following:

With deep concern they viewed the divisions and party spirit among professing Christians, principally owing to the adoption of human creeds and forms of government.   While they were united under the name of a presbyter, they endeavored to cultivate a spirit of love and unity with all Christians, but found it extremely difficult to suppress the idea that they themselves were a party separate from others.   This difficulty increased in proportion to their success in the ministry. Jealousies were excited in the minds of other denominations; and a temptation was laid before those who were connected with the various parties to view them in the same light.   At their last meeting they undertook to prepare for the press a piece entitled, "Observations on Church Government," in which the world will see the beautiful simplicity of Christian Church government, stript of human invention and lordly traditions.

As they proceeded in the investigation of that subject, they soon found that there was neither precept nor example in the New Testament for such confederacies as modern church sessions, presbyteries, synods, General Assemblies, etc.   Hence they concluded that while they continued in the connection in which they then stood, they were off the foundation of the apostles and prophets of which Christ himself is the chief cornerstone.   However just, therefore, their views of church might have been, they would have gone out under the name, the precious cause of Jesus, and dying sinners who are kept from the Lord by the existence of sects and parties in the church, they have cheerfully consented to retire from the din and fury of conflicting parties—sink out of the view of fleshly minds, and die the death.   They believe their death will be great gain to the world.   But though dead, as above, and stript of their mortal frame, which only served to keep them too near the confines of Egyptian bondage, they yet live and speak in the land of gospel liberty; they blow the trumpet of jubilee, and willingly devote themselves to the help of the Lord against the mighty.   They will aid the brethren, by their counsel, when required; assist in ordaining elders or pastors, seek the divine blessing, unite with all Christians, commune together, and strengthen each others' hands in the work of the Lord.

We design, by the grace of God, to continue in the exercise of those functions which belong to us as ministers of the Gospel, confidently trusting in the Lord, that he will be with us.   We candidly acknowledge that in some things we may err, through human infirmity; but he will correct our wanderings and preserve his Church.   Let all Christians join with us in crying to God day and night to remove the obstacles which stand in the way of his work, and give him no rest till he make Jerusalem a praise in the earth.   We heartily unite with our Christian brethren of every name in thanksgiving to God for the display of his goodness in the glorious work he is carrying on in our western country, which we hope will terminate in the universal spread of the Gospel. (Biography of B. W. Stone, pages 51-55.)

PRACTICES MODIFIED IN MANY PARTICULARS

The stand they now took drove them to modify their practices in many particulars. Among the first things to which they turned their attention was infant baptism. Previous, indeed, to the great excitement in 1801, Robert Marshall had become satisfied that infant baptism was not taught in the Word of God; upon which Stone tried to set him right, but in the course of the discussion he became so thoroughly convinced of its unscripturalness that he discontinued the practice entirely. The religious awakening, however, soon engrossed the minds of all, and for some years baptism was left out of view. At length, many becoming dissatisfied with their infant baptism, a meeting was convened to thoroughly consider the subject, and, after a friendly investigation, and discussion, it was decided that each member should act in accordance with his convictions. As none among them had been immersed, it was a question whether any one was qualified to administer baptism, which was finally settled upon the ground that authority to preach carried with it the authority to baptize. In the performance of this newly-discovered duty, the ministers first baptized each other, and then their congregations. The practice of immersion soon prevailed generally among the churches.

Shortly after having reached the conclusion that the immersion of believers is the only Scriptural baptism, at a great meeting at Concord, when mourners were daily invited to collect around for prayer, as was their custom then, and many persons were prayed for without receiving the expected comfort, the words of Peter rolled through Stone's mind—"Repent, and be baptized every one of you in the name of Jesus Christ for the remission of sins, and ye shall receive the gift of the Holy Spirit"—and he thought, "were Peter here he would thus address these mourners." So he quickly arose and addressed them in the same language and urged them to comply with this demand. The effect, however, was the reverse of what he intended. Instead of comforting the mourners, it only perplexed and confused them by directing their attention to an untried course of procedure utterly unknown to "revivals," and for which they were wholly unprepared. "While their hearts were filled with ardent desires for special operations of the Holy Spirit and of fire, this unexpected presentation produced a chilling effect, and tended to cool the ardor of their excited imagination. Mr. Stone himself, indeed, quoted Peter's language on this occasion evidently more from his anxiety to suggest some means of relief, and from his unbounded confidence in the Word of God, than from any proper understanding of the relation of baptism to remission of sins."

The independent stand that Stone took on the Bible alone greatly increased his labors. Kindred spirits speedily rallied to his support. The Presbyterians forbade their people to associate with them in their worship, on pain of censure or exclusion, but this caused many to cast their lot with them. Churches quickly sprang up over a wide region, rejecting all standards but the Bible and refusing to wear any name but that of "Christians." Stone and his co-laborers now devoted themselves to encouraging and strengthening these widely-scattered churches.

"SHAKERISM"

Scarcely had the work been inaugurated, however, before the very life of the churches was threatened by the appearance of a strange delusion. A semi-religious, socialistic movement, known as "Shakerism," had some years before this established several communities in the State of New York. Its leaders, hearing of the revolt against Calvinism led by Stone, sent three missionaries—Bates, Mitchum and Young—among them. They were eminently qualified for their work, and soon made sad havoc of the newly-planned churches. Stone thus describes them and their work:

Their appearance was prepossessing, they were grave and unassuming at first in their manners; very intelligent and ready in the Scriptures, and of great boldness in their faith. They informed us that they had heard of us in the East, and greatly rejoiced in the work of God among us—that as far as we had gone we were right, but we had not gone far enough into the work—that they had been sent by their brethren to teach the way of God more perfectly, by obedience to which all should be led into perfect holiness. They seemed to understand all the springs and avenues of the human heart. They delivered their testimony and labored to confirm it by the Scriptures. They promised the greatest blessings to the obedient, but certain damnation to the disobedient. They urged the people to confess their sins to them, especially the sin of matrimony, and to forsake all immediately—husbands must forsake their wives and wives their husbands. . . . Many said they were the great power of God, confessed their sins to them and forsook their marriage state. Among them were three of our preachers—Matthew Houston, Richard McNamar and John Dunlavy. Several more of our preachers and pupils, alarmed, fled from us, and joined the sects around us. (Biography, page 62)

It was only by the great effort of Stone that the churches were saved from this vortex of ruin. He labored day and night, far and near, among the churches where the Quakers went. By this means the evil influence was checked and their broken ranks were rallied, and soon led once more to victory.

THE WORK PROSPERS

Soon after the trouble with the Quakers had been quelled and the churches were once more in a prosperous condition, another trouble arose which threatened their entire overthrow. Two of the preachers, who with Stone had thrown off the yoke of Presbyterianism, abandoned the movement, reaffirmed their faith in the Westminster Confession of Faith, and returned to the Presbyterian fold. "Of the five of us," as he wrote at a later date, "that left the Presbyterians, I only was left, and they sought my life." Conscious of the integrity of his purpose, and convinced of the scripturalness of his position, Stone continued to preach to the churches far and near, to any who would listen to him, rendering his services gratuitously, and earning as best he could the support of his family out of his little farm. Preaching the Gospel as he now understood it, multitudes flocked to his standard, and many flourishing churches were established by him in Ohio, Kentucky and Tennessee.

As an evangelist among the pioneer population of newly-settled States he was without a rival. His large, generous nature quickly won the confidence of the hardy inhabitants. His zeal and originality awakened their interest and fixed their attention. His warm sympathies and strong emotions melted them to repentance and led them to obedience. Seldom did he preach a sermon that did not result in conversions, sometimes scores coming forward at the close of a single address. At other times the wayside cabin with its lonely occupant received with gladness the message of life. Here is a scene as he describes it:

> One day as I was riding along slowly to an appointment at night, I was passing by a small hut, when a woman ran out and called to me. I stopped my horse. She told that she had heard me preach the day before, and with a heavenly countenance thanked God for it. "For," said she, "the Lord has blessed my soul. Will you stop and baptize me?" "Yes," said I, "gladly will I do it." I dismounted, and walked into the hut. "Oh," said she, "will you wait till I send for my sister, a short distance off. She was with me, and the Lord has blessed her, too. She wants also to be baptized." "Oh, yes," said I; "I will gladly wait." She quickly dispatched a little boy to call her husband from the field near the house, and to tell the sister to come. In the meantime she was busy preparing dinner for me. It was no doubt the best she had, but such as I had never seen before. I never more thankfully, more happily, and more heartily dined. The husband soon came in, and the wife beckoned him out, and informed him of her intention of being baptized. He obstinately opposed it. In tears and distress she informed me. I talked mildly with him of the impropriety of his conduct, and at length gained his consent. Her countenance brightened with joy, and her sister came in shortly.

There, in the depths of the forest, in a stream that flowed near by, was witnessed a scene that rivals in picturesqueness and simple beauty any recorded in the Word of God.

On another occasion as he was returning from an appointment he was overtaken by a gentleman returning from the same meeting, and the two continued the journey together. Stone introduced the subject of religion, which was found not to be disagreeable to the stranger, though he made no profession of religion.   He urged him with many arguments to a speedy turning to the Lord.   It was very evident that his mind was deeply troubled and that he was vacillating as to his choice of life or death.   At length they came to a clear running stream, when he said to Stone: "See, here is water.   What doth hinder me to be baptized?" To which he replied in the language of Philip to the Eunuch: "If thou believest with all thine heart, thou mayest."   The ready response came: "I believe that Jesus Christ is the Son of God, and am determined hereafter to be his servant."   Without anything further passing between them, they dismounted and Stone baptized him.

About 1812 Stone filled an appointment of long standing in Meigs County, Ohio.   The Separate Baptists, by previous appointment, held their annual association at the same time and place.   They agreed to worship together.   The crowd of people was great, and early in the meeting Stone baptized William Caldwell, a Presbyterian preacher, in the Ohio River.   This drew the cords of friendship more closely between him and the Baptists.   By this united effort the excitement became very great.   The elders and members of the association met daily in a house near the stand, where they transacted their business, while worship was carried on at the stand.   Stone was asked and urged to assist them in their deliberations in the association, and frequently requested to give his opinion on certain points, which he did to their acceptance and approbation.   They had a very difficult case before them, on which they could come to no decision.   He was urged to speak on it, and to speak freely. He spoke freely and fully on the point, showing it to be a party measure, and unscriptural, at the same time exerting himself against sectarianism, formularies and creeds, laboring all the while to establish the scriptural ground of union among Christians, and the name they should wear, and that until Christians were united in spirit on the Bible there would be no end to such difficult cases as now confronted them.   Having closed his speech, he went at once to the stand.

The mind of the association was withdrawn from any

further consideration of the knotty cases before them to the consideration of what had been presented to them in the speech which they had just heard, with the result that they agreed to forever lay aside their formularies and creeds and take the Bible alone for their rule of faith and practice—to drop the name "Baptist" and take the name "Christian"—and to disband their association and join Stone and others in their efforts to return to apostolic Christianity. They then marched to the stand, shouting the praises of God and proclaiming aloud what they had done. They embraced each other with Christian love, by which the union was cemented. This gave a mighty impetus to the work and multitudes were added to the Lord.

CHAPTER III.

THOMAS CAMPBELL

For the present I turn from the work of Stone to that of the Campbells. Chiefly because of failing health, Thomas Campbell, an humble, but intellectually and spiritually-gifted minister of the Seceder Presbyterian Church in the parish of Ahory, Armaugh County, Ireland, determined to seek for himself and for his family a home in this country. He came alone, intending to send for his family as soon as he had established himself. He arrived in Philadelphia May 27, 1807. The Seceder Synod of North America was in session in that city when he landed. He at once presented his credentials to that body, was cordially received, and at once assigned to the Presbytery of Chartiers, in Southwestern Pennsylvania. As soon as he became settled in his new home he began in a very earnest way to exercise his ministry as a member of the presbytery, which embraced a number of counties. He had come to this country as a zealous missionary of the cross, filled with the love of souls. Already in Ireland, through various influences, he had learned to cherish a liberal religious spirit, to esteem as of little value the barriers that separate into sects.

CONFLICT WITH THE SECEDERS

The Seceders constitute one of the "straitest sects" of the Calvinistic faith, and even to this day they will not affiliate in full fraternal fellowship with other Presbyterians. It was in the matter of the communion that the severe test of fellowship was applied. Thomas Campbell had come to this country with his heart filled with a burning zeal to labor in the Lord's vineyard, and in largest charity for all communions, while still maintaining sincerely and fully his relations to his particular communion. He believed that in this freest land men's hearts would necessarily be emancipated from the unyielding sectarian prejudices and animosities of the Old World. While eminently prudent and peace-loving, he was a man of heroic temper.   He would not temporize nor bow to the tyrannous dictates of human traditions or human policy.   "This grave spirit he had already shown in his early youth, when he decided from conviction not to follow the religion of his father, who was attached to the Church of England, and preferred, as he used to say, 'to worship God according to act of Parliament.'   'The law of the Lord, in the word and spirit of the Gospel, which is 'the law of liberty,' was Thomas Campbell's supreme rule of life."

It is interesting to unfold the events which led to the final crisis that inaugurated actually and in a formal manner the restoration movement.   The Seceders were not very numerous within the limits of the Chartiers Presbytery; the power of expansion was not in them.   Mr. Campbell at once gained a wide and strong influence.   His natural ability, his scholarship and literary culture, made him much superior to the preachers in that region; and his deep religious fervor and zeal and his rare courtesy of manner won the hearts of the people.   He did not respect in his labors the narrow spirit and strict, illiberal rules and habits of the Seceder Church.   Besides this, he had found near him a number of excellent people who had come over from Ireland, Presbyterians and Independents, some of whom had been his acquaintance and cherished friends in his native land. These gathered around him, and he promptly took them to his heart in his ministrations as brethren.   This kind of freedom, however, was not in harmony with "the usages" of the Seceders.   Later on he took a step which went even further than this, and thus in a very decided way transgressed the established custom of the Church.

He was sent on a missionary tour with a young preacher, a Mr. Wilson, up the Allegheny Valley, above Pittsburgh, "to hold a celebration of the sacrament among the scattered Seceders of that then sparsely-settled region.   He found there many members of other Presbyterian bodies who had not for a long time enjoyed the privilege of these by them so highly-cherished occasions.   His heart urged him to deplore in his introductory sermon the existing divisions among

Christians, and to invite all the pious among his hearers, who were prepared for it, to unite in the participation of this sacred feast of God's people; and many accepted the invitation. This was a bold infraction of Seceder custom." Campbell could have no fellowship with such bigotry. Mr. Wilson soon discovered that Campbell had no regard for sectarian differences and prejudices and that he was not sound in the Seceder faith. "His conduct of inviting those not of his Church to partake of the communion was an overt act of extreme transgression that could not be overlooked;" but he made no objection at the time this grave offense was committed. He felt it his duty, however, to bring the matter before the presbytery at its next meeting. The charge contained several complaints, but the principal one was this public act in regard to the communion. It recited, moreover, that "Campbell had expressed his disapprobation of things in the 'Standards' and of the practical application of them."

The presbytery, already much dissatisfied with his liberal course, readily took up Wilson's charges. But they had before them a man who, although ever remarkably inclined to peace and warmly attached to the Seceder Church, would, nevertheless, not yield to any human authority against his convictions in matters of serious import. The present was a decisive moment in his life, reaching in its effects far beyond what was then thought.

After an investigation, which called from him a most earnest plea in behalf of Christian liberty and fraternity, he was found deserving of censure. In vain did he protest the treatment he had received at the hands of his brethren. In vain did he appeal from the presbytery to the synod. Party spirit was unyielding. He had expressed sentiments, it insisted, which were "very different from sentiments held and professed by the Church." This, it held, was an altogether sufficient ground of censure. From that time many of his fellow ministers became inimical to him and were disposed to inflict on him at every opportunity their petty persecutions.

Unjust as he felt the censure of the synod to be, yet so

strong was his love of peace and his desire to continue to live and labor with his brethren that he submitted to it; the condition, however, expressed in a written form to this tribunal "that his submission should be understood to mean no more, on his part, than an act of deference to the judgment of the court; that by so doing he might not give offense to his brethren by manifesting a refractory spirit." After this concession he hoped that he would be permitted to continue his labors in peace; but, much to his regret, the hostility of his opponents continued. Misrepresentations, calumny, anything that would detract from his influence, were employed against him. Spies were employed to attend his meetings, that, if possible, they might find fresh ground of accusation in his utterances. At last, worn out with these efforts, and having satisfied himself that corruption, bigotry and tryanny were inherent in existing clerical organizations, he decided to sever his connection with the religious body to which he had given life-long support, renouncing the authority of the presbytery and synod. That this final decisive step caused him much grief can not for a moment be doubted; but it is certain, also, that the freedom which it gave him, as a servant of God, must have been to him a genuine joy and an impartation of a strength of soul he never knew before.

These painful experiences soon led to important consequences. By his forced withdrawal from the presbytery he found himself without church affiliations. But this only quickened his zeal in the efforts to extend Christ's kingdom. He had gained a wide and strong influence in the region in which he lived. No meeting houses were at his command; but he held his assemblies, after the pioneer fashion, in private dwellings, barns, schoolhouses and under green trees. In these labors it was no part of his plan to organize a separate religious party. Such parties were already too numerous. At first it seems that he had no definite plan of action. He had simply determined to use his strength in such ways as Providence should open to him, in putting an end to partyism, by inducing the different denominations to unite together on the Bible. In this purpose many of his neighbors heartily sympathized with him, though shrinking from the conclusions to which they were being irresistably driven.

At last the time seemed ripe for some forward movement. He therefore determined to adopt what he believed to be the best course to promote the interest of his Master's cause. He saw that many of his hearers sincerely, some ardently, had accepted the principles he was advocating and were constant in attendance on his ministry. He consequently proposed to them that they meet together and consult on the best method to give more order, definiteness and permanency to their efforts. This met with ready and general approbation. A day was named and at the appointed hour a large company assembled in an old farmhouse in the neighborhood. The company was composed of thoughtful men and women, deeply conscious of the importance of the occasion. They were plain, hard-working pioneers, but they were men and women of faith, whose hearts were pained at the division into warring sects and parties. Though belonging to different religious parties, they had met to seek a pathway of closer fellowship.

A feeling of deep solemnity pervaded the entire assembly, when at length Mr. Campbell arose to address them. The theme of the occasion had grown to be the burden of his heart. He gave a clear exposition of the situation and of the object of the assembly. The events that had led to the calling of this meeting, well understood by all, had made a deep impression upon them. The discourse was a strong argument against sectarian divisions and in behalf of Christian unity on the Bible as the only infallible standard of doctrine and practice, to the rejection of all human traditions. He concluded this remarkable discourse by urging with great earnestness the adoption of the following principles as the rule of their future action and life as Christians: *"Where the Scriptures speak, we speak; where the Scriptures are silent, we are silent."* This bold maxim was so just that no one of the audience, prepared as they were by previous teaching, could for a moment hesitate to accept it as right. These people could not help seeing the effect of this law on some of the most familiar practices of the denominations to which most of them belonged.

THE DECLARATION AND ADDRESS

Ths discourse to which reference has been made, closed with: "Where the Scriptures speak, we speak; where the Scriptures are silent, we are silent," and produced a profound impression on the audience. The majority of the audience were ready, unhesitatingly, to give a hearty assent to this great declaration. But the troublesome question arose, "Where will it lead us?"

When Mr. Campbell had concluded, opportunity was given for free expression of views, whereupon Andrew Munro, a shrewd Scotch Seceder, arose and said: "Mr. Campbell, if we adopt that as a basis, then there is an end of infant baptism." This remark and the manifest conviction that it carried with it, produced a great sensation, for the whole audience was composed of pedo-baptists who cherish infant baptism as one of their cardinal doctrines. "Of course," said Mr. Campbell, in reply, "if infant baptism is not found in Scripture we can have nothing to do with it." This bold declaration came like a new revelation to the audience. Thomas Acheson, one of Mr. Campbell's closest friends, in a very excited manner arose and said: "I hope I may never see the day when my heart will renounce that blessed saying of the Scripture, 'Suffer the little children to come unto me, and forbid them not, for of such is the kingdom of heaven!'" Upon saying this he burst into tears, and was about to retire to the adjoining room when James Foster, well informed in the Scriptures, called out, "Mr. Acheson, I would remark that in the portion of Scripture you have quoted there is no reference to infant baptism." Without offering a reply Mr. Acheson passed into the adjoining room to weep alone.

This new turn of things, so unexpected to them, did not lessen their confidence in the position they had taken, or in the man who was leading them onward. At the end of the conference the great principle was adopted without any real opposition. It would have been difficult for them to object to a profession so manifestly loyal to God and so impregnably founded in the Holy Scriptures. The principle, so universal in its application, and its controlling authority in all things that concern the faith and practice of the followers of the Lord Jesus Christ, became henceforth the watchword and directive law of action of those endeavoring to restore apostolic Christianity. Some of those who started out in this great movement, when they saw more clearly the inevitable, logical result of the great principle now adopted, one after another broke off all connection with this work.

They now began to feel that in order to carry out with successful effect this noble purpose they must organize themselves into a well-ordered, permanent association. At a meeting held August 17, 1809, it was decided that they would formally unite themselves into a regular body, under the name of "The Christian Association of Washington." They then appointed twenty-one of their number to meet and confer together, and, with the assistance of Thomas Campbell, to determine upon the proper means to carry into effect their purposes. At it was found to be very inconvenient to hold meetings in private houses, it was deemed advisable to provide some regular place of meeting. The neighbors, as was customary in those days, all moved by good will for the excellent man and his purposes, assembled and erected a log building three miles from Mount Pleasant, Washington County, Pa. This building was designed, also, for the purpose of a common school, which was much needed in that neighborhood. No ecclesiastical aspirations, no sectarian ambition, no party purpose or name, entered into the erection of this humble building. The name and cause of Christ alone prompted and sanctified the act of these honest souls.

Near by, in the house of Mr. Welch, a worthy farmer who was friendly to the association, Mr. Campbell had a home. A little chamber upstairs was assigned to him as his apartment. Here he spent his leisure time in quiet study, for he felt that he needed these days of undisturbed retirement to prepare himself to meet, in wisdom and the fear of God, the crisis through which he and those united with him were passing. The writing with which he was at this time engaged was designed to set forth to the public at large, in a clear and definite manner, the character and purposes of the association. In the "prophet's chamber" Thomas Campbell wrote the "Declaration and Address" which became so famous in the early history of the effort to restore apostolic Christianity. When it was finished he called a special meeting of the chief members and read it to them for their approval and adoption. This meeting unanimously approved it and ordered its publication September 7, 1809.

This production is, in its substance and spirit, as well as in its vigorous and scholarly style, the most notable historical production of the initiatory period of the effort to restore the apostolic church in its doctrine and practice, and is worthy of diligent and thoughtful study at the present day. It is proper, therefore, that I should note the essential principles therein set forth. The admirable introduction setting forth and deploring the divided state among the professed followers of the Savior concluded as follows:

Our desire, therefore, for ourselves and our brethren would be that, rejecting human opinions and the inventions of men as of any authority, or as having any place in the Church of God, we might forever cease from further contentions about such things, returning to and holding fast by the original standard, taking the divine Word alone for our rule, the Holy Spirit for our teacher and guide to lead us into all truth, and Christ alone as exhibited in the Word for our salvation; and that by so doing we may be at peace among ourselves, follow peace with all men and holiness, without which no man shall see the Lord.

Then follows a statment of the purpose and program of the association: To form a religious association for promoting simple and evangelical Christianity, under the name of the "Christian Association of Washington"; to contribute a certain sum to support a pure Gospel ministry and supply the poor with the Scriptures; to encourage the formation of similar associations; to consider itself not a church, but as a church reformation society; to countenance only such ministers as adhere closely to the example and precept of Scripture in conduct and teaching; to entrust the management of the association to a standing committee of twenty-one; to hold two meetings a year; to open each meeting with a sermon; and to look to the friends of genuine Christianity for the support of their work.

This is followed by the address, with the following dedicatory heading: "To all that love our Lord Jesus Christ, in sincerity, throughout all the churches, the following address is most respectfully submitted." After an arraignment of the evils of divisions and an indictment of sectarianism, he pleads with his "dearly beloved brethren" of "all the churches" "to unite in the bonds of an entire Christian unity—Christ alone being the head, the center, his word the rule; and explicit belief of and manifest conformity to it in all things—the terms." Thus to "come firmly and fairly to original ground, and take up things just as the apostles left them." In this way they could become "disentangled from the accruing embarrassments of intervening ages," and stand "upon the same ground on which the church stood at the beginning." "Here, indeed, was the startling proposition to begin anew—to begin at the beginning; to ascend at once to the pure fountain of truth, and to neglect and disregard, as though they had never been, the decrees of popes, cardinals, synods and assemblies, and all the traditions and corruptions of an apostate church. Here was an effort not so much for the reformation of the church as was that of Luther and of Calvin and of Haldanes, but for its complete restoration at once to its pristine purity and perfection. By coming at once to the primitive model and rejecting all human imaginations; by submitting implicity to the divine authority as plainly expressed in the Scriptures, and by disregarding all the assumptions and dictations of fallible men, it was proposed to form a union upon a basis to which no valid objection could possibly be offered. By this summary method the church was to be at once released from the controversies of eighteen centuries, and from conflicting claims of all pretenders to apostolic thrones, and the primitive Gospel of salvation was to be disentangled and disembarrassed from all those corruptions and perversions which had heretofore delayed or arrested its progress."

There were certain "fundamental truths" of the nature of "first principles," "truths demonstrably evident in the light of Scripture and right reason," which *underly* the proposal for a union of the professed followers of Christ. These are so interesting and important that I deem it wise to give them, for they need to be diligently and profoundly studied by the present generation.   They are summed up in the following propositions:

1.   That the Church of Christ upon earth is essentially, intentionally and constitutionally one; consisting of all those in every place that profess their faith in Christ and obedience to him in all things according to the Scriptures, and that manifest the same by their tempers and conduct, and of none else; as none else can be truly and properly called Christians.

2.   That although the Church of Christ upon earth must necessarily exist in particular and distinct societies, locally separate one from another, yet there ought to be no schisms, no uncharitable divisions among them.   They ought to receive each other as Christ Jesus hath also received them, to the glory of God.   And for this purpose they ought all to walk by the same rule, to mind and speak the same thing, and to be perfectly joined together in the same mind and in the same judgment.

3.   That in order to this nothing ought to be inculcated upon Christians as articles of faith, nor required of them as terms of communion, but what is expressly taught and enjoined upon them in the Word of God.   Nor ought anything to be admitted as of divine obligation, in their church constitution and management, but what is expressly enjoined by the authority of our Lord Jesus Christ and his apostles upon the New Testament Church, either in express terms or by approved precedent.

4.   That although the Scriptures of the Old and New Testaments are inseparably connected, making together but one perfect and entire revelation of the divine will, for the edification and salvation of the Church, and therefore in that respect can not be separated, yet as to what directly and properly belongs to their immediate object, the New Testament is as perfect a constitution for the worship, discipline and government of the New Testament Church, and as perfect a rule for the particular duties of its members, as the Old Testament was for the worship, discipline and government of the Old Testament Church, and the particular duties of its members.

5. That with respect to the commands and ordinances of our Lord Jesus Christ, where the Scriptures are silent as to the express time or manner of performance, if any such there be, no human authority has power to interfere, in order to supply deficiency by making laws for the Church; nor can anything more be required of Christians in such cases, but only that they so observe these commands and ordinances as will evidently answer the declared and obvious end of their institution.   Much less have any human authority power to impose new commands or ordinances upon the Church, which our Lord Jesus Christ has not enjoined.   Nothing ought to be received into the faith or worship of the Church, or be made a term of communion among Christians, that is not as old as the New Testament.

6. That although inferences and deductions from Scripture premises, when fairly inferred, may be truly called the doctrine of God's holy Word, yet are they not formally binding upon the consciences of Christians farther than they perceive the connection, and evidently see that they are so; for their faith must not stand in the wisdom of men, but in the power and veracity of God.   Therefore no such deductions can be made the terms of communion, but do properly belong to the after and progressive edification of the Church.   Hence, it is evident that no such deductions or inferential truth ought to have any place in the Church's confession.

7. That although doctrinal exhibitions of the great system of divine truths and defensive testimonies in opposition to prevailing errors be highly expedient, and the more full and explicit they be for those purposes the better; yet, as these must be in a great measure the effect of human reasoning, and of course must contain many inferential truths, they ought not to be made terms of Christian communion, unless we suppose, what is contrary to fact, that none have a right to the communion of the Church, but such as possess a very clear and decisive judgment, or are come to a very high degree of doctrinal information; whereas the Church from the beginning did, and ever will, consist of little children and young men, as well as fathers.

8. That as it is not necessary that persons should have a particular knowledge or distinct apprehension of all divinely-revealed truths in order to entitle them to a place in the Church, neither should they, for this purpose, be required to make a profession more extensive than their knowledge; but that, on the contrary, their having a due measure of scriptural self-knowledge respecting their lost and perishing condition by nature and practice, and of the way of salvation through Jesus Christ, accompanied with a profession of their faith in the obedience to him, in all things, according to his Word, is

all that is absolutely necessary to qualify them for admission into his Church.

9. That all who are able through grace to make such a profession, and to manifest the reality of it in their tempers and conduct, should consider each other as the precious saints of God, should love each other as brethren, children of the same family and Father, temples of the same Spirit, members of the same body, subjects of the same grace, objects of the same divine love, bought with the same price, and joint-heirs of the same inheritance.   Whom God hath thus joined together no man should dare put asunder.

10. That divisions among the Christians is a horrid evil, fraught with many evils.   It is anti-Christian, as it destroys the visible unity of the body of Christ; as if he were divided against himself, excluding and excommunicating a part of himself.   It is anti-scriptural, as being strictly prohibited by his sovereign authority, a direct violation of his express command. It is anti-natural, as it excites Christians to condemn, to hate and oppose one another, where bound by the highest and most endearing obligation to love each other as brethren, even as Christ has loved them.   In a word, it is productive of confusion and of every evil work.

11. That (in some instances) a partial neglect of the expressly revealed will of God, and (in others) an assumed authority for making the approbation of human opinions and of human inventions a term of communion, by introducing them into the constitution, faith or worship of the Church, are, and have been, the immediate, obvious and universally acknowledged causes of all corruptions and divisions that ever have taken place in the Church of God.

12. That all that is necessary to the highest state of perfection and purity of the Church upon earth is, first, that none be received as members, but such as, having that due measure of scriptural self-knowledge described above, do profess their faith in Christ and obedience to him in all things according to the Scriptures; nor, secondly, that any be retained in her communion longer than they continue to manifest the reality of their profession by their temper and conduct. Thirdly, that her ministers, duly and scripturally qualified, inculcate none other things than those very articles of faith and holiness expressly revealed and enjoined in the Word of God.   Lastly, that in all their administrations they keep close by the observance of all divine ordinances, after the example of the primitive Church, exhibited in the New Testament, without any additions whatever of human opinions or inventions of men.

13. Lastly, that if any circumstantials indispensably necessary to the observance of divine ordinances be not found

upon the pages of express revelation, such, and such only, as are absolutely necessary for this purpose should be adopted under the title of human expedients, without any pretense to a more sacred origin, so that any subsequent alteration or difference in the observance of these things might produce no contention nor division in the Church. ("Memoirs of Thomas Campbell," pages 48-52.)

CHAPTER IV.

ALEXANDER CAMPBELL

Alexander Campbell, the son, arrived in this country September 29, 1809, just as the proof sheets of the Declaration and Address were coming from the press, and as a matter of the first concern with him, Thomas Campbell gave a full detail of the events already related to his son, and desired especially that he should read and consider the Declaration and Address. This Alexander did, and fell in heartily with the action of his father and the principles set forth therein. A new world of thought and life was now opened to him. He had spent one of the two years of separation in study at the University of Glasgow, where his father had formerly studied, and while there came more intimately under the influence of the new ideas and move‧ments of the country. There he had met Greville Ewing, the Haldanes, and other religious leaders of the time who were pressing for larger liberty of religious service under the rule of a stricter conformity to the Scriptures, and had in a large measure imbibed these principles. He had not had the courage to write to his father of his change of convictions from the old church, and now feared that his changed course would bring him deep pain. In this attitude of mind the meeting between father and son took place. Happy was the surprise when each learned that the other no longer adhered to the old religious party in which they had been reared.

SUBJECT AND ACT OF BAPTISM SETTLED

While reading the proof sheets of the Declaration and Address, Alexander Campbell had a conversation on the principles set forth therein with a Mr. Riddle, of the Presbyterian Church, whom he accidentally met. When the proposition that "nothing should be required as a matter of faith or duty for which a 'Thus saith the Lord' could not be produced either in express terms or by approved precedent," was introduced, Mr. Riddle very promptly replied that the words, however plausible in appearance, were not sound; for if that were followed it would be necessary to abandon infant baptism. To which he replied, "Why, sir, is there in the Scriptures no express precept nor precedent for infant baptism?" "Not one, sir," was the prompt reply.

This reply startled and mortified Mr. Campbell, and shortly afterward he mentioned the suggested difficulty to his father, who replied, "We make our appeal to the law and the testimony. Whatever is not found therein must of course be abandoned." Not willing to remain in uncertainty on the subject, he procured all the books and tracts he could favorable to the practice. On reading them he was disgusted with the assumptions and fallacious reasonings to sustain the practice, and threw them aside with the faint hope of finding something more convincing in the Greek New Testament. "This, however, only made the matter worse, and upon again entering into a conversation with his father on the subject he found him entirely willing to admit that there were neither 'express terms' nor 'precedent' to authorize the practice. 'But,' said he, 'as for those who are already members of the church and participants of the Lord's Supper, I can see no propriety, even if the scriptural evidence for infant baptism be found deficient, in their unchurching or paganizing themselves, or in putting off Christ, merely for the sake of making a new profession; thus going out of the church merely for the sake of coming in again.'"

From this it seems that he was disposed only to concede that they ought not to teach nor practice infant baptism without divine authority, and that they should preach and practice scriptural baptism in regard to all who were to make, for the first time, a profession of faith. In deference to his views, the son dismissed the subject for the time, "seemingly satisfied with the fallacious reasoning imposed by circumstances, which prevented his father from seeing then the real position which baptism occupied in the Christian economy, and consequently from making, in regard to it, a practical application of his own principles." With this

Alexander Campbell seems to have suspended his investigation of the subject, and to have foreborne giving to it that impartial and continued attention necessary to the discovery of truth.   In a discourse delivered June 5, 1811, on Christ's commission to his apostles (Mark 16: 15, 16), he said, in reference to baptism: "As I am sure it is unscriptural to make this matter [baptism] a term of communion, I let it slip.   I wish to think and let think on these matters."

But circumstances came up later which compelled him to give it a most painstaking examination.   He was married March 12, 1811, and on March 13, 1812, his first child was born.   Soon after this event a great change took place in his views in regard to baptism.   His wife, with her father and mother, was still a member of the Presbyterian Church, and, as the child grew, it was natural that the subject of infant baptism should become one of immediate practical interest.   As viewed from the viewpoint of his early education, infant baptism was a rite justified, inferentially at least, and not to be neglected; but viewed from the principles set forth in the Declaration and Address it possessed no divine authority, yet as an ancient and venerated practice, and for the sake of peace, it seemed to his father and to himself expedient to allow its continuance in the case of such members as conscientiously believed it proper.   Most of the members of the church, furthermore, supposed themselves to have been baptized into the church in their infancy.   From the occasional discussions of the subject among the members of the Brush Run Church, there was an increasing conviction on the part of many that baptism was a matter of much more importance than had been generally supposed, and now his changed relationship caused him to share in this conviction.   Admitting that infant baptism is without divine warrant assumed a very different aspect, and was no longer, "May we safely reject infant baptism as a mere human invention?" but, "May we omit believers' baptism, which all admit to be divinely commanded?"   In other words, if infant baptism is without divine warrant, it is invalid, and they who receive it are as a matter of fact still unbaptized. "When they come to know this in after years, will God accept the credulity of the parent for the faith of the child?" "Men may be pleased to omit faith on the part of the person baptized, but will God sanction the omission of baptism on the part of the believer, on the ground that in his infancy he had been the subject of a ceremony which had not been enjoined?" "On the other hand, if the practice of infant baptism can be justified by inferential reasoning on any sufficient evidence, why should it not be adopted or continued by common consent, without further discussion?"

Such were some of the thoughts which at this time passed through the mind of Alexander Campbell. Desiring to maintain "a conscience void of offense toward God and men," and sensible of the responsibilities resting upon him in the new relationship which he sustained as a father, he was led to think more earnestly and seriously upon the whole subject, so that he might not come short in any duty that God had placed upon him. At this point he parted company with all uninspired authorities and turned to the Greek New Testament and diligently applied himself to the meaning of the words translated into the English by the words "baptize" and "baptism," and soon became thoroughly satisfied that the act indicated by them could not be performed short of a burial of the subject in water. By further investigations he was led to the strong conviction that believers, and believers only, were the scriptural subjects of the ordinance. "He now fully perceived that the rite of sprinkling to which he had been subjected in infancy was wholly unauthorized, and that he was, consequently, in point of fact, an unbaptized person, and hence could not consistently preach a baptism to others of which he had never been a subject himself." The subject was of such serious and anxious inquiry that he frequently conversed with his wife on the subject; she also became interested in it, and finally reached the same conclusion.

Having now reached such a definite conclusion in regard to the matter, he could not long refrain from putting his convictions into practice, so he resolved to obey what he now found to be a positive, divine command. Some time prior to this he had formed an acquaintance with Matthias Luce, a Baptist preacher, who lived some thirty miles distant, to whom he now decided to apply to perform the rite. On his way to see him he called to see his father and the family. Soon after his arrival his sister, Dorothea, took him aside and told him that she had been in great trouble for some time in regard to the validity of her baptism, as she could find no authority whatever in the New Testament for infant baptism, and as she had received nothing else, could not resist the conviction that she had never been baptized, and requested him to lay her difficulties before her father. To this unexpected announcement he responded that he also had reached the same conclusion and was then on his way to arrange with Mr. Luce to immerse him, and that he would lay the whole matter before their father. Accordingly he sought and obtained an interview with him; discussed the subject at some length, and concluded with these words: "I now fully and conscientiously believe that I have never been baptized, and consequently I am, in point of fact, an unbaptized person; and hence can not consistently preach baptism to others, as I have never submitted to it myself." To this his father responded, "I have, then, nothing further to add. You must please yourself."

As Alexander was leaving the next morning, his father said: "When, where, and by whom do you intend to be immersed?" To which Alexander replied: "As to the place, I prefer to be baptized near home, among those who are accustomed to hear my preaching; as to the time, just as soon as I can make arrangements with a suitable Baptist preacher. I will let you know as soon as I make the necessary arrangements." The interview with Mr. Luce was satisfactory and everything was satisfactorily arranged. Mr. Richardson gives the following interesting account of the baptism:

Wednesday, June 12, 1812, having been selected, Elder Luce, in company with Elder Henry Spears, called at Thomas Campbell's on their way to the place chosen for the immersion, which was the deep pool in Buffalo Creek, where three members of the Association had formerly been baptized. Next morning, as they were setting out, Thomas Campbell simply remarked that Mrs. Campbell had put up a change of raiment for herself and him, which was the first intimation that they also intended to be immersed. Upon arriving at the place, as the greater part of the Brush Run Church, with a large concourse of others, attracted by the novelty of the occasion, were assembled at David Bryant's house, near the place, Thomas Campbell thought it proper to present, in full, the reasons which had determined his course. In a long address he reviewed the entire ground which he had occupied, and the struggles that he had undergone in reference to the particular subject of baptism, which he had earnestly desired to dispose of, in such a manner that it might be no hindrance in the attainment of that Christian unity which he had labored to establish on the Bible alone. In endeavoring to do this he admitted that he had been led to overlook its importance, and the very many plain and obvious teachings of the Scriptures on the subject; but having at length attained a clearer view of duty, he felt it incumbent upon him to submit to what he now saw an important Divine institution. Alexander afterwards followed with an extended defense of their proceedings, urging the necessity of submitting implicitly to all God's commandments, and showing that the baptism of believers only was authorized by the Word of God.

In his remarks, he had quoted, among other scriptures, the command of Peter to the believers on the day of Pentecost: "Repent and be baptized, every one of you, in the name of Jesus Christ, for the remission of sins, and you shall receive the gift of the Holy Spirit;" and had dwelt at length upon the gracious promises of God to all who should obey him. When he had concluded, James Hanen, who, with his wife, had also concluded to be baptized, took his child from its mother's arms and requested her to walk aside, asked her what she thought of the declaration of Peter, "You shall receive the gift of the Holy Spirit," and how she understood it. Mrs. Hanan, being well acquainted with the Scriptures, soon gave a satisfactory reply, and both were accordingly baptized along with the rest, consisting of Alexander Campbell and his wife, his father and mother, and his sister—in all, seven persons. Alexander had stipulated with Elder Luce that the ceremony should be performed precisely according to the pattern given in the New Testament, and that, as there was no account of any of the first converts being called upon to give what is called "a religious experience," this modern custom should be omitted, and that the candidates should be admitted on the simple confession that "Jesus Christ is the Son of God." These points he had fully discussed with Luce during the evening spent at his house when he first went up to request his attendance, and they had been arranged as he desired.   Elder Luce had, indeed, at first objected to these changes, as being contrary to Baptist usage, but finally consented, remarking that he believed they were right, and he would run the risk of censure.   There were not, therefore, upon this occasion, any of the usual forms of receiving persons into the Church upon a detailed account of religious feelings and impressions. . . . All were, therefore, admitted to immersion upon making the simple confes·sion of Christ required of the converts in the apostolic times. The meeting, it is related, continued seven hours. (Memoirs of A. Campbell, Vol I, pages 396-398.)

Within a week of the immersion of the Campbells and their group, thirteen other members of the Brush Run Church asked to be immersed, and it was done by Thomas Campbell, upon a simple confession of their faith in Jesus Christ as the Son of God.   It was not long before the entire church of thirty or more members were immersed, for those who did not accept immersion withdrew from the church and united with some of the denominations in the community.   Immersion became a condition of union and communion with the Brush Run Church.   Its conversion into a company of immersed believers did not bring them any favor from the pedobaptist churches of the community.

The Brush Run Church had come to its position under the guidance of primitive apostolic example and its application to every item of faith and practice which is adopted in its order.   It was not seeking agreement with any religious body, but "the old paths," agreement with the "original standard," "that it might come fairly and firmly to original ground upon clear and certain premises, and take up things just as the apostles left them."   It was feeling its way and making sure of its ground as it went.   It knew of no religious body that stood upon original ground; none that dared to return to the original standard.   The sense of freedom which it enjoyed in being bound only by the New Testament with respect to all doctrines and practices, was equaled only by the sense of certainty it enjoyed in being infallibly guided by the New Testament to the true conditions of unity and communion.

THE REDSTONE ASSOCIATION

As was to be expected, the attitude of the Brush Run Church in becoming a body of immersed believers awakened a storm of opposition from the pedobaptist ranks, and its members became the subjects of no little persecution. Misrepresentations of all kinds, were freely circulated among the people. Family and friendship ties were broken, and the common civilities of society were denied to this new order of "heretics." It is related that Alexander Campbell, returning after nightfall from one of his appointments about this time, was overtaken by a violent storm. Calling at the house of a member of the Seceder Church, he asked for shelter from the violence of the storm. Before granting his request she desired to know his name. On being informed she promptly refused him admittance, giving as her reason her hostility to his religious views. So he was forced to continue his journey through an almost trackless forest, until he reached his home. These trials, so far from discouraging this feeble band of earnest searchers for the truth, served rather to strengthen their faith and zeal. Convinced of the correctness of their course, they were drawn more closely to each other by the petty persecutions which they were now called upon to suffer. "They often visited each other's houses, frequently spending the greater portion of the night in social prayer, in searching the Scriptures, asking and answering questions, and singing hymns of praise." Thus was laid, in obscurity and adversity, the foundation of the great work of returning to the "example of the primitive Christians exhibited in the New Testament; without any addition whatever of human opinions or inventions of men."

A new situation now confronted them. When the Baptists heard of the action of the Brush Run Church in submitting to immersion and adopting it in their practice, they were highly elated and began to urge the church to join the Redstone Association, which embraced all the Baptist churches of that region. Alexander Campbell had not been favorably impressed with the Baptists, either as ministers

or people, and had no idea of uniting with them. He, however, liked the people better, and the preachers less, the
more he became acquainted with them. He did not press
himself upon their attention, but they knew his power as a
preacher and often sent for him to preach for them. He
visited their association which convened at Uniontown, Pa.,
in the autumn of 1812. He went as a spectator, and returned more disgusted than when he went. He was invited
to preach, but he declined, except one evening in a private
family, "to a dozen preachers and twice as many laymen."
He returned home not intending ever to visit another association. Later on he learned that the Baptists themselves
did not appreciate the preaching or the preachers of that
association. They regarded the speakers as worse than
usual, and their discourses as not at all edifying. Then
they pressed on Mr. Campbell from every quarter to visit
their churches, and preach for them. He often spoke to
Baptist congregations for sixty miles around.

The matter of joining the Redstone Association was laid
before the Brush Run Church in the fall of 1813. They
discussed the propriety of the measure. After much discussion and earnest desire to be directed by the wisdom that
cometh down from above, they finally concluded to make
an overture to that effect, and to write out a full view of
their sentiments, wishes and determinations on the subject.
They did so, exhibiting their remonstrance against all human
creeds as bonds of communion and union among Christians,
and expressing a willingness, upon certain conditions, to
co-operate or unite with that association, provided always
that they should be allowed to teach and preach whatever
they learned from the Holy Scriptures, regardless of any
creed or formula in Christendom.

The proposition was discussed at the association, and,
after much debate, was decided by a good majority in favor
of their being received. Thus a union was formed. But
the party opposed, though small, began early to work, and
continued with a perseverance worthy of a better cause. But
for three years they could do nothing. The situation in

which Mr. Campbell found himself, soon after his connection with the Redstone Association of the Baptist churches, was not at all inviting. The originality of his method in dealing with the Scriptures, and his utter disregard for customs, however time-honored, which were not sanctioned by primitive precept or example, awakened the suspicion of the more narrow-minded of the Baptist preachers, who were not slow in manifesting their disapproval. His popularity among the churches of the association no doubt added to their displeasure, and at every opportunity he was made to feel the sting of their resentment. This hostility, which at first manifested itself in slights and little annoyances, at last led to an open attack upon his teachings.

When the association met at Cross Creek in August, 1816, in spite of the intrigues of his enemies he was appointed as one of the speakers, on which occasion he preached his great "Sermon on the Law." In that discourse he sharply discriminated between the law of Moses and the Gospel, showing that the former had served its purpose, and that its authority had passed away when the kingdom of the Messiah was established. This marked another important advance in the progress of the efforts to return to apostolic Christianity. The distinction between the law and the Gospel, the old covenant and the new, the letter and the spirit, the Jewish commonwealth and the kingdom, had been greatly obscured in popular thought. It was claimed that the law was still alive, and that Christians come under its provisions as such, with the exception of its strictly ceremonial parts, and that the church under the Christian dispensation is the same that existed under the Jewish dispensation. The sermon, though containing but plain Scripture teaching, was such a bold assault upon the theology and style of preaching current among the Baptists that it created a great sensation in the association, and raised a storm of persecution. The common people were, for the most part, pleased with his simple, natural presentation of the truth, but this only added fuel to the flame of bitterness which some of the preachers cherished against him. "This will never do," they said, "this is not our doctrine."

In consequence of the views presented in this sermon, Mr. Campbell was "brought up for trial and condemnation" at the next meeting of the association in the autumn of 1817. At that time but few were ready to accept the conclusion in the sermon, and the actual adherents of the teaching, scattered among the Baptists of three States, did not number more than one hundred and fifty persons; but notwithstanding this feeble support, upon investigation he was acquitted of the charge made against him.   Opposition to him increased in the Redstone Association, and some of the preachers determined to manufacture a sentiment that would thrust him out when the association should meet in September, 1823.   In pursuance of this purpose certain influential men canvassed all the churches and secured the appointment of messengers who were in sympathy with themselves in opposition to Mr. Campbell; and when the association met all things were in readiness to exclude the author of the "Sermon on the Law" from the fellowship of the association.   But to the astonishment and chagrin of the plotters, when the letter from the Brush Run Church was read, Mr. Campbell, though present, was not mentioned as a messenger.   This cooled the ardor of his enemies who had hoped to close Baptist ears against him by a decree of excommunication, and crush his influence generally by putting him in the discreditable position of one expelled from the association.   A motion being made to invite him to a seat in the body, his enemies opposed it, and demanded to know why he had not been sent as a messenger.   After much discussion Mr. Campbell relieved the situation by stating that the church of which he was then a member did not belong to the Redstone Association.   In describing the chagrin of his enemies when this announcement was made, Mr. Campbell says:

Never did hunters, on seeing the game unexpectedly escape from their toils at the moment when its capture was sure, glare upon each other a more mortifying disappointment than that indicated by my pursuers at that instant, on hearing that I was out of their bailiwick, and consequently out of their jurisdiction. A solemn stillness ensued, and for a time all parties seemed to have nothing to do.

Foreseeing the storm that was gathering, and learning, just a few weeks before the time for the association to convene, the plans that were being so industriously laid to exclude him from the association, he determined to defeat the project in a way which his enemies little expected, but which was in strict accordance with Baptist usage. As he had been frequently solicited by Adomson Bently to leave the Redstone Association and unite with the Mahoning, and as a number of the members of the Brush Run Church lived in Wellsburg and vicinity, he decided this was an opportune time to form a separate congregation in which he would have his membership, and which might afterward unite with the Mahoning Association. He announced, therefore, to the church at Brush Run that he desired from them letters of dismission for himself and some thirty other members in order to constitute a church at Wellsburg. This request was granted and a congregation was at once formed in the town of Wellsburg, and continued to assemble regularly ever afterward in the house which had been previously erected for that purpose. Thus were the unrighteous attempts of wicked men defeated.

A WIDER FIELD

Shortly before the events already mentioned, Mr. Campbell was very unexpectedly drawn into a discussion with John Walker, a minister of the Seceder Presbyterian Church. It came about in this way: The jealousy of rival religious parties at Mount Pleasant, Ohio, led to a controversy between Mr. Walker and Mr. Birch, a Baptist preacher, which ended in a challenge by Mr. Walker to meet any Baptist preacher of good standing in the public discussion of the question of baptism. The high opinion entertained throughout that region for Mr. Campbell's ability led to his selection as the most suitable champion of the Baptist cause. Owing to the circumstances under which he was placed, he did not give an immediate answer. In the meantime Mr. Birch renewed the appeal, and finally made it more urgent by stating that it was the unanimous wish of all the Baptist churches throughout that region that he should be their representative in the discussion.   Being thus called upon by the church, and urged by personal friends, he could no longer refuse to yield to his own convictions of public duty.

His hesitancy was not due to his own disinclination, but in deference to his father, who did not regard "public debates the proper method of proceeding in contending for the faith once delivered to the saints."   He, however, finally succeeded in convincing his father that, however much the usual unprofitable debates upon human theories were to be deplored and avoided, no objection could lie against a public defense of revealed truth, for which the Scriptures afforded abundant precedent.   Having gained this point with his father, he finally informed Mr. Birch of his willingness to enter the discussion.

All preliminaries having been arranged, the discussion began on Monday morning, June 19, 1820, at Mount Pleasant, Ohio.   It was attended by a large concourse of people and created great interest.   Mr. Walker's first speech was very brief, and as it gives the gist of his whole contention throughout the debate, I will give it in full:

> My friends, I do not intend to speak long at one time, perhaps not more than five or ten minutes, and will, therefore, come to the point at once: I maintain that baptism came into the room of circumcision; that the covenant on which the Jewish Church was built, and to which circumcision is the seal, is the same with the covenant on which the Christian Church is built, and to which baptism is the seal; that the Jews and the Christians are the same body politic under the same lawgiver and husband; hence the Jews were called the congregation of the Lord; and the bridegroom of the church says, "My love, my undefiled is one"—consequently the infants of believers have a right to baptism.

In response to this speech Mr. Campbell said that the pedobaptists acted as if they did not themselves believe infant baptism to be true, since, in point of fact, they did not put baptism in the room of circumcision, as they did not confine it to males only and extend it to servants as well as to children, perform it on the eighth day, etc.; and then proceeded to point out various differences between the two institutions which rendered the supposed substitution of the one for the other impossible. Among these he particularizes the fact that circumcision required only carnal descent from Abraham, but that baptism demanded faith in Christ as its indispensable prerequisite; and that baptism differed from circumcision in the nature of the blessings it conveyed, which were spiritual and not temporal: "Baptism is connected with the promise of the remission of sins and the gift of the Holy Spirit." This utterance is his first public recognition of the importance of baptism. While he then distinctly perceived and asserted a scriptural connection between baptism and remission of sins, he seems at this time to have viewed it only in the light of an argument and to have but a faint conception of its great practical importance in the economy of grace.

As the discussion proceeded, all recognized that he was an invincible defender of what he believed the Scriptures taught. His whole training had fitted him for such an arena. His liberal education, his extensive reading, his wonderful memory, his faultless diction, his remarkable self-control, sustained as they were by deep earnestness of purpose, gave him at once a vantage ground which he never relinquished. But such was the originality of his method in handling the truth and his freedom from the accepted terms of the theological schools that even the victory, which was universally admitted to be with him, was not accepted by many of the Baptists as an unmixed blessing. The opportunities and issues of the debate were such as to convince Mr. Campbell of its practical utility in disseminating the truth and he gave the following challenge in his concluding speech.

> I this day publish to all present that I feel disposed to meet any pedobaptist minister of any denomination, of good standing in his party, and I engage to prove in a debate with him, either orally or with the pen, that infant sprinkling is a human tradition and injurious to the well-being of society, religious and political.

Such a challenge was well calculated to make a deep impression on all who heard it, and this was what he designed it to do.   In the frankness of his independent spirit he, from that time forward, held himself in readiness to meet in public discussion any worthy champion who might rise in opposition to the truths he taught, or in defense of popular religious error.

The effect of this discussion, however, was to aid Mr. Campbell's growing reputation.   His fame was widely extended by the publication of the debate, which was read by thousands, and began soon to produce results far beyond his fondest hopes.   The printed debate circulated very widely among the Baptists, who felt that they had the best of the argument.   While some Baptists "remained extremely dubious in regard to the orthodoxy of their champion," others took grateful pride in him, and felt, as one Baptist declared, that "he had done more for the Baptists in the West than any other man."

The printing and circulation of the debate opened the eyes of Mr. Campbell to the power and usefulness of the press.   From that time forward he cherished the hope that he might do something upon a more extended scale to rouse the people from their spiritual lethargy.   Step by step he had been brought to an eminence from which he could survey the wide field in which he was destined to labor, and he now nerved himself for the undertaking.   After maturing his plans, he conferred with his father and others concerning the advisability of issuing a monthly publication in the interest of religious truth.   They heartily approved his plan, and he issued in the spring of 1823 a prospectus for the work which he proposed to call "The Christian Baptist." In this prospectus the nature and objects of the publication were candidly and clearly stated, as follows:

The "Christian Baptist" shall espouse the cause of no religious sect, excepting that ancient sect "called Christians first at Antioch."   Its sole object shall be the eviction of the truth and the exposing of error in doctrine and practice.   The editor, acknowledging no standard of religious faith or works other than the Old and New Testament, and the latter as the only standard of the religion of Jesus Christ, will, intentionally at least, oppose nothing which it contains, and recommend nothing which it does not enjoin.   Having no worldly interest at stake from the adoption or reprobation of any articles of faith or religious practice, having no gift nor religious emolument to blind his eyes or to pervert his judgment, he hopes to manifest that he is an impartial advocate of truth.

He dedicated the work "to all those, without distinction, who acknowledge the Scriptures of the Old and New Testaments to be a true revelation from God, and the New Testament as containing the religion of Jesus Christ; who, willing to have all religious tenets and practices tried by the divine Word, and who, feeling themselves in duty bound to search the Scripture for themselves in all matters of religion, are disposed to reject all doctrine and commandments of men, and to obey the truth, holding fast the faith once delivered to the saints."

The Campbell-McCalla Discussion

While making preparations to issue The Christian Baptist, he received a letter from Mr. McCalla, a Presbyterian preacher of Augusta, Ky., accepting his challenge given at the conclusion of the Walker debate. Mr. McCalla had been a lawyer and had gained a high reputation among the Presbyterians for his polemical powers. It was therefore greatly desired by his friends and the pedobaptists of the community that he should have an opportunity to retrieve, if possible, the injury which had been done to their cause by the generally-admitted failure of Mr. Walker. After having ascertained his standing, Mr. Campbell agreed to meet him, and arrangements were made for the discussion to take place at Washington, Ky., beginning October 15, 1823. As the Ohio River was too low for navigation at the time, Mr. Campbell made the entire distance of about three hundred miles on horseback.

Here, as in his former discussion, the entire bearing of the baptismal question was carefully canvassed. Each controverted point was hotly contested in the presence of a vast assemblage, which had been drawn together by Mr. Campbell's reputation and their own interest in the question at issue. During this discussion, which continued seven days, in addition to his defense of the scriptural act and subject of baptism, the design and importance were set forth and

examined in a systematic form, and with such critical ability
as to astonish his hearers.   In the discussion with Walker
he barely touched the design of baptism, but either during
that debate or while transcribing it for publication, an impression was made on his mind that it had a very important
meaning and that it was in some way connected with remission of sins, but he was so engaged in other matters that it
passed out of his mind till he received the challenge to meet
McCalla in debate, when he resolved to settle its true import
before he ever debated the subject again.   In the investigation, he examined the New Testament with great care
and discussed the subject with his father for several months,
and formed his conclusion after thorough examination and
reflection, and after he saw that it was the way marked out
by the Holy Spirit he had no hesitancy, on the second day
of the debate with McCalla, in saying:

Our third argument is deduced from the design or import
of baptism.   On this topic of argument we shall be as full as
possible, because of its great importance, and because perhaps neither Baptists nor Pedobaptists sufficiently appreciate
it.   I will first merely refer to the oracles of God, which
show that baptism is an ordinance of the greatest importance
and of momentous significance.   Never was there an ordinance
of so great import or design.   It is to be but once administered.
We are to pray often, praise often, show forth the Lord's
death often, commemorate his resurrection every week, but
we are to be baptized but once.   Its great significance can
be seen from the following testimonies: The Lord saith, "He
that believeth and is baptized shall be saved" (Mark 16: 16).
He does not say, "He that believeth and keeps my commandments shall be saved," but he saith, "He that believeth and
is baptized shall be saved."   He placeth baptism on the right
hand of faith.   Again, he tells Nicodemus that "unless a man
be born of water and of the Spirit he can not enter into the
kingdom of God."   Peter, on the day of Pentecost, places baptism in the same exalted place.   "Repent," says he, "and be
baptized, every one of you, for the remission of sins" (Acts
2: 38).   Ananias saith to Paul, "Arise and be baptized and
wash away thy sins, calling upon the name of the Lord" (Acts
22: 16).   Paul saith to the Corinthians, "Ye were once forni-
cators, idolaters, adulterers, effeminate, thieves, covetous,
drunkards, rioters, extortioners, but ye are washed in the name
of the Lord Jesus," doubtless referring to their baptism.   He
tells Titus, "God our Father saved us by the washing of
regeneration and renewing of the Holy Spirit" (Titus 3: 5).

See again its dignified importance.   Peter finishes the grand climax in praise of baptism: "Baptism doth now also save us . . . by the resurrection of Jesus Christ from the dead" (I Peter 3: 21).

It was this view of baptism misapplied that originated infant baptism.   The first errorists on this subject argued that if baptism was so necessary for the remission of sins, it should be administered to infants, whom they represented as in great need of it on account of their "original sin."   Affectionate parents, believing their children to be guilty of "original sin," were easily persuaded to have them baptized for the remission of "original sin," not for washing away sins actually committed.   Faith in Christ is necessary to forgiveness of sins, therefore baptism without faith is an unmeaning ceremony.

Our argument from this topic is, that baptism being ordained to be to a believer a formal and personal remission of all his sins, can not be administered unto an infant without the gravest perversion and abuse of the nature and import of this ordinance.   Indeed, why should an infant that never sinned—that, as Calvinists say, is guilty only of "original sin," which is a unit—be baptized for the remission of sins?" ("Campbell-McCalla Debate," pages 116, 117, 136.)

For a number of years prior to the debate Mr. McCalla had taken great delight in assailing the distinctive tenets of the Baptists, and gave them no little annoyance.   As the debate progressed his defeat became more and more manifest and raised Mr. Campbell to great popularity among them; but as it was not his intention to seek popularity among them by catering to their admiration, by fostering their favorite but defective views of the Gospel and its institutions, he deemed it wise on the evening of the fifth day of the debate to candidly inform the principal Baptist preachers present of the exact position which he occupied. Being assembled in a room where he had called them together, he introduced himself fully to their acquaintance in the following manner, as related by himself:

Brethren, I fear that if you knew me better you would esteem and love me less.   For let me tell you that I have almost as much against you Baptists as I have against the Presbyterians. They err in one thing and you in another; and you are each nearly equidistant from original apostolic Christianity." I paused; and such a silence as ensued, accompanied by a piercing look from all sides of the room,I seldom before witnessed. Elder Vardeman at length broke the silence by saying: "Well, sir, we want to know our errors or your heterodoxy.   Do let us hear it. Keep nothing back." I replied: "I know not where to begin; nor am I in health and vigor after the toils of the day to undertake so heavy a task; but I am commencing a publication called The Christian Baptist, to be devoted to all such matters, a few copies of which are in my portmanteau, and, with your permission, I will read you a few specimens of my heterodoxy." They all said: "Let us hear—let us hear the worst error you have against us." I went upstairs and unwrapped the first three numbers of the Christian Baptist that ever saw the light in Kentucky. I had just ten copies of the first three numbers. I carried them into the parlor and read a sample, the first essay on the clergy—so much of it as respected the "call to the ministry" as then taught in the "kingdom of the clergy," and especially among the Baptists. This was the first essay ever read from it in Kentucky. After a sigh and a long silence, Elder Vardeman said: "Is that your worst error, your chief heterodoxy? I do not care so much about that, as you admit that we have a providential call, without a voice from heaven or a special visit from some angel or spirit. If you have anything worse, for my part I wish to hear it." The cry was, "Let us hear something more." On turning to and fro, I read an article on "Modern Missionaries|" This, with the "Capital Mistake of Modern Missionaries," finished my reading for the evening. On closing this essay, Elder Vardeman said: I am not so great a missionary man as to fall out with you on that subject. I must hear more before I condemn or approve." I then distributed my ten copies among the ten most distinguished and advanced elders in the room, requesting them to read these numbers during the recess of the debate, and to communicate freely to me their objections. We separated. So the matter ended at that time. ("Memoirs of A. Campbell," Vol. II, page 88.)

At the close of the debate the Baptist preachers were so much pleased with the results, and so tolerant of what they found in the "Christian Baptist," that they requested Mr. Campbell to furnish them with the printed proposals for its publication, in order to extend its circulation, and urged him to make an immediate tour through the State.

Previous engagements prevented, and he could only comply with their wishes so far as to visit Bryan's Station, Mayslick, and Lexington; promising, if possible, to make a more extended tour through the State the following year.

As Mr. McCalla's character for ability was well established and equally well sustained by his Presbyterian brethren, the results of the discussion were less damaging to his reputation than to the cause which he advocated, which to this day has never recovered from the withering defeat which it then suffered. But Mr. McCalla labored for some time after the debate to change public sentiment by preaching on the subjects discussed in various parts of Kentucky, endeavoring at the same time to prejudice the minds of the people in advance against the report of the debate which Mr. Campbell was soon to publish.

Mr. Campbell was fully satisfied with his part in the discussion, and was now thoroughly satisfied that debates were a great means of reaching the people with the truth, for he wrote:

Public discussion, is, we are convinced, one of the best means of propagating the truth and of exposing error in doctrine or practice. We now reap the benefits of public debates of former times, and we have witnessed the beneficial results of those in our own time. And we are fully persuaded that a week's debating is worth a year's preaching, such as we generally have, for the purpose of disseminating truth and putting error out of countenance. There is nothing like meeting face to face in the presence of many witnesses and "talking the matter over"; and the man that can not govern his spirit in the midst of opposition and contradiction is a poor Christian indeed. (Christian Baptist, Vol. 1, page 189.)

VISITS THE KENTUCKY BAPTISTS

The debate was attended by great crowds of people from far and near. Mr. Campbell's reputation as one of the first pulpit orators of the day was fully established; and wherever he could be induced to speak he was met by throngs of hearers. His most important reception on this trip was at Lexington, where he spoke in the Baptist meetinghouse, of which Dr. Fishback was minister. At the hour for the meeting the house was crowded to its utmost capacity. When Mr. Campbell rose he was not able to stand erect during the delivery of his discourse. "This was based on the first chapter of Hebrews, and led him to dwell upon the divine glory of the Son of God—a theme on which he was almost surpassingly eloquent. It lasted two hours, during which the audience sat in rapt attention." He made a very profound impression on the entire audience. They recognized in him the mightiest intellect that had ever visited their city.   The freshness of his thoughts, the extent and accuracy of his Biblical knowledge and his grand generalizations of the wonderful fact of redemption opened up trains of reflection wholly new, and presented the subject of Christianity in a form so simple and yet so comprehensive as to fill every one with admiration; so that from this time forward Mr. Campbell was esteemed by the people of Kentucky as great among the greatest of her public men, and without a rival in the department to which he had devoted his powers.

Immediately after the close of the debate with Mr. McCalla, Mr. Campbell made preparations for its publication.   This was done from his own notes and those taken by Sydney Rigdon during the debate, and notwithstanding Mr. McCalla's effort to discredit it before its appearance, its general accuracy was attested by those who heard the discussion.   Its publication and circulation proved the severest blow that pedobaptism ever received.

In the fall of 1824 Mr. Campbell made his promised visit to Kentucky, visiting a large portion of the State, addressing everywhere large audiences, and extending his acquaintance and influence with the Baptists.   This more intimate acquaintance led him to esteem them very highly, and to regard them as much nearer the apostolic model than any other of the denominations with which he had formed acquaintance, and he felt that it would not be difficult to eliminate from the Baptist churches such erroneous theories and usages as had gained currency among them.   With these convictions in mind, he now visited the Baptists in Kentucky, to impart to them, as well as to the community at large, those clearer views of the Gospel to which he had been led by diligent and prayerful study of the Bible.   These he had, to some extent, already presented through the pages of The Christian Baptist, which, since the debate, had been read throughout Kentucky with interest and had produced intense excitement among the churches.   "Some individuals were favorably impressed with the plea for reform; others remained in perplexity and doubt, while not a few were disposed to cling tenaciously to their cherished opinions."

CHAPTER VII.

JOHN SMITH

Among the Baptist preachers whom Mr. Campbell met on this visit was John Smith, who, on account of the prominent part he afterwards had in presenting apostolic Christianity to the people, deserves more than a passing notice. He was born October 15, 1784, in a log cabin in East Tennessee, whither his parents had moved a short time before his birth on account of religious persecution. His father and mother had espoused the Baptist faith. But as Virginia, at that time, had an established form of religion, the Episcopal, Baptists were a despised, hunted, persecuted people. They were described by their persecutors as "schismatical persons, so averse to the established religion, and so filled with new-fangled conceits of their heretical inventions, as to refuse to have their children baptized." To escape from this galling oppression and to secure religious privileges which were so dear to him, George Smith took his little flock into the wilderness, seeking mercy at the hands of the savage tribes of the forest, which was not accorded him by the savage spirit of religious intolerance. In his new home he was at least free to work out the great problem of his own destiny in harmony with "the dictates of conscience" and the leadings of Providence. He was humble-minded and earnestly pious. He held firmly every dogma of the Philadelphia Confession of Faith as it was expounded in his day. "He conscientiously sought, too, to impress his own severe faith on the minds of his children. To labor for their daily bread and to wait, with humbleness of heart, for the Holy Ghost, were the two great commandments on which hung all his precepts and admonitions. He exhorted them to seek after God, if, haply, they might find him; yet to esteem themselves dead and to abide the good time when, unless predestinated to eternal wrath, the mysterious Spirit would give them life and open their eyes to the beauties of the Saviour."

When John was in his twelfth year the migratory spirit again seized George Smith, who determined to plunge into the wilderness once more, with a view of securing cheap lands and providing for the future of his growing family. Having sold his Tennessee farm, he set out, in the autumn of 1795, accompanied by John and an older brother, on the trail that led across the Cumberland Mountains in the unsettled territory of Kentucky, in search of a "goodly spot where he might build a cabin, plant a patch of corn, and prepare as well as he could for the family" that was to join him in the coming summer.

In the new home the life of the boy continued its developments along such lines as its rude surroundings stimulated. Of work there was plenty, and from his daily tasks he never shrank.   Of opportunity for intellectual development there was none, and the thirst of the ambitious youth was unquenched.   At this period John Smith's spiritual nature gave promise of being as untamed as the forest that surrounded his home.   Unhallowed sports crept into the backwoods.   Sunday horse races and card-playing became the pastime of the young men.   For the latter John had a fondness, and would creep away on Sundays to spend the day with idle companions in his favorite game; but the grief and patience of the father at last touched his heart, and he threw away his cards, saying, "It is wrong to distress so good a father as ours; it is a sin and a shame!"

SOUL STRUGGLES

This proved to be the turning point in the young man's career, and with it came the question of religion demanding his consideration.   Indeed the subject had been kept before him in some form from his earliest recollection.   But the doctrine taught at that time was not very attractive to young hearts.   Calvinism in its severest type was prevalent.   It taught a "hell of the most appalling type, into which even little children might be cast; an unalterable destiny for every one, regardless of his conduct or his creed, as God might have chosen him for heaven or doomed him to hell before he was born; a dread uncertainty that rested on his fate;

his utter inability to understand the Scriptures, to believe or repent, to love God or to obey him, until endued with power from on high; the necessity of some supernatural sign or sensation, some miraculous voice or vision, as an evidence of pardon and acceptance with God."

It was natural that John should imbibe the spirit of his father's creed and for him to expect, should he be among the elect, that some visible or audible manifestation of divine approval should be given him.   The great revival which swept the country in the beginning years of the nineteenth century was at its height as he began seriously to think upon the subject of religion.   It was the theme he heard discussed on every hand, and he determind to investigate it as far as his limited resources would permit.   Failing to find the way to assured salvation, he at last appealed to a Baptist preacher, Isaac Denton, a friend of the family, for light upon the subject which was beginning to agitate his mind. According to the prevailing notion, conversion was a change of a mysterious nature wrought out in the soul by super-natural agency.   This change young Smith now most sin-cerely desired to experience.   With this in mind the follow-ing conversation took place:

Smith—What must I do in order to have this change of which you speak?

Denton—Nothing, John; God's grace is sovereign and un-conditional.   If you are his sheep you will be called, and you will hear his voice and follow him.

Smith—But when, Mr. Denton, will the Lord call?

Denton—In his own good time, John.   He has worked out your whole life, and determined your destiny according to his own wise, but hidden and eternal, purpose.

Smith—How then may I know whether I am one of his sheep or not?

Denton—You will know it by your change when it comes; till then you can only wait on the Lord and hope.

Smith—If I am left to perish I know it will be on account of my sins; but if I should be saved, will it not be on account of my goodness?

Denton—The Lord sees no goodness in you, John.   If you are ever brought to life, it will be solely because it was his good pleasure to choose you before the foundation of the world, and that, too, without any reference to your character or works foreseen by him.   True, if you should be lost, if you perish, it will be on account of your sins, and to the praise of his glorious justice.

Smith—My destiny, you say, is fixed and I can not change it. I need not, then, give myself any concern; I have nothing to do.

Denton—Ah, great is the mystery of godliness. There is something for you to do.

Smith—What is it, Mr. Denton?

Denton—You must pray, pray, pray in the dust and ashes to the Lord.

Smith—Pray for what, sir?

Denton—That the blinding scales may fall from your eyes, and that you may see and feel what you really are in the sight of God; for you are yet in the gall of bitterness and the bonds of iniquity.

It is not strange that a young man with keen intellect of John Smith should have turned from such instruction, saying, "Since my destiny is fixed and I can not change it, I need not, then, give myself any concern. I have nothing to do."

But his heart was not to be stifled by the forbidding theology. While stoutly for a season he maintained his unbelief, his position was not satisfactory to himself, and he resolved at last to examine the subject in the light of the Scriptures. Though failing to find proof of the doctrines taught, he became convinced of his duty to be a Christian, and, knowing no way to approach to Christ, he began earnestly and persistently to seek religion after the manner of the times. The illness and death of his venerable father in the spring of 1804, deepened his interest in personal salvation, and from that time through many weary months he sought for assurance of saving grace. In his fruitless search his agony was indescribable.

He had been taught that an indispensable step to salvation was to feel himself the greatest of sinners. This he desired to do, and then despaired of salvation, simply because he could not feel that he was "too wicked to be saved." A gloomy cloud overshadowed his sunny temper. His nights were sleepless and his days filled with torment. In vain he prostrated himself alone in the forest and prayed for the blessed assurance of his pardon. Finally, after a night spent in agonizing prayer, his heart seemed to throw off its burden, and he was happy. Returning home and relating his experience to his brother William, the latter replied with joy, "You are converted, John, at last." He went to a meeting, expecting to offer himself for membership, but the weird experience of others sent him away in sorrow and disgust. His mind was again beclouded by doubts and despair, and he prayed the Lord to keep his poor heart from error and to lead him by the right way into the everlasting kingdom.

Religious friends who had watched with solicitude the long and painful struggle of the young man believed that a work of grace had already been wrought in his heart, and urged him to relate the facts before the congregation. This he did on December 26, 1804, giving a plain statement of his religious struggles, and though his experience was lacking in the marvelous element which characterized the conversion of that time, the congregation unanimously voted him the subject of a work of grace. The next day he was baptized, and at once entered into the active service of the Master to find in doing the peace he had failed to receive in seeking.

DESIRES TO PREACH

No sooner had John Smith been received into the Baptist Church than he became exceedingly anxious to preach the unsearchable riches of Christ. But two obstacles rose before him which seemed an insurmountable barrier to the realization of his desires. One was his ignorance. In his brief term of schooling he had barely learned to read and his surroundings and occupation had left him without further means of self-improvement, as he looked with yearning heart toward the ministry, he "wept at the thought that he was now a man without an education." No less was the hindrance which the popular sentiment of the day threw across his pathway. It was regarded as an almost unpardonable act of presumption to stand before the people as an expounder of the Scriptures without a supernatural call, and yet he was without evidence of such a call to preach the gospel. No voice spoke to his listening ear. No answer came to his earnest prayer. No sign met his expectant vision.

In the face of these obstacles the way seemed completely blocked, so nothing remained for him to do but to continue in his labors on the farm. At last circumstances opened up before him for larger usefulness for God. His widely scattered neighbors were pious people, and, in the absence of churches and ministers, often gathered at night after a day of toil, in each other's cabins, to sing and pray, and talk about their religious interests. At these meetings he was present, when circumstances would permit, and his native ability, gave him pre-eminence among them. As they met from house to house they often constrained him to lead in prayer. In these religious meetings his confidence increased, his heart warmed, and he greatly desired to enter into more active service. But still he waited for some audible call which should assure him of the Lord's will. His brethren urged that when God gave man a talent, he gives the right to use it. He was finally persuaded to lay aside his scruples, and at the prayer meeting he consented to make a short talk. The appointment was made, the people came together, filling the house to its utmost capacity, the light from the fire fell full upon his face as he arose and stood near the table, but as he looked into the faces of his neighbors, he was seized with stage fright, and forgot everything he had hoped to say. He fled from the house and sought the darkness outside, but in his hurried flight he stumbled and fell to the ground. As he arose his mind cleared, and he returned and delivered a thrilling address, and from that time he continued in his humble way to lead those who were as sheep without a shepherd.

He waited anxiously for the call, but it came not. But the call from his brethren was so strong that he continued to exercise the gift of exhortation, with increasing desire to devote his life to the work of proclaiming the Gospel to his fellowmen. In deference to the judgment of his brethren, who urged him to lay aside all scruples and become their preacher, he at last consented to be ordained, and entered at once upon the duties of his new calling, while continuing to provide for his family by his labors on the farm. He was marvelously endowed for the work of a pioneer preacher. "His well-toned voice and earnest manner, his fine common sense and unaffected piety, rendered him pre-eminently popular as a speaker; his genial humor, too, threw its sunny influence on all around him and made him the delight of every fireside." As his reputation spread flattering offers came to him from the more favored portions of Kentucky, through which he was induced to travel on a preaching tour. Wealthy congregations, pleased with his originality and genius, offered him what was then regarded as a handsome salary to labor with them. But, conscious of his lack of education and culture, he declined these offers, while his soul, for the time lifted up with pride, planned ambitiously for the future.

TERRIBLE CALAMITY

Just here occurred the saddest episode of his life. The South was being opened up, and many were drawn thither by what seemed to be a most promising picture. He sold his farm and stock for $1,500, with which he hoped to enter ten thousand acres of land, which, with the advance in price, he was sure would make him a wealthy man. In the fall of 1814, he located his family in a log hut, in what is now Madison County, Alabama, and went out to select his land. During his absence, in one awful night, his hopes and happiness were dashed to pieces. The house which contained his possessions and wife and children, was burned to the ground, and two of his children and all his money were consumed in the flames of that awful night. His poor wife escaped, only to die of a broken heart and be buried with the ashes of her children. The husband, though a strong man, was so shocked that he was at last stricken with fever, and for weeks lingered near the grave. But he finally recovered, and with a sad heart, he retraced his steps, empty-handed and alone, to the old home in Kentucky.

PREACHES AT CRAB ORCHARD

Immediately after his return to Kentucky he began preaching again; but he was from that time harassed by doctrinal difficulties which gave him no rest until he turned from his creed to the Bible in its primitive simplicity. His appearance, as he joined his brethren in the meeting of the Baptist Association, shortly after his return, is thus described by his biographer:

He reached Crab Orchard on Saturday, with the dust of the journey thick upon him. He wore a pair of homespun cotton pantaloons, striped with coperas—loose enough, but far too short for him—and a cotton coat, once checked with blue and white, but now of undistinguishable colors; these had been given him in Alabama. His shapeless hat was streaked with sweat and dust. His socks, too large for his shrunken ankles, hung down upon his worn shoes. His shirt was coarse and dirty and unbottoned at the neck; his white cravat was in the coffin with his wife. (Life of John Smith, page 96.)

But if the exterior of this vessel was rough, within it was garnished and adorned with all the graces of truth. He was pressed upon to speak on the occasion. He lifted his head and sat erect, he arose, and, with firm step, walked to the stand and stood up before the people. As he looked around upon them his eyes kindled and his spirit was stirred within him. The multitude stared curiously for a moment at the uncouth figure before them. Some laughed out right, while others were withdrawn from the assembly. His first work was to stop them. Raising his voice so that all could hear, he said: "Stay, friends, and hear what the Great Augustine said. Augustine wished to see three things before he died: Rome in her glory, Paul on Mars' Hill, and Jesus in the flesh." A few sat down, but many moved on.

In louder tones he cried: "Will you not stay and see what the great Cato said. Cato repented of three things before his death: First that he had ever spent an idle day; second, that he had ever gone on a voyage by water when he might have made the same journey by land; and, third, that he had ever told the secrets of his bosom to a woman." Many more were seated.

But he continued: "Come, friends, and hear what the great Thales thanked the gods for. He thanked the gods for three things: First, that he was endowed with reason, and was not a brute; second, that he as a Greek, and not a barbarian; and third, that he was a man, and not a woman." By this time all were seated and the sermon began.

His theme was redemption. His analysis was three-fold: (1) Redemption as conceived; (2) Redemption as applied; (3) Redemption as completed. He seemed inspired for the occasion. His voice like a trumpet reached and thrilled the most distant hearer, and his thought swept the audience like the storm sweeps the sea. The people crowded closer to hear him, and some who could find neither sitting nor standing room, climbed the trees, so that even the forest swayed to and fro as if under the magic spell in the third division, and portrayed the final glory of the redeemed, every heart was filled with emotion, every eye as weeping, every face was radiant with hope, and at the close one loud "Amen" ascended to the heavens.

In the course of time he again married, choosing as a companion a sensible and consecrated woman who lived in the neighborhood where he ministered, and who cheerfully joined him in all his plans for the betterment of human society.

THE CHRISTIAN BAPTIST

Though preaching the doctrine of the Philadelphia Confession of Faith, he now found himself ill at ease. The strange inconsistency of his position embarrassed him. Why urge sinners to repent if they were already safe, and if among the non-elect they could not repent. As the situation flashed upon him in the midst of an impassioned exhortation, he immediately closed his remarks and sat down, saying: "Brethren, something is wrong; I am in the dark —we are all in the dark; but how to lead you to the light, or to find the way myself, before God I know not." Retiring on his knees he prayed that he would take God's Word as his only guide, examine it carefully, and follow its teachings wherever they might lead him. In the keeping of this pledge he began anew to study the Bible. When his day's work in the field was done, he would sit by his candle with his Bible upon his knees, and often spend the whole night in solemn meditation in his search for light.

It was while in this state of mind that the prospectus of The Christian Baptist fell into his hands, and he read it with profound interest.   He ordered the paper sent to that Mr. Campbell's discussion of scriptural themes would him and induced others to subscribe for it.   He hoped greatly assist him in solving his own doctrinal difficulties. The first numbers were read with great interest, and through them light began to break along his darkened pathway.   He read each succeeding number with great care to ascertain to which of the contending parties Mr. Campbell belonged, and soon found himself in a realm of truth entirely beyond the range of the popular systems.   Among other things that specially appealed to him as the following from the trenchant pen of Mr. Campbell:

> We have no system of our own, nor of others, to substitute in lieu of the reigning systems.   We only aim at substituting the New Testament in lieu of every creed in existence; whether Mohametan, Pagan, Jewish or Presbyterian. We wish to call Christian to consider that Jesus Christ has made them kings and priests to God.   We neither advocate Calvinism, Arminianism, Arianism, Socinianism, Trinitarianism, Unitarianism, Deism, or Sectarianism, but New Testamentism.   We wish, we cordially wish, to take the New Testament out of the abuses of the clergy, and put it into the hands of the people.   (Christian Baptist, Vol. 1, page 90.)

FETTERS CAST OFF

So thorough did these views accord with his that he determined at the first opportunity to meet Mr. Campbell and learn from him by personal interview more of the new order that he was advocating.   During his visit to Kentucky in 1824, to which I have already referred, the opportunity presented itself.   Mr. Campbell was to speak at Flemingsburg, and Smith rode twenty miles on horseback that he might see and hear him.   He reached the town on the day that Mr. Campbell was to preach.   Shortly after his arrival he met William Vaughn, a Baptist preacher, with whom he was well acquainted, when the following conversation took place:

> Vaughn—Brother John, have you met Bro. Campbell yet?
> Smith—No, sir, I have not.   Have you seen him?

Vaughn—Why, I have been with him for eight days and nights, through Mason and Bracken counties, and have heard him every day.

Smith—Do, then, tell me what his views are on doctrinal points. Is he a Calvinist or an Arminian, or Arian, or a Trinitarian?

Vaughn—I do not know. He has nothing to do with any of these things.

Smith—Well, I can tell when I hear him just what he is.

Vaughn—How?

Smith—If a man of sense and takes a position, even though he should not run it out into any ism, I can do it for him, and tell exactly where he would land. But tell me, Bro. Vaughn, does he know anything about heartfelt religion?

Vaughn—Lord bless you, he is one of the most pious, godly men that I was ever in company with in all my life.

Smith—But do you think he knows anything about a Christian experience?

Vaughn—Bless you, he knows everything. Come, I want to introduce you to him.

Of this meeting with Mr. Campbell he afterward said: "I then felt as if I wanted to sit down and look at him for one hour, without hearing a word from any one. I wanted to scan him who had been so much talked of, and who had in *The Christian Baptist* and in his debates introduced so many new thoughts." But the hour appointed for the address had come, and they walked into the house together. Smith was determined now to ascertain the theory of religion to which he held, if, indeed, he held to any; for he was still full of doubt and suspicion.

Mr. Campbell read the fourth chapter of Galatians. After giving a general outline of the whole epistle, he took up the allegory of Sarah and Hagar, and in a simple, plain and artless manner, leaning with one hand on his cane, he delivered his discourse. "He seemed," as Smith afterward remarked, "to move in a higher sphere or latitude than that in which the isms of the day abounded." At the conclusion of the services Smith remarked to Mr. Vaughn, "Is it not hard, Bro. Vaughn, to ride twenty miles, as I have done, just to hear a man preach thirty minutes?" "You are mistaken," said Mr. Vaughn; "look at your watch, for it certainly has been longer than that." He looked at his watch, and, to his surprise, saw that the discourse had been

two hours and a half long.   On discovering this he said,
"I have never been more deceived.   Two hours of my life
are gone, I know not how, though wide awake, too, all the
time !"   On being questioned as to whether he had ascertained whether he was a Calvinist or an Arminian, he replied : "No, I know nothing about the man; but be he
saint or devil, he has thrown more light on that epistle, and
on the whole Scripture, than I have received in all the sermons that I have ever heard before."

RESOLVES TO PREACH THE SIMPLE GOSPEL

For several days he accompanied Mr. Campbell from
place to place, an enraptured listener to every discourse, and
earnestly engaged him in conversation as they traveled along
the way or sat under some hospitable roof.   At last his
mind cast off its fetters.   The way hitherto so clouded
became plain, and he left the company of Mr. Campbell,
resolved henceforth to devote his life to preaching the simple Gospel as exhibited in the New Testament.

The step was, as he had anticipated, attended with great
sacrifices.   Old friends forsook him.   He had always stood
high among his preaching brethren, but now he was regarded
with undisguised suspicion.   Soon the storm gathered furiously about him.   At the annual meeting of the association
in which he held his membership charges were preferred
against him, among the most serious of which was that,
instead of the King James translation of the Scriptures, "he
had on two or three occasions in public, and often in his
family, read from Alexander Campbell's translation."   Without being given an opportunity to defend himself, he was
placed under censure, and given a year in which to correct
his views and change his ways.

Returning to his home, the way for a time seemed to
close before him.   The little farm was covered with a
heavy mortgage.   The churches that had obligated themselves to pay his debt in compensation of his services, now
refused to make further payment.   Nothing apparently
remained but for him to cultivate his farm with his own
hands, and for a time to abandon the work of the ministry.
Taking his ax he went into the forest with the heroic pur-

pose, first to free himself from debt, and then to return to the defense of the faith which he now felt to be the teaching of the Word of God. But one day as he was bending to his labors he thought of the cause that he loved, and remembered that there was no one in all the land to advocate it but himself. He also thought of the construction that would be put on his silence by his enemies. He dropped the ax, went to the house, and threw down his coarse apron at the feet of his wife, exclaiming:

Nancy, I shall work no more! Get whom you please to carry on the farm, but do not call on me! In all the land there is not one soul to open his mouth in defense of the best cause under the sun! I am determined, from this time forth, to preach the Gospel, and leave the consequences to God.

With the courage of his convictions, he immediately began to preach the truth as he now felt it and saw it. No personal consideration was allowed to interfere with the course he had marked out for himself. His heroic wife readily caught his spirit and as cheerfully accepted the responsibilities of her new position—agreeing to take the oversight of the farm, care for the family, and to relieve him of every temporal care, while he should give himself wholly to the ministry of the Word.

But from a course so radical and perilous his friends earnestly sought to dissaude him. They argued: "Your more influential brethren will abandon you; you will get nothing for your preaching; your debts will press you to the earth, and your farm and house eventually given up." "Conscience," said he, "is an article that I have never yet brought into the market; but should I offer it for sale, Montgomery County, with all its lands and houses, would not be enough to buy it, much less that farm of one hundred acres."

As he now went from house to house, and neighborhood, to plant the cause of Christ, his zeal knew no bounds. His heart was all aglow with his new-born knowledge of the truth, and with tireless effort he sought to win men to respect and obey the simple claims of the Gospel. So intense was his desire that he scarcely allowed himself time to eat and sleep.   After a busy day he would often spead a greater part of the night answering questions or meeting objections which his public discourses had aroused, or in helping some half-persuaded inquirer to a full acceptance of the Gospel; often going the same hour of the night to some near-by stream to administer baptism, when a surrender had been made.   Or, if at home, the burden that was upon his heart, and his thirst for the knowledge of the Word of God, would often interfere with his sleep, and he would arise and light his candle at midnight "to examine some word or text not yet understood, and which, perhaps, had confused him in his dreams."

The preaching of John Smith, so different from that of the times, so far removed from the conventional forms, and so new and strange in doctrine, at once awakened new interest in languishing churches.   Calls now came to him from so many quarters that he seldom had an opportunity to enjoy the fellowship of his family, to which he was warmly attached.   He endeavored, if possible, to visit his home once a week; but this purpose he was not always able to accomplish.   "He would tarry at some distant place, preaching and baptizing till the week was nearly gone, and then, dismissing the people at a late hour, ride hurriedly through the darkness, sometimes through mud and cold and tempest, in order to keep his promise with his wife.   At other times, when going from one part of the district to another, he would pass along by his own house, but, too much hurried to stop and rest, would linger a while at the gate, and, gathering strength from her words of cheer, press on to his distant appointment."   On one occasion, as he thus hurried from one appointment to another, he stopped at home just long enough to change his soiled linen for clean. As he was about to leave his wife remarked with a touch of sadness in her tone, "Is it not time that you were having your washing done somewhere else?   We have attended to it for you a long time."   "No, Nancy, I am pleased with your way of doing things, and I do not wish to make any change."   After a kind good-bye to her and a few playful words to the little ones, he passed on to meet the congregation that would wait for him that day in some young convert's house, or perhaps, in some hospitable grove.

The patient heroism of faith finds few better illustrations than in the wife of this tireless pioneer. Upon Nancy Smith rested the burden of the family and the farm. When help could not be secured, she would go forth herself into the busy field to tend the growing crop, or to superintend the gathering of the harvest, that her faithful husband might devote all his energies to the cause to which they were both so much devoted. His preaching brought no material recompense to relieve their pinching poverty. Though he labored incessantly for the salvation of his fellow men, no one ever thought of contributing to his support, or if they felt inclined to minister to him in temporal things were probably too poor. During the years 1825-1830, in which he laid the foundation of primitive Christianity in Kentucky, he never received a dollar for his services, or compensation of any kind, save the remittance to a friendly merchant in a neighboring town for a small bill of goods.

The result of such zeal, such labor, such sacrifice, brought its reward to this devoted messenger of truth in a richer blessing than any that material prosperity had to offer. His message was gladly received. Multitudes gathered to hear him, and many received with joy the glorious Gospel of the Son of God which he now felt himself commissioned to preach. A revival of religious interest began to follow the track of his ministry, and he had the satisfaction of seeing hundreds, who had held aloof from the religious systems of the day, now turn to the Lord. So fruitful were his labors that within a short period of six months he was able to report seven hundred conversions and five new churches organized. But greater still, he had established a great cause in the hearts of the people.

Although he had renounced the Calvinistic theory of conversion, and had laid aside its unyielding creed for the New Testament, he still considered himself a Baptist, and lived in fellowship with those who "stood resolutely by the old church covenant", hoping that his brethren would one day accept the primitive Gospel. But his genial fraternal spirit was far from being reciprocated by the Baptist preachers with whom he associated. Once, meeting an old acquaintance, Smith said to him, kindly, "Good morning, my brother." To which the other scornfully replied, "Don't call me brother, sir! I would rather claim kinship with the devil himself." "Go, then," said Smith, "and honor thy father."

But the bitterness of opposition did not always end in harmless railery. It too frequently resorted to misrepresentations and other unchristian means to check his growing popularity and influence. Churches were closed against him, compelling him to take his audience to some neighboring house, or hall, or, in fair weather, to a grove. But, whatever the discouragement or hindrance, he continued to preach. "Usually he divided his discourses, which were two or three hours long, into three divisions, according to the objects he had in view; in the first he corrected misrepresentations; in the second he exposed popular errors, and in the third he presented the simple Gospel to the people." Having taken his stand upon the Bible, he felt himself secure. The truth made him fearless, and his courage at last won respect for the unpopular position to which he held.

"ANCIENT ORDER OF THINGS" AMONG THE BAPTISTS IN KENTUCKY

The years 1828-1830 were great years in the ministry of John Smith. In them was witnessed the fruition of years of self-sacrificing labor, and the triumph of the ancient Gospel on the soil of Kentucky. The year 1828 was a notable one among the Baptist associations. At the meetings of three of the largest associations the Reformers were in control, due in a very large degree to Smith's preaching. As we have already seen, his influence over the people was tremendous. The churches for which he preached regularly —Spencer's Creek, Grassy Lick and Mount Sterling—reported in their annual letters of 1828 to the North District Association of which they were members, the baptism of 392 persons during the year. The twenty-four churches of the Association reported the baptism of about nine hundred persons, "the greater part of whom had been immersed by Smith." Five new churches had been organized by Smith on the Bible alone and became members of the Association.

The North District Association met in July, 1828. At its meeting the previous year the Lulbegrud Church had sent the following charges aimed at John Smith, but veiling the object of their charge under the designation, "one of their preachers." The accusations were:

1. That, while it is the custom of Baptists to use as the Word of God the King James translation, he had on two or three occasions in public, and often privately in his family, read from Alexander Campbell's translation.

2. That while it is the custom in the ceremony of baptism to pronounce, "I baptize you", he, on the contrary, is in the habit of saying, " immerse you".

3. That in administering the Lord's Supper, while it is the custom to break the loaf into bits, small enough to be readily taken into the mouth, yet he leaves the bread in large pieces, teaching that each communicant shall break it for himself.

Without waiting for himself to be singled out, Smith arose and said, "I plead guilty to them all." After bitter debating and wrangling over the charges it was finally voted that they be laid over for another year. The meeting of 1828 was the time when these charges should be brought up. Smith had been unceasingly engaged in preaching, and marvelously successful in winning men to Christ during the years. Still, when the Association met, he was in doubt at first as to which side had the majority of messengers. In the registration of messengers, it was soon found that the majority were favorable to him. The messengers, from the five new churches he had established turned the scale in his favor. The charges were not mentioned on the floor of the Association. In 1830 this Association divided, ten churches voluntarily withdrawing and forming a new association on Baptist principles. The North District Association met for the last time as an advisory council in 1831, and was dissolved one year later. Fourteen churches and four parts of churches were enrolled on the occasion of the dissolution. On the same day the churches that had withdrawn from the Association two years before met and formed a new association under the same name.

The Bracken Association was the next to meet, in 1828. Licking Association, rigidly Calvinistic and devoted to the Philadelphia Confession of Faith, desired to enter into mutual correspondence with Bracken, but had determined as a condition of it to require from Bracken a pledge to support the Philadelphia Confession of Faith, which no doubt would have been given in 1827; but in the meantime Smith had gone into that district, and preached among the churches; and such men as Walter Warden and Jesse Holton, already moved by the plea of Alexander Campbell, and encouraged by the boldness and success of Smith, were already favoring the return to the "ancient order of things." The letter came from Licking requiring the pledge and was read before the Association. After a prolonged discussion by various members, during which Smith sat in silence, he finally saw his opportunity to speak. This opportunity was given when James Arnold, a messenger from the North Bend Association, moved that the terms proposed by Licking be rejected, and that all further correspondence with that body be dropped. Smith supported the proposition, and as he rose to do so took from his saddle bags a copy of the Confession of Faith, and said.

Brethren, Licking requires of Bracken an utter impossibility. No one can maintain inviolate the doctrine of grace as revealed in the Scriptures, and at the same time, defend that which is taught in the Philadelphia Confession of Faith; for the doctrine of the creed is not the doctrine of the Bible. No two books in the world differ more than these; and in no point do they differ more widely than on the doctrine of salvation by grace.

He then contrasted the teaching of the New Testament with that of the Confession of Faith, and his argument was so convincing that practically all seemed satisfied that the terms proposed by Licking were contradictory, and when the vote was taken the proposition to reject was carried almost unanimously. A prominent witness of these events said:

It was John Smith that gave impulse and tone to the reformation in Bracken, as he had already done in North District, Boone's Creek and other associations.

It was decided while the Association was in session that Bracken would recommend no creed or confession of faith but the New Testament. Bracken did not, however, remain long of this mind; but went back into regular fellowship in 1830; yet not without great loss by defection to the side of those contending for the "ancient order of things". Benedict, the Baptist historian, informs us that "the number of members was reduced from 2,200 to 900 on account of the sweeping inroads of the Reformers."

The next association to take action in 1828 was the Boone's Creek. The letter sent out by the Association in 1827 said to the churches composing it: "We hear from some of the churches that they are endeavoring to return to 'the ancient order of things', and they recognize the Scriptures alone as an entire and sufficient rule of faith and practice." During the spring and summer of 1828 there was an increase of about 870 members by immersion, many of whom had been brought in through the preaching of John Smith. The Association, composed of thirteen churches, met on the third Sunday in September. The question before it, raised in letters of two churches, was concerning an amendment to the constitution to bring it into harmony with the Word of God. The following action was taken by the Association and reported back to all the churches:

We, therefore, recommend to the churches an abolition of the present constitution, and, in lieu thereof, an adoption of this resolution: Resolved, That we the Churches of Jesus Christ, believing the Scriptures of the Old and New Testament to be the Word of God, and the only rule of faith and obedience given by the great Head of the Church for its government, do agree to meet annually on every third Saturday, Lord's day, and Monday in September of each year, for the worship of God, and on such occasions voluntarily communicate the state of religion amongst us by letter and messenger. (Christian Baptist, Vol. 6. page 420.)

Such men as John Smith, William Morton, Jeremiah Vardeman and Jacob Creath, Jr., all under the influence of the restoration movement, were the leading spirits in this meeting. The report of the action of churches with reference to the resolution was made a year later. The result showed that seven churches voted to retain the constitution, six voted to abolish it. At the meeting in 1830 these six churches were dropped from the Association, and both the North District and Tate's Creek messengers were rejected.

In 1829 Tate's Creek Association was under the controlling influence of the restoration movement. A minority of orthodox Baptist churches withdrew and called a meeting for the month of June, 1830, at which they drew up a bill of errors against certain preachers and churches of the Association. This Association was composed of delegates from ten of the twenty-six churches. They organized and proceeded to meet as the "Tate's Creek Association", and resolved to cut off correspondence with the churches that "tolerated the heresy of Campbellism". Thus we see that the majority of this Association was in line with the effort to restore the "ancient order of things".

The Franklin and Elkhorn Associations were, however, not friendly to the movement, though there was a strong and influential minority committed to those principles. In 1829 Franklin Association adopted decrees rejecting as heretical all those who sought to return to apostolic Christianity and all churches were warned not to harbor any such errors. The Elkhorn Association at its meeting in 1830 dropped from further correspondence two churches, and refused to recognize the messengers from the North District, thus excluding from Baptist fellowship eighteen churches and 1,427 members.

The Russell Creek and South Concord Associations took action against "Campbellite heresy", the latter passing a resolution advising all churches to lock their doors against "the followers of Alexander Campbell, who deny the agency of the Spirit". Very few of the Kentucky Baptist Associations escaped the influence of the effort to return to primitive Christianity.

The success of the movement only increased the bitterness and hate of the opposition. No longer satisfied with misrepresentation, and with closing the doors of their meeting places against Smith, the leaders of the Baptist churches formulated measures for the forcible expulsion of all who gave heed to the teaching of Smith and his co-workers. As this purpose spread from church to church and from association to association, Smith threw himself fearlessly into the breach, and with his rugged eloquence sought to stay any attempt at disruption, and to preserve the peace and order of religious society. As the heat of this controversy grew intense, his genial spirit and good-fellowship were only the more manifest. In the excitement of the times he alone was calm. Amidst the cloud of angry faces that often denied him a hearing, his countenance alone was lit up with a friendly smile. When the doors were locked against him by some unfriendly hand, he would speak to those who gathered to hear him on such occasions in the woods, refusing to sanction any act of violence by which admittance might be gained. Though from this time in the thickest of the fight, he was a man of peace; and while others "gnashed on him with their teeth", he only replied in pleasantries. The principles for which he now contended were the right of free speech and private judgment. As railing accusations were brought against him and those who shared his views, he would usually seek the opportunity of replying, but was invariably refused the simple privilege claimed.

The effort of John Smith, therefore, to main the unity of the Baptist Church on the broad platform which he had framed for himself was soon found unavailing. The unyielding policy of those who were antagonistic to apostolic Christianity was to deny fellowship to those who joined in the search to learn the way of the Lord more perfectly. "Seek first to reclaim these reformers from their error", was the method now suggested; "if your efforts should fail, invite them to leave you, and to practice their reformation to themselves. If they will not go at your request, separate them from you in the best way you can."

Henceforth his whole energy and strength were consumed in setting in order the things lacking and strengthening the faith of the brethren.   At this time there were about eight thousand intelligent, pious men and women in the State standing with Smith.   During the winter and spring of 1831 he gave himself unreservedly to the rejected churches of the old North District Association, organizing them after the New Testament model, and pressing the claims of the primitive Gospel of larger conquest.

CHAPTER VIII.

WALTER SCOTT

Inasmuch as the name of Walter Scott is inseparably linked with the movement to restore apostolic Christianity, I now give a sketch of his life and work. He was born in Dumfriesshire, Scotland, October 31, 1796. He was carefully trained in the Scotch Presbyterian Church by his mother. At the very early period in his life he gave evidence of a decided talent. Though the resources of the family were only moderate, his watchful parents gave him every educational advantage, the mother praying that the church might enjoy the service of his rare gift of mind and heart. The Scotch family of the old school sought no greater honor than to have a son at the university. Though a collegiate education at that time was regarded within the reach of the sons of the wealthy only, in his devoted family the slender resources were so husbanded as to enable Walter, after a preparatory course at the academy, to enter the University of Edinburgh. Here he pursued his studies with a zeal and success that fully justified the labors and sacrifices of his parents. After completing his university course, while casting about for a place to plant his feet and enter the service of his race, an unexpected turn of affairs changed the channels of his life. His mother's brother, George Innis, had some years before emigrated to this country, and by faithfulness and integrity advanced himself to a place of responsibility in the governmental service in New York City. Anxious to assist his relatives still in Scotland, he wrote his sister to send one of her sons, promising what assistance he could render in his advancement. Walter, as the best fitted by education for the opportunities of a new country, was the one selected to go; and as the plan was in perfect harmony with his own wishes, he at once started on the voyage, reaching New York on July 7, 1818, and on his arrival was kindly welcomed by his uncle, through whose influence he soon obtained a posi-

tion as Latin tutor in a classical academy, for which he was
eminently qualified.   But in this position he did not long
remain.   He had made some acquaintances in the city, and
from them heard glowing reports of the West, as all the
region beyond the Allegheny Mountains was then called;
and had resolved to see for himself the land of which he
had heard so much.   On foot, with a light heart and a
light purse, with a young man about his own age as a traveling companion, he set out for the regions beyond.   After
a long journey he reached Pittsburgh in the early spring
of 1819.   He sought employment, and soon had the good
fortune to fall in with George Forrester, a fellow countryman, and the principal of an academy, by whom he was
immediately engaged as an issistant in his school.   Somewhat to the surprise of young Scott, he soon made the discovery that his employer, though a deeply religious man,
differed very much in his views from those which he himself had been taught to regard as true.   Mr. Forrester's
peculiarity consisted in making the Bible his only authority
and guide in religious matters, while Scott had been trained
to regard the Presbyterian Standards as the true and
authoritative exposition and summary of Bible truth.

A SINCERE TRUTH SEEKER

Mr. Forrester had been trained under the Haldanes of
Scotland before coming to this country, and had in connection with his school duties, built up a small congregation
who shared his views.   Differing, as they did, they were,
nevertheless, both lovers of the truth, and the frequent and
close examinations which they made of the Scriptures resulted in convincing Scott that human standards in religion
were, like their authors, imperfect; and in impressing him
deeply with the conviction that the Word of God is the
only true and sure guide.   Better soil for the planting was
not to be found than that presented in the heart of Walter
Scott.   He was a sincere truth seeker.   He loved the Bible
and was ready to accept whatever it clearly taught.   No
sooner, therefore, did he learn of this new religious movement than he set about diligently to test the correctness of

his employer's views. Together they made an earnest, prayerful search of the Scriptures. Often, after the labors of the day had closed in the school room, they would prosecute their examinations of the Scriptures far into the night; not in the spirit of controversy, however, but with an earnest desire to know the will of God, and a determination to follow wherever his Word, the expression of his will, should lead.

The result of this painstaking search was that in a few weeks he turned his back upon his past religious training, convinced that human standards of belief were without the sanction of God's Word. This conclusion was not reached without much anguish of spirit. He further discovered that though he had adhered, in all strictness, to the church traditions, he had not obeyed some of the important commands of the Bible. Among his first discoveries, in his conscientious search of truth, was the absence of scriptural authority for infant baptism, and his need of personal obedience to a command so repeatedly enforced as that of baptism into Christ. He, therefore, announced his purpose to reject all authority but that of Christ, and in obedience to the divine command he was immersed by Mr. Forrester and immediately entered into hearty co-operation with the small congregation planted by Mr. Forrester.

He at once proved himself a valuable addition to this struggling congregation. Although he did not immediately take a public part in the services, his genial presence, zealous devotion, and Christian culture were an inspiration to the whole congregation. He humbly accepted the position of learner, continued his diligent search of the Scriptures and rejoiced in his new-found faith. In the meantime Mr. Forrester, desiring to devote himself exclusively to religious work, turned over the management of the school to his talented assistant.

Mr. Scott's original methods of instruction, his pleasing manner and faultless character won for his school a wide reputation and patronage. Had success in this line been the goal of his ambition, his situation would have proved eminently satisfactory; but this was not his ambition. The more he studied the Bible the more he felt drawn toward the ministry of the Word.   A new world of religious truth was gradually unfolding before him.   He soon found that even his teachers in this new religious school but partially apprehended the divine purpose and method in the world's salvation.   From his study of the Bible, especially Acts of Apostles, which now enlisted his attention, the plan of redemption began to take form in his mind.   Conversion had always been a perplexing subject to him, but in the light of this book all mystery fled.   He now found that all who heard, believed and obeyed the glad message of salvation were filled with peace and joy in believing.

While pursuing this line of investigation a small tract, sent out by an obscure congregation in New York, fell into his hands.   The views expressed in it so perfectly coincided with its authors, feeling that such an association would add with those he now held that he determined to get acquainted greatly to his Christian knowledge.   He, therefore, at once severed his connection with the school and set out in search for more light upon the great religious problems that now consumed his thought.   The visit proved a keen disappointment.   He found the practice of the church much different from what he had been led to expect from their publication. So after a short sojourn in the city, with a heavy heart he continued his journey, visiting Baltimore and Washington, in each of which he had learned of small congregations of independent believers; but these visits only added to his disappointment.   These early attempts at religious reformation were not always successful and frequently resulted in a caricature of the thing attempted.   In describing his fruitless journey he said:

I went thither, and having searched them up I discovered them to be so sunken in the mire of Calvinism that they refused to reform; and so finding no pleasure in them I left them.   I then went to the Capitol, and, climbing up to its lofty dome, I sat myself down, filled with sorrw at the miserable desolation of the Church of God.

His drooping spirit was cheered by his return to Pittsburgh, after a journey on foot of three hundred miles.   He received a warm welcome from those who had learned his true worth, and, as a suitable successor in the school room had not been found, a handsome salary was pledged to secure his services once more. Broken in spirit and purse, he accepted the position and continued in the management of the school for several years with remarkable success. But his chief delight now was to minister to the little church, which, deprived of its leader by the sudden death of Mr. Forrester, looked to him for leadership. This period marks his growth in spiritual things. His reverence for Christ and his Word led to the constant study of the Bible. His chief delight was in the Holy Scriptures. It was in these hours with the Spirit of truth that he made the final dedication of himself to God, promising "that if he, for Christ's sake, would grant him just and comprehensive views of his religion he would subordinate all his present and future attainments to the glory of his Son and his religion."

TURNING POINT IN HIS LIFE

It was while thus engaged singlehanded in working out the problem of human redemption as revealed in the Word of God that he first met Alexander Campbell, with whom his own history and efforts in the future were to be so intimately blended. They possessed many elements in common, had been reared in the same school of religious thought, had been driven by the same burning thirst for truth to the Bible, and through its message were led to pursue a similar path in their search for acceptance with God. The following, from the pen of Dr. Richardson, beautifully presents the predominating characteristics in contrast at the time of their first meeting:

The different hues in the characters of these two eminent men were such as to be, so to speak, complimentary to each other, and to form, by their harmonious blending, a completeness and a brilliancy which rendered their society, peculiarly delightful to each other. Thus, while Mr. Campbell was fearless, self-reliant and firm, Mr. Scott was naturally timid, diffident and yielding; and, while the former was calm, steady and prudent, the latter was excitable, variable and precipitate. The one, like the north star, was ever in position, unaffected by terrestrial influences; the other, like the magnetic needle, was often disturbed and trembling on its center, yet ever returning or seeking to return to its true direction. Both were nobly endowed with the powers of higher reason—a delicate self-consciousness, a decided will and a clear conception of truth. But, as it regards the other departments of the inner nature, in Mr. Campbell the understanding predominated, in Mr. Scott the feelings; and, if the former excelled in imagination, the latter was superior in brilliancy of fancy. If the tendency of one was to generalize, to take wide and extended views and to group a multitude of particulars under a single head or principle, that of the other was to analyze, to divide subjects into their particulars and consider their details. . . . In a word, in almost all those qualities of mind and character, which might be regarded differential or distinctive, they were singularly fitted to supply each other's wants and to form a rare and delightful companionship. (Memoirs of A. Campbell, Vol. 1, p. 510.)

They at once recognized in each other kindred spirits and joined hands, and, with Thomas Campbell, fromed a trio of unsurpassed genius, eloquence and devotion to truth.

WALTER SCOTT

The turning point in the life of Walter Scott came in 1827, when Alexander Campbell, on the way to the annual meeting of the Mahoning Association, visited him at his home in Steubensville, Ohio, and pervailed upon him to attend the meeting at New Lisbon. Scott, though not a member of the Association, was chosen evangelist.

The Association was organized in 1820 and was composed of ten Baptist churches. The number was doubled later, seventeen of whom were represented at the New Lisbon meeting. These churches in the main were in eastern Ohio, near the Pennsylvania line, and between the Ohio River and Lake Erie, and were known as the Western Reserve. One of the churches—Wellsburg—was in Virginia. Spiritually they were almost dead This, perhaps, was the result of extreme Calvinistic teachings and their elaborate man-made creeds. At this association fifteen churches reported only thirty-four baptisms, and eleven of these were at Wellsburg, the church home of Alexander Campbell.

The new evangelist threw the full force of his ardent nature into the work. He had long been an earnest, faithful, and prayerful student of the Word of God. He had drunk deep into its spirit, and became fully convinced of the weakness and inefficiency of modern systems, in all of which "there seemed to be a link wanting to connect an avowed faith in Christ with an immediate realization of the promises of the gospel. These seemed placed at an almost infinite distance from the penitent, bowed down under a sense of guilt, and longing for some certain evidence of acceptance, which he often vainly sought in the special spiritual illuminations upon which men were taught to rely."

The Association had imposed upon him no particular course whatever, and it was his duty, therefore, to consider how the proclamation of the gospel could be rendered most effective for the conversion of sinners.

In view of all the circumstances, this was a very difficult and perplexing question with which to grapple. He was aware of the fact that Mr. Campbell had spoken of baptism in his debate with McCalla as a pledge of pardon, but in this point of view it was, as yet, contemplated only *theoretically.* However, his knowledge of the Scriptures led him to think that baptism was in some way intimately connected with the personal enjoyment of the blessings of the gospel, but as yet he was unable to perceive just what position it occupied in relation to other requirements.

After a more diligent and prayerful study of the Word of God, and many conferences with other pious and godly men, it became clear to Scott that the Gospel contained facts to be believed, commands to be obeyed, and promises to be enjoyed. But in its specific application it was five-fold: (1) Faith to change the heart; (2) Repentance to change the life; (3) Baptism to change the state; (4) Remission of sins to cleanse from guilt; (5) The gift of the Holy Spirit to help in the Christian life and make one a partaker of the divine nature. This arrangement of these items was so manifestly in harmony with the Scriptures that he was transported with the discovery. The key of knowledge was now in his possession. The things that before were dark and perplexing were now clear and he resolved to preach the same Gospel preached by inspired men, and to preach it in the same way From his present viewpoint the Word of God was for the salvation of the world, and the inspired teachers made no mistake in their method of preaching it.

This was a bold and novel thing to do, but he believed it to be right, and he had the courage of his convictions, and proceeded to do it.

Fearing that he might give cause of offense to the churches which had employed him, he sent an appointment outside the limits of the Association, and with some misgivings, but in an earnest and interesting manner, laid before the audience his analysis of the Gospel, and at the close he gave a formal invitation to any one so disposed to come forward, confess his faith in Christ and be baptized for the remission of sins; but no one came. To his audience this was like the proclaration of a new religion, so different did it seem from the orthodoxy of the day. They regarded him as an amiable but deluded enthusiast, and looked upon him with wonder, pity, and even scorn. This result was not unexpected, for the whole community was filled with the idea that something supernatural had to occur before any one could become a fit subject for baptism. Instead of giving way to this traditional prejudice, he said to himself "This way is of God, and ought to succeed, and with his help it shall." He was right, and God gave him success, as he gives to all such men. He accordingly announced that he would deliver a series of discourses on the Ancient Gospel at New Lisbon, Ohio, the place at which he had been selected as evangelist by the Association a few months before. Here he was to witness the removal of the barriers and the triumph of the cause that was so near his heart.

When he arrived on Sunday to begin the series of meetings every seat in the building was literally packed, soon even standing room was at a premium, and the doorway was blocked up by the eager throng. Scott was just the man to be moved to the highest point by such an occasion. The following is a vivid descriptiontion of the events of that day:

His theme was the confession of Peter, "Thou art the Christ, the Son of the living God" (Matt. 16: 16), and the promise which grew out of it, that he should have entrusted to him the keys of the kingdom of heaven. The declaration of Peter was a theme upon which he had thought for years; it was a fact which he regarded the four gospels was written to establish; to which type and prophecy had pointed in all the ages gone by; which the Eternal Father had announced from heaven when out of the waters of Jordan and the Spirit descended and abode upon him, and which was repeated again amid the awful grandeur and solemnity of the transfiguration scene. He then proceeded to show that the foundation truth of Christianity was the divine nature of the Lord Jesus—the central truth around which all others revolved, and from which they derived their efficacy and importance—and that the belief of it was calculated to produce such love in the heart of him who believed as would lead him to true obedience to the object of his faith and love. To show how that love and faith were to be manifested, he quoted the language of the great commission (Matt. 28: 18-20; Mark 16: 15, 16), and called attention to the fact that Jesus had taught his apostles "that repentance and remission of sins should be preached in his name unto all the nations, beginning from Jerusalem (Luke 24: 47). He then led his hearers to Jerusalem on the memorable Pentecost and bade them listen to an authoritative announcement of the law of Christ, now to be made known for the first time by Peter to whom Christ had promised to give the keys of the kingdom of heaven (Matt. 16: 16), which he represented as meaning the conditions upon which the guilty might find pardon at the hands of the risen, ascended, and glorified Son of God, and enter his kingdom.

After a rapid yet graphic review of Peter's discourse, he pointed out its effect on those that heard him, and bade them mark the inquiry which a deep conviction of the truth they had heard forced from the lips of the heart-pierced multitudes, who, in their agony at the discovery that they had put to death the Son of God, their own long-expected Messiah, "said unto Peter and the rest of the apostles, Brethren, what shall we do?" and then with flashing eyes and impassioned manner, as if he fully realized that he was but re-echoing the words of one who spake as the Spirit gave him utterance, he gave the reply, "Repent ye, and be baptized every one of you in the name of Jesus Christ unto the remission of your sins; and ye shall receive the gift of the Holy Spirit." He then, with great force and power, made his application; he insisted that the conditions were unchanged, that the Word of God meant what it said, and that to receive and obey it was to obey God and to imitate the example of those who, under the preaching of the apostles, gladly accepted the gospel message. His discourse was long, but his hearers marked not the flight of time. the Baptists forgot, in admiration of its scriptural beauty and simplicity, that it was contrary to much of their own teaching and practice; some of them who had been, in a measure, enlightened before, rejoiced in the truth the moment they perceived it; to others, who had long been perplexed by the difficulties and contradictions of the discordant views of the day, it was light like light to weary travelers long benighted and lost.

The man of all others, however, in that community who would most have delighted in and gladly accepted those views, so old and yet so new, was not there, although almost in hearing of the preacher, who, with such eloquence and power, was setting forth the primitive gospel. This was William Amend, a pious, God-fearing man, a member of the Presbyterian Church, and regarded by his neighbors as an "Israelite indeed." He had for some time entertained the same views as those Mr. Scott was then preaching in that place for the first time, but was not aware of the fact that any one agreed with him. He was under the impression that all the churches—his own among the number—had departed from the plain teachings of the Word of God. He had discovered, some time before, that infant baptism was not taught in the Bible, and, consequently, that he was not a baptized man; the act of baptism seemed also to him to have been changed, and he sought his pastor, and asked to be immersed. His pastor endeavored to convince him that he was wrong, but finding that he could not be turned from his purpose, he proposed to immerse him privately, lest others of his flock might be unsettled in their minds by his so doing, and closed by saying that baptism was not essential to salvation. Mr. Amend regarded everything that Christ had ordained as being essential, and replied that he should not immerse him at all; that he would wait until he found a man who believed the gospel, and who could, without any scruple, administer the ordinance as he conceived it to be taught in the New Testament.

He was invited a day or two before to hear Mr. Schott, but knowing nothing of his views, he supposed that he preached much as others did, but agreed to go and hear him. It was near the close of the services when he reached the Baptist Church and joined the crown at the door, who were unabl to get into the house. The first sentence he heard aroused and excited him; it sounded like the gospel which he had read with such interest at home, but never had heard from the pulpit before. He now felt a great anxiety to see the man who was speaking so much like the oracles of God, and pressed through the throng into the house.

Mr. Dibble, the clerk of the church, saw him enter, and knowing that he had been seeking and longing to find a man who would preach as the Word of God read, thought within himself, "Had Mr. Amend been here during all this discourse I feel sure that he would have found what he has so long sought in vain. I wish the preacher would repeat what he said before he came in." Greatly to his surprise Mr. Scott did give a brief review of the various points of his discourse, insisting that the Word of God meant what it said, and urging his hearers to trust that Word implicitly. He rehearsed again the Jerusalem scene, called attention to the earnest, anxious cry of the multitude, and the comforting reply of the apostle, "Repent ye, and be baptized every one of you in the name of Jesus Christ unto the remission of your sins; and ye shall receive the gift of the Holy Spirit." He invited any one present who believed with all his heart to yield to the terms proposed in the words of the apostle. and show by a willing obediness his trust in the Lord of life and glory. Mr. Amend pressed his way through the crowd to the preacher and made known his purpose; made a public confession of his faith in Jesus Christ as the Son of the living God and expressed his desire to obey him, at once, and on the same day, in a beautiful, clear stream which flows on the southern border of the town, in th presence of a great multitude, he was baptized in the name of Jesus Christ for the remission of sins. (Life of Walter Scott, pages 104-108.)

From that day the meeting continued with increasing interest. Seventeen persons, "hearing, believed, and were baptized." The whole community was aroused and began to search the scriptures, some in the same spirit of the Bereans of old to see whether these things were so; others with no higher purpose than to file objections to that which was so boldly proclaimed, and many of these were forced to admit that if the teaching were false the Bible could not be true, for the preacher could read everything that was demanded from the Word of God.

It was a fortunate thing that a man with such an unsullied character and reputation as that of Mr. Amend should be the first to render obedience to the apostolic teaching at New Lisbon He was a man with more than ordinary intelligence, and his scriptural knowledge was far beyond that of most men in his station in life. His action was not the result of an impulse produced by Mr. Scott's discourse, for that he had not heard; but from a careful study of the Word of God. He was not aware of the fact that there was another person in the world who held similar views to his own.

Although Mr. Scott was pleased with the initial success, it was still a mystery to him why his first discourse had failed to convince any one, and that at the close of the second, Mr. Amend, who had heard neither of them, should come forward so intelligently; hence he wrote a letter requesting him to state the facts which induced him to respond to the invitation so promptly, to which he replied:

Now, my brother, I will answer your questions. I was baptized November 18, 1827, and I will relate to you a circumstance which occurred a few days before that date. I had read the second chapter of Acts when I expressed myself to my wife as follows: "Oh, this is the gospel—this is the thing we wish—remission of our sins! Oh, that I could hear the gospel in these same words—as Peter preached it! I hope I shall some day hear it; and the first man I meet who will preach the gospel thus, with him will I go." So, my brother, on the day you saw me come into the meeting-house, my heart was open to receive the Word of God, and when you cried, "The scriptures no longer shall be a sealed book. God means what he says. Is there any man who will take God at his word, and be baptized for the remission of sins?" at that moment my feelings were such that I could have cried out, "Glory to God! I have found the man for whom I have long sought." So I entered the kingdom where I readily laid hold of the hope set before me. (Life of Walter Scott, page 113.)

Within three weeks after the close of the meeting at New Lisbon, Mr. Scott returned and found the interest there greater than when he left, and seven others were baptized. Soon after this he visited there again, and baptized more than thirty others. The members of the Baptist Church gladly accepted the truth, and resolved that thenceforth the Bible should be their only rule of faith and practice

The ice was now broken, and a new era was inaugurated which was marked by a quiet thoughtfulness, and an unwonted searching of the Scriptures, "whether these things were so," and a final decision to obey the personal Christ, expressed in public confession of faith in Christ and baptism. The country was aroused as never before. The conversion of Mr. Amend confirmed Mr. Scott in his conviction that the way preached and practiced by God's inspired messengers at Pentecost was the right way. His labors and success aroused much inquiry and great opposition, and the wildest rumors were circulated concerning his preaching and work. The interest in the public mind swelled to a torrent which swept everything before it. Not only individuals by the hundreds became obedient to the faith, but often entire congregations would wheel into line with the "ancient order of things." Baptist congregations voted out the Philadelphia Confession of Faith and substituted the New Testament in its place. And not only the Baptists, but Presbyterians, Universalists, Lutherans, Christian Connectionists, Methodists, and Episcopalians in large numbers were reached. The Deerfield Methodist Church came in as a whole.

Exaggerated reports concerning the teaching and practice of Mr. Scott reached Mr. Campbell and he became fearful lest his zeal and youthful inexperience should lead him into serious error. He therefore decided that it would be well for his father, Thomas Campbell, to visit his field of labor and ascertain the truth concerning the state of affairs. Upon arriving, he heard Mr. Scott's presentation of the gospel and witnessed his method of procedure with surprise and great pleasure. It at once became apparent to him that what he and his son had taught was now reduced to practice, and that the rumors that had reached him were untrue. He therefore remained in this promising field some time, and by his earnest and efficient labors gave great assistance to the work. On April 9, 1828, from New Lisbon, he wrote to his son giving his impressions of the work, as follows:

I perceive that theory and practice in religion, as well as in other things, are matters of distinct consideration. It is one thing to know the art of fishing—for instance the rod, the line, and the hook, and the bait, too; and quite another thing to handle them dextrously when thrown into the water, so as to make it take. We have spoken and long known the former (the theory), and have spoken and published many things correctly concerning the ancient gospel, its simplicity and perfect adaptation to the present state of mankind, for the benign and gracious purpose of his immediate relief and complete salvation; but I must confess that, in respect to the direct exhibition and application of it for that blessed purpose, I am at present for the first time upon the ground where the thing has appeared to be practically applied to the proper purpose. "Compel them to come in, saith the Lord, that my house may be filled."

Mr. Scott has made a bold push to accomplish this object, by simply and boldly stating the ancient gospel, and insisting upon it; and then by putting the question generally and particularly to male and female, old and young: "Will you come to Christ and be baptized for the remission of your sins and the gift of the Holy Spirit? Don't you believe this blessed gospel? Then come away." This elicits a personal conversation; some confess faith in the testimony, beg time to think; others consent, give their hand to be baptized as soon as convenient; others debate the matter friendly; some go straight to the water, be it day or night, and upon the whole none appear offended. (Life of Walter Scott, pages 158, 159.)

By the end of the first year many languishing churches had been brought into living activity, many new ones had been organized, and a thousand persons had been baptized into Christ. Mr. Scott was unanimously chosen to continue in the work, and he consented, stipulating only that he should have William Hayden, a zealous young preacher and sweet singer, to assist him. But his second year was one of great conflict. By this time, those bound by sectarian traditions began to realize if Scott were allowed to continue preaching what they called "heresy" unopposed as he had been allowed to do during the preceding year, sectarianism was doomed, hence the opposition became extremely fierce. That you may have some idea of the conflict that ensued all over the country, I give a brief history of the introduction of the ancient gospel at Sharon, Pa. Just a short distance over the state line in Ohio, the Baptist churches at Warren and Hubbard had accepted it almost in a body, so generally indeed, that both houses of worship passed quietly out of the hands of the Baptists; and in the case at Warren, not only the greater part of the congregation, but the preacher also accepted the truth so ably and eloquently urged by Scott, and became himself an earnest and successful advocate of the same. Some of the Baptists had heard of the great changes that had taken place in the two churches mentioned; some of the members had even gone so far as to visit them, and could find no well-founded objections to what they had heard stigmatized as heresy; nay, it even seemed to them like the things they had read in the Bible; and some of them went so far as to sit down at the Lord's table with them. Such an element in the church, of course, soon made itself felt. The Scriptures were closely searched, and the light began to spread. Suspicion was aroused—was the hated "heresy" about to break out among them and destroy their peace? Several were soon marked men; the views they held were assailed and loudly condemned, when some one suggested that, as it was not the custom to condemn without a hearing in ancient time, they had better send for the public advocates of the new doctrine and learn the best or worst at once. This suggestion prevailed and Scott and Bently were invited to preach at Sharon. They came and Scott preached every night for three weeks. The curiosity which at first characterized many who attended soon deepened into sincere interest, and some began to inquire, "Brethren, what shall we do?" The inspired answer was given, and, in response to the gospel invitation, several persons presented themselves and were immediately, on a confession of their faith in Christ as the Son of God, baptized.

Shortly after this meeting closed the cry was raised that what had been done was not according to "Baptist usage." Those who had been baptized had not been required to relate an experience of grace prior to baptism, and the church had not been allowed to pass on their fitness for membership, and so they were not received as members. But there was another serious trouble that could not be so easily settled They could refuse to receive into their fellowship those baptized by Mr. Scott; but what was to be done with those who received with gladness the message delivered by him as the word of God? Some of these were the most influential members, and to make the case more perplexing, were tolerant of the views held by the Baptists. As they had formerly held the same, they desired that the others should see as they did; but they did not attempt to force their views upon the church; they wished to hold them in peace, however, but at the same time did not want to be bound by the creed and church articles. All this class sympathized with those who had been refused membership. In their view, if the Lord, as they believed, had accepted them, why should the church reject them?

Those who were still attached to the Baptist views were of a different spirit. And they were fully determined that all who even sympathized with those whom they regarded as heretics should either repent or be excluded from their fellowship. This naturally produced serious trouble, and many of the leading members left the church and cast their lot with those endeavoring to restore the apostolic church. But the opposition only stirred the evangelists to greater zeal and power, and created for them a sympathy which opened the doors to thousands of hearts hitherto closed to their message. Like fighting fire in the stubble, the stroke of the flail only increased the flame. Throughout the country they went "turning the country upside down," like the apostles of old. So great was their influence that, when the Mahoning Association met in 1830, it disbanded, and ceased its connection with the Baptist Church, that church having repudiated all who were set for a return to apostolic simplicity.

The three years spent by Mr. Scott in the Western Reserve; the great audiences that greeted him, and the marvelous success that crowned his labors, stimulated his fervent nature to the highest and drew from his rich soul the rarest wealth. His mind was filled with truth, and his thought was illuminated with the finest imagery. He knew the Bible as few men, and loved it with a passionate love. His life was wholly given to the Savior, and never was a sacrifice more unreservedly made. No wonder that a preacher like this should revolutionize the hearts of men

REFORMERS IN OTHER STATES

JOHN WRIGHT

In our study so far we have learned of several independent movements, in widely separated localities, making strenuous efforts to throw off the shackles of sectarianism and to stand wholly on apostolic ground, and it is fitting that I should give a brief sketch of others.

John Wright was born in Rowan County, North Carolina, December 12, 1785. When he was about twelve years old his father moved into Powell's Valley, Va., where he grew to manhood. From Virginia the whole family emigrated to Wayne County, Ky., where he was joined in marriage to Miss Nancy Beeler, who proved to be a most excellent helpmeet, ever ready with him to make any sacrifice for the cause of Christ. In the latter part of 1807, he moved from Kentucky into Clark's Grant, Indiana.

In August, 1808 he and his wife were baptized by William Summers, and they immediately united with the Baptist

Church, and in the latter part of the same year he began to preach. This was long before the current Reformation was heard of by the inhabitants of the West. He was, therefore among the very first to break the stillness of Indiana's forest with the glad tidings of salvation. In January, 1810, he moved to Blue River, four miles south of Salem, and was shortly afterwards joined by his father, where they organized a congregation of Free-Will Baptists. They exerted great influence in behalf of Christianity, and it was not long until they had organized ten Baptist Churches which they organized into what was called Blue River Association.

From the very first, John Wright was of the opinion that all human creeds were heretical and schismatical, and in that region there has not come after him a more persistent contender for the word of God as the only and all-sufficient rule of faith and practice. He labored to destroy all divisions and promote union among all professed followers of the Lord; and in this difficult and most important service he was very successful. Though at first he tolerated the name Baptist, he afterwards waged a war of extermination against all party names. This war was declared in the year 1819, when he offered at the church at Blue River a resolution in favor of discarding all party names. As individuals, he contended that they should be called "friends," "disciples," "brethren," "saints," "Christians;" and, as a body, "Church of Christ," or "Church of God." He opposed the term "Christian" as applied to the church, because it is not so applied in the writings of the apostles.

The resolution was adopted, and, having agreed, also, to lay aside their speculative opinions and contradictory theories, they were prepared to plead consistently for Christian union, and to invite others to stand with them upon the one broad and sure foundation They then began in earnest the work of reformation, and with such success that by the year 1821 there was not a Baptist Church in all that region.

About this time a spirited controversy over the subject of Trine Immersion was being waged among the Tunkers, of whom there were fifteen congregations in that section of country. The leading spirits in opposition to that doctrine were Abram Kern, of Indiana, and Peter Hon, of Kentucky. At first they contended against great odds, but so many of their opponents finally surrendered that they finally gained a decisive victory in favor of one immersion. At the close of the contest, while both parties were exhausted by the conflict, Mr. Wright recommended to his brethren that they should send a letter to the Annual Conference of the Tunkers, proposing a union of the two bodies on the Bible alone. The letter was written and John Wright, his brother, Peter, and several others, were appointed as messengers to convey it to the conference and there advocate the measures it proposed. So successful was the effort that at the first meeting the union was permanently formed.

About the same time Mr. Wright proposed a correspondence with the Newlights, for the purpose of forming with them a more perfect union. He was appointed to conduct the correspondence on the part of his brethren, which he did with so much ability and discretion, that a joint meeting was assembled at Edinburg, where the union was readily consummated.

A few years subsequent to this, the work of reformation began to progress rapidly among the Regular Baptists of the Silver Creek Association. This was directly through the influence of Absolom and J. T. Littell, and Mordecai Cole, the leading spirits of that locality. Through their teaching hundreds of individuals and some whole churches renounced all human creeds and boldly took a stand on the Bible alone. But still there was a shyness existing between them and those who had done the same thing under the labors of Mr. Wright. The former having held Calvinistic opinions, stood aloof through fear of being called Arians; while the latter feared to make any advances lest they should be stigmatized as "Campbellites." Thus the two parties stood when Mr. Wright became their mediator communicating the sentiments of each to the other. By this means it was soon ascertained that they were all endeavoring to preach and practice the same thing. The only important difference between them was in regard to the design of baptism, and on this point Mr. Wright yielded as soon as he was convinced of his error.

This move resulted in the permanent union of these two large and influential bodies of believers. In consequence of this effort at peace making, more than three thousand united in the bonds of peace, agreeing to stand together on the one foundation and to forget all minor differences in their devotion to the great interests of the Redeemer's kingdom. This was the greatest achievement of Mr. Wright's long and eventful life; and he deserves to be held in high esteem for his love of truth, for his moral courage in carrying out his convictions of right, and for the meek and affectionate spirit which gave him such power in leading people out of sectarianism and uniting them together in the bonds of love in Christ Jesus.

HERMAN CHRISTIAN DASHER

The parents of Herman Christian Dasher came to this country from Salzburg, Germany, to escape the persecution of the Roman Catholic Church, and located near Savannah, Georgia. They were Lutherans and had Herman christened in infancy and brought up in that faith. When he arrived at manhood and began to be impressed with the importance of uniting with a church, and of living the Christian life, he was deeply perplexed by the existence, and by the proclaiming of so many contradictory doctrines. Fortunately, instead of becoming an infidel, as so many do under like circumstances, he turned to the Holy Scriptures for light. He soon became thoroughly convinced that immersion is baptism, and that affusion is not, and that therefore he ought to be immersed.

He could not cast his lot with the Baptists, as he could not tell an experience of grace which they required, for he had seen no marvelous light, neither had he heard any marvelous sounds. He was by no means convinced "that God had for Christ's sake forgiven his sins," though he did not then understand the doctrine of baptism for remission of sins, as he afterwards did; nor did he think that God demanded any such experience as a prerequisite to baptism and church membership. But he desired most earnestly to become a Christian, believing in his heart that Jesus is the Christ the Son of the living God, the Savior of sinners.

This brought before him a new difficulty, for within the whole range of his acquaintance, there was not one who would immerse him on a simple confession of his faith in Christ. All demanded that he should profess to have a miraculous and mysterious work of the Holy Spirit within him, in taking away his heart of stone and giving him a heart of flesh.

Providentially, about this time, while he was most earnestly engaged in studying the Bible, he was thrown into the company of a Mrs. Threadcraft, of Savannah, who informed him that in her city a Mr. S. C. Dunning, who had formerly been a Baptist preacher, but had recently seceded from that body, because he did not believe it taught and practiced as the Word of God required. In this movement he had been accompanied by eight or ten others. This lady further informed him that Mr. Dunning preached the Scriptures as he did, and that at his hands he could obtain baptism upon a simple confession of his faith in Jesus Christ as the Son of God. This information filled him with such great joy that he did not delay in making the journey into Savannah to see Mr. Dunning, who baptized him without further delay. This was during the year 1819.

Immediately after returning to his home he immersed his wife, her sister and her husband. These "continued steadfastly in the apostles' teaching and fellowship, in the breaking of bread and the prayers," meeting every Lord's Day in the house of Mr. Dasher. The little church grew and prospered, being occasionally visited by Mr. Dunning, who assisted in building it up by his teaching and exhortatons.

Some time after this, Mr. Dasher, accompanied by a number of the members of the church, moved into Lowndes County, and located where the vity of Valdosta now stands In this new field he continued the work of preaching the word and built up a congregation which met in his own residence. This was the beginning of the work in Valdosta and the region around about. It was many years after the baptism of Mr. Dasher before he knew that there were any others in any place contending for the "truth as is in Jesus," as he and those associated with him were doing.

CHAPTER IX.

THE CHRISTIANS AND REFORMERS UNITE

A new period has now dawned in the movement for the union of all Christians by the restoration of primitive Christianity. The Baptists had thrust from their fellowship those who had embraced it and they were forced into a separate existence. Every preacher among them was filled with a zeal to plant churches after the primitive order wherever they could get a large enough company together.

The work spread principally from two centers, Ohio and Kentucky. From Ohio it was carried into New York and Pennsylvania; and westward into Michigan, northern Ohio, and Indiana, and Wisconsin. From Kentucky it was carried eastward and southward into Virginia, Maryland, the Carolinas, Tennessee, and Alabama; and westward into Indiana, Illinois and Missouri. The movement spread chiefly in a westward direction from Kentucky and Tennessee along the lines of emigration. Very often a sufficient number of emigrants to establish themselves into a congregation after the primitive order found themselves together in the same neighborhood and began at once to meet together for mutual edification and the spread of the truth.

While it was well known that there were many things received and practiced in common there had been no special effort to bring about a union between them. In 1824, at Georgetown, Ky., Mr. Stone and Mr. Campbell first met When they compared views, it seemed that there were irreconcilable differences between them. Stone thought Campbell was heterodox on the Holy Spirit, and Campbell suspected Stone's soundness on the divinity of Christ. But on a more careful investigation, they found these differences more imaginary than real, and they joined hearts and hands and God blessed them with the most important work since the apostolic age. With the kindly feelings towards each other, the work of union between their brethren was well on the way when it was begun. And so, after a number of friendly conferences, it was decided to have a meeting of representative men at Georgetown, Ky., to continue for days, including December 25, 1831. The results of this conference were so satisfactory that another was convened in Lexington, January 1, 1832. In these gatherings the spirit of the Master was supreme.

At the Lexington meeting, at an early hour the house was crowded. Stone, John T. Johnson, Samuel Rogers, G. W. Elley, Jacob Creath, "Raccoon" John Smith, and many other worthy men were there, all guarded in thought and purpose against any compromise of truth, but all filled with the spirit of the Master: "That they may all be one; even as thou, Father, art in me, and I in thee, that they also may be in us: that the world may believe that thou didst send me." It was decided that one man from each party should speak, setting forth clearly the grounds of union, and Smith and Stone were selected as the speakers   After this had been announced, the two brethren went aside, and conferred in private. Neither knew what the other would say in the critical hour which had now come upon the churches; nor did either, in the moment of solemn conference, ask the other to disclose his mind, touching their differences, more fully than he had already done. It was decided between them that Smith should speak first.

The occasion was to Smith the most important and solemn that had occurred in the history of the reformation. "It was now to be seen whether all that had been written and said and done in behalf of the simple gospel of Christ and the union of Christians was really the work of the Lord, or whether the prayers of Stone and Johnson were but the idle longings of pious, yet deluded hearts; whether the toils and sacrifices of Smith were but the schismatic efforts of a bold enthusiast, and whether the teachings of Campbell were only the speculations of a graceless and sensuous philosophy. The denominations around mocked, and declared that a church without a constitution could not stand, and that a union without a creed was but the chimera of a dreamy and infatuated heresy."

At the appointed hour, Smith, realizing the tremendous importance of the occasion, arose with simple dignity, and stood before the mingling brotherhoods. He felt the weight that rested upon him. Every eye turned upon him, and every ear leaned to catch the slightest tones of his voice. He said:

God has but one people on the earth. He has given to to them but one Book, and therein exhorts and commands them to be one family. A union such as we plead for—a union of God's people on that one Book—must then be practicable. Every Christian desires to stand complete in the whole will of God. The prayer of the Savior, and the whole tenor of his teaching, clearly show that it is God's will that his children should be united. To the Christian, then, such a union must be desirable. But an amalgamation of sects is not such a union as Christ prayed for and God enjoins. To agree to be one upon any system of human invention would be contrary to his will, and could never be a blessing to the church or the world: therefore the only union practicable or desirable must be based on the Word of God as the only rule of faith and practice. There are certain abstruse and speculative matters—such as the mode of the divine existence and the ground and nature of the atonement—that have for centuries, been themes of discussion among Christians. These questions are as far from being settled now as they were in the beginning of the controversy. By a needless and intemperate discussion of them much feeling has been provoked, and divisions have been produced. For several years past I have tried to speak on such subjects only in the language of inspiration, for it can offend no one to say about those things just what the Lord himself has said. In this scriptural style of speech all Christians should be agreed. It can not be wrong. it can not do harm. If I come to the passage, "My Father is greater than I," I will quote it, but will not stop to speculate upon the consubstantial nature of the Father and the Son. "Have this mind in you, which was also in Christ Jesus: who existing in the form of God, counted not the being on an equality with God a thing to be grasped," I will not stop to speculate upon the consubstantial nature of the Father and the Son. I will not linger to build a theory on such texts, and thus encourage a speculative and wrangling spirit among my brethren. I will present these subjects only in the words which the Lord has given me. I know he will not be displeased if we say just what he has said. Whatever opinions about these and similar subjects I may have reached in the course of my investigation, if I never distract the church of God with them or seek to impose them on my brethren, they will never do the world any harm.

I have the more cheerfully resolved on this course, because the gospel is a system of facts, commands, and promises; and no deductions or inferences from them, however logical or true, forms any part of the gospel of Jesus Christ. No heaven is promised to those who hold them, and no hell is threatened to those who deny them. They do not constitute, singly or together, any items of the ancient and apostolic gospel. While there is but one faith, there may be ten thousand opinions; and hence if Christians are ever to be one, they must be one in faith, and not in opinion. When certain subjects arise, and even in conversation or social discussion, about which there is a contrariety of opinion and sensitiveness of feeling, speak of them in the words of the Scriptures, and no offense will be given, and no pride of doctrine will be encouraged. We may even come, in the end, by thus speaking the same things, to think the same things.

For several years past I have stood pledged to meet the religious world, or any part of it, on the ancient gospel and order of things as presented in the words of the Book. This is the foundation on which Christians once stood, and on it they can, and ought to, stand again. From this I can not depart to meet any man, or set of men, in the world. While, for the sake of peace and Christian union, I have long since waived the public maintainance of any speculation I may hold, yet not one gospel fact. commandment, or promise will I surrender for the world. Let us, then, my brethren, be no longer Campbellites or Stoneites, New Lights or Old Lights, or any other kind of lights; but let us all come to the Bible, and to the Bible alone, as the only book in the world that can give us all the light we need.

When Smith had concluded, Stone arose, with his heart filled with love and hope, said:

I will not attempt to introduce any new topic, but say a few things on the subject presented by my beloved brother. Controversies in the church sufficiently prove that Christians can never be one in their speculations upon these mysterious and sublime subjects, which, while they interest the Christian philosopher, can not edify the church. After we have given up all creeds and taken the Bible, and the Bible alone, as our rule of faith and practice, we met with so much opposition that I was led to deliver some speculative discourses upon these subjects. But I never preached a sermon of that kind that really feasted my heart; I always felt a barrenness of soul afterwards. I perfectly accord with Bro. Smith that these speculations should never be taken into the pulpit; and when compelled to speak of them at all, we should do so in the words of inspiration.

I have not one objection to the ground laid down by him as the true Scriptural basis of union among the people of God, and I am willing to give him, now and here, my hand.

And as he spoke these words, he extended his hand to Smith, and it was grasped by a hand full of the honest pledges of love and fellowship, and the union of these two bodies was virtually accomplished. It was then proposed that all who felt willing to unite on the principles enunciated should signify it by giving to each other the hand of fellowship, and at once the audience joyfully joined hands in joyful accord. A song was sung, and, amid tears of inexpressible happiness, the union was confirmed.

Following this meeting, some further friendly conferences were held by means of committees, and by arrangement the members of both churches communed together on February 19, agreeing to consummate the formal and public union of the two churches on the following Lord's day. During the week, however, some began to fear a difficulty in relation to the choice of elders and the practical adoption of weekly communion, which they thought would require the constant presence of an ordained administrator. The person who generally ministered to the Christian Church at Lexington at this time was Thomas Smith, a man of more than ordinary abilities and attainments, and long associated with the movement of Barton W. Stone. He was at first, apprehensive that the proposed union was premature, and that disagreements might arise in regard to questions of church order. The union was therefore postponed, and matters remained for a short time stationary, but it soon became apparent to the Christians that there were no exclusive privileges belonging to the preacher as it concerned the administration of the ordinances, and Thomas M. Allen, who enjoyed the esteem and confidence of the entire brotherhood, induced them to complete the union and to transfer to the new congregation, thus formed under the title of the "Church of Christ;" the comfortable church house which they had previously held under the designation of "the Christian Church." This wise measure secured entire unanimity, and the formal and public union was consummated on February 26, as had been previously arranged, when they again broke bread together, and in that sweet and solemn communion again pledged to each other their brotherly love.

At Paris, Mr. Allen also effected a union of the two churches and the union at Georgetown, Lexington, and Paris soon led to union throughout the state. This desire for unity was greatly furthered by the efforts of John Smith and John Rogers, who had been appointed at the Lexington meeting to visit all the churches and hold meetings in conjunction with each other. Their work was wonderfully successful throughout Kentucky in uniting the two bodies. The effect of this union was very great on those who had never made any profession of religion. Multitudes became obedient to the faith throughout Kentucky, and an impetus was given to the cause by the union of the two peoples, which served to illustrate the overwhelming power which the gospel would exert upon the world if all the sad divisions among those who claim to follow Christ were healed. The sectarians of Kentucky, who had foretold a speedy disruption of the union, were surprised to find their prophecies unfulfilled, and not less grieved at the inroads continually made upon their own power, which, from this period steadily and rapidly declined. It is worthy of mention that at the time these events were happening in Kentucky, the spirit of union was prevailing over sectarianism in a number of other states also. Every preacher among them was a missionary and traveling evangelist.

"This union of the Christians and Reformers was not a surrender of one party to the other; it was an agreement of such as already recognized and loved each other as brethren to work and worship together. It was the union of those who held alike the necessity of implicit faith and of unreserved obedience; who accepted the facts, commands, and promises as set forth in the Bible; who conceded the right of private judgment to all; who taught that opinions were no part of the faith delivered to the saints; and who were now pledged that no speculative matters should ever be debated to the disturbance of the peace and harmony of the church, but when compelled to speak on controverted subjects, they would adopt the style and language of the Holy Spirit." It was an equal and mutual resolution to meet on the Bible as on common ground and to preach the gospel rather than to propagate opinions.